Voices That Matter

Voices That Matter

Kurdish Women at the Limits of Representation in Contemporary Turkey

MARLENE SCHÄFERS

The University of Chicago Press

Chicago and London

The University of Chicago Press, Chicago 60637
The University of Chicago Press, Ltd., London
© 2023 by The University of Chicago
Published 2023
Printed in the United States of America

32 31 30 29 28 27 26 25 24 23   1 2 3 4 5

ISBN-13: 978-0-226-81980-8 (cloth)
ISBN-13: 978-0-226-82305-8 (paper)
ISBN-13: 978-0-226-82303-4 (e-book)
DOI: https://doi.org/10.7208/chicago/9780226823034.001.0001

Library of Congress Cataloging-in-Publication Data

Names: Schäfers, Marlene, author.
Title: Voices that matter : Kurdish women at the limits of representation in
    contemporary Turkey / Marlene Schäfers.
Description: Chicago : University of Chicago Press, 2023. |
    Includes bibliographical references and index.
Identifiers: LCCN 2022014514 | ISBN 9780226819808 (cloth) |
    ISBN 9780226823058 (paperback) | ISBN 9780226823034 (ebook)
Subjects: LCSH: Women, Kurdish—Turkey—Social conditions. |
    Women, Kurdish—Civil rights—Turkey. | Kurds—Songs and music—History
    and criticism. | Singing—Political aspects.
Classification: LCC HQ1726.7.Z8 K877 2023 | DDC 305.409561—dc23/eng/20220404
LC record available at https://lccn.loc.gov/2022014514

♾ This paper meets the requirements of ANSI/NISO Z39.48-1992
(Permanence of Paper).

To Gazîn

Contents

Note on Language, Naming, and Musical Notation

This book proceeds from the observation that the Kurdish voice constitutes an overdetermined object of concern and debate, hope and promise, in contemporary Turkey. Setting Kurdish voices into writing—as I do in this book—does not escape these tensions. I carried out the fieldwork that my account is based on in both Turkish and the Kurmanji variant of Kurdish, which is spoken by most Kurds living in Turkey and northern Syria, as well as in parts of northern Iraq, western Iran, and the Caucasus. Given that Kurdish does not have official status in Turkey, the language has not been standardized to the extent that other national languages have. Regional variations abound, as do ideas about how to accommodate them. To give readers a sense of the sonic articulation of these voices, I have decided to stay close to my interlocutors' spoken language when transcribing their songs and citing original phrases. This means that while I rely on the standard Kurdish Latin orthography that is commonly used by Kurds in Turkey, Syria, and Europe, my transcriptions occasionally deviate from standard orthography that readers may encounter elsewhere. I write, for instance *min go* or *mi go* (I said), rather than *min got*. Where terms from the region's local languages have entered into common use in English, I use the English spelling rather than adhering to Kurdish orthography (e.g., I write Yezidi rather than the Kurdish *êzidî*, Ajam rather than *acem*, or Kurmanji rather than *kurmancî*).

Staying close to the spoken language of my interlocutors also means acknowledging the extent to which Turkish and Kurdish routinely intersect and intermingle in everyday speech. In order to allow readers not familiar with the two languages to recognize whether original phrases are in Kurdish or Turkish, I italicize *Kurdish* words and expressions while italicizing and underlining *Turkish* ones. I apply this only where spoken language or primary written sources are concerned. Where I provide original terms, names, or titles, I use simple italics for either language. Unless otherwise stated, all translations are my own, though based on generous assistance by Ergin Öpengin where song texts are concerned. Needless to say, I am responsible for any mistakes that may remain.

In Turkey, non-Turkish place-names have been systematically replaced by Turkish ones. In the attempt to undo some of that colonial hold over Kurdish geographies, I prioritize Kurdish place-names rather than Turkish ones, which I place in brackets upon first mention. Where more than one designation is used in Kurdish, I employ the one most commonly used by my interlocutors. For instance, rather than Amed (Tk. Diyarbakır) I use Diyarbekir.

For the same reason, I refer to the part of Kurdistan that lies within Turkish national borders as northern Kurdistan (Bakur in Kurdish) rather than Turkish Kurdistan (or Turkey's Kurdistan). While northern Kurdistan refers to Kurdish areas under Turkish rule, southern Kurdistan (Başûr) refers to Kurdish areas within Iraq, eastern Kurdistan (Rojhilat) to those in Iran, and western Kurdistan (Rojava) to those in Syria.

As will become clear throughout the book, for Kurdish women raising their voices and claiming them as their own is both an attractive and a risky undertaking. This has consequences for how I have decided to deal with my interlocutors' identities. While some of the women I encountered were keen to have their names recorded, many others only talked to me on the condition that I would maintain their anonymity. Ultimately, I have decided to err on the side of caution and replace my interlocutors' personal names with pseudonyms except where individuals are publicly well known. This decision has not been easy, particularly where individuals explicitly asked me to mention their names. The anthropological convention of anonymizing interlocutors all too easily contributes to patterns of erasure and renders individuals unable to lay claim to their achievements. At the same time, my interlocutors live in highly precarious situations, saturated with political and gendered forms of violence, which makes it difficult to gauge the long-term consequences of exposure. While choosing anonymity in response is perhaps not ideal, I believe that caution is warranted in light of the potential harms involved.

Given that this book makes an argument about the significance of the voice's sonic form, readers may expect to see the sung narrative that forms the object of the ethnography rendered in musical notation. However, the central genre of this book, the *kilam*, is not well suited to doing so. Its irregular meter and rhythm mean that standard notation is unable to comprehensively capture its acoustic and musical qualities. Not all readers, moreover, may be trained to read musical notation. I have therefore decided to rely on prose in order to convey some of the key aspects of the vocal aesthetics at stake and give readers a sense of the quality of the soundscapes created by my interlocutors' voices. I also rely on transcriptions of kilams' lyrics in order to discuss narrative structure and poetic form where this helps me make my arguments. Transcriptions obviously have their own shortcomings. They fail, for instance, to reflect the live qualities of a performance, and they do not represent sonic characteristics, including patterns of melody and intonation or speed of delivery. Nonetheless, I hope that transcriptions will prove useful for conveying to readers some of the narrative, poetic, and linguistic qualities of my interlocutors' voices.

Well aware that rendering sound in writing can never substitute for the embodied experience of listening, I point interested readers to the online collection of audio(visual) recordings that accompanies this book at www .marleneschafers.com. While I am not able to share all of my fieldwork recordings, the listening examples I have curated online will allow readers to get a better sense of the repertoires described and analyzed in the pages that follow.

Introduction

"Our voices can no longer be hidden," Gazîn proclaimed with firm resolution. "Today it is no longer like it used to be. Now we can say, 'This is me, this is us.' We can show our existence to the world." I was impressed by the proud insistence of this middle-aged Kurdish woman on the power of her voice, particularly since I knew something of what it had cost her to raise it. Gazîn had just been telling me about the lifelong struggle she had waged for her voice—a struggle that had involved major conflicts with her family and wider social circle, confrontations with Turkish state authorities, and that had been beset by violence, loss, and fear. I had met Gazîn only a few days earlier at a women's demonstration in the center of Wan (Tk. Van), a sprawling Kurdish town of several hundred thousand inhabitants situated at the eastern edge of the Turkish republic. Organized by a coalition of local women's rights organizations, the demonstration was held to protest the increasing number of femicides in Turkey, one of which had just recently occurred in a neighboring province. It took place on a warm evening in late August 2011 in a small public park right in the center of town. At the rally, Gazîn proudly introduced herself to me as the director of a newly founded NGO supporting women singers and artists and invited me to come visit their office sometime soon. When I did so the following week, I found myself welcomed into two tiny rooms inside a bland and dusty office block just off one of Wan's busy intersections in the city center. While the front room, with its large black desk and office chair, conveyed a sense of official business, in the back room to which Gazîn directed me we sat on low benches draped with colorful rugs and cushions, arranged around a large millstone and several copper jugs. Historical Kurdish women's dresses with vibrant patterns adorned the walls, alongside framed images of iconic female singers.

That day, the association's office was bustling with visitors, mainly elderly men who prided themselves on being knowledgeable *dengbêj*s. At once poets and singers, historians and storytellers, Kurdish dengbêjs perform different forms of sung narrative, including epic tales of war and battle, stories of tragic love and courageous deeds, and personal accounts of painful experience. Sipping tea from small tulip-shaped glasses, the men shared local news, discussed Kurdish politics—including the recent collapse of yet another ceasefire agreement between the Turkish state and the guerrilla forces of the Kurdistan Workers' Party (Partiya Karkerên Kurdistanê, PKK)—and challenged each other to perform one or another oral tradition. Gazîn, though, wanted to take me away from this busy scene, keen to confide in a more intimate setting how her own life as a singer had unfolded. It was thus in the quieter back room that I was to learn about the trajectory that had taken Gazîn to where she stood today, the proud director of a freshly inaugurated NGO, a woman who felt she no longer had to hide her voice. Gazîn was one of the few female dengbêjs to reach this level of success. By the time we met, she had recorded over a dozen albums and produced several video clips to accompany her most popular pieces, which were regularly broadcast on various Kurdish TV channels. She was frequently invited to perform at festivals across the Kurdish region and had even traveled to France to give a concert. These were major achievements for a woman who hailed from a rural background, had not attended school, and had learned to make do with the most modest of economic means while raising five children.

Getting to this point had clearly not been easy. As Gazîn explained to me, in northern Kurdistan many people considered it immodest ('*eyb*, *şerm*) for a woman's singing voice to be heard in public. Even though many women knew the rich repertoires of oral tradition that are today widely celebrated as key aspects of Kurdish cultural heritage, performing them in public was often met with severe opposition from families, kin, and the wider society. Zehra, a younger female singer of Kurdish pop genres who had joined our conversation, agreed. She recounted how she had published her first cassettes under a pseudonym for fear of her family's reaction. When they nonetheless discovered her pursuit of a singing career, they pressured her to give it up. Gazîn similarly spoke of years of fierce arguments and conflict with her family over her public appearances.

In addition, there were the political consequences. In a country where Kurdish linguistic and cultural expression has been suppressed for decades, Kurdish voices continue to attract suspicion and surveillance. Although the formal ban on the Kurdish language was lifted in the early 1990s, when I conducted field research for this book two decades later Kurdish sounds remained heavily policed, perpetually suspected of indicating disloyalty toward the Turkish nation. Outside Turkey's Kurdish heartlands, the sounds of Kurdish easily incited public anger, while Turkish courts, for their part, regularly issued rulings declaring spoken or sung Kurdish a threat to what the constitution proclaims as the indivisible unity of the nation. Becoming audible in and through Kurdish was a risky undertaking in Turkey. Gazîn knew this only too well: at the time we met, she had been freshly indicted on the grounds that two public performances of hers constituted acts of promoting separatism.

Against these stories of patriarchal restriction, political subjection, and different forms of violent disciplining, Gazîn, Zehra, and the other women at the singers' association displayed remarkable perseverance. Determined to raise their voices despite all opposition, they stubbornly negotiated with the authority figures in their extended families to let them participate in the association's activities. They risked not only straining domestic relations but also legal sanctioning to perform at concerts and on television. Notwithstanding the precarity of their everyday lives and the challenges of having to run multigenerational households with modest financial means, they dreamed of fame and popularity, of being celebrated on stage and screen, and of the financial gain that such fame might bring. They also insisted that not being able to raise their voices would condemn them to suffocate amid experiences of restraint and memories of loss. And despite the routine frustrations they encountered—when once again a husband or father-in-law intervened to prevent them from attending a performance, a music producer withheld their rightful profits, or yet another promised concert invitation was withdrawn—they radiated a resolute optimism. As women and as Kurds, they knew they had important stories to tell. The time had come for them to raise their voices.

In the stories that Gazîn, Zehra, and the other women at the association told me about their passionate investment in their voices and the struggles they had waged in order to raise them, the voice functioned as a powerful index of emancipation and empowerment. In a context rife with political subjection and gendered disciplining, it held outstanding liberatory potential. Freely circulating voices signaled free subjects, unencumbered in their urge to express their desires, opinions, and inner selves. Such voices spoke of social progress and political advancement, suggesting avenues for overcoming both personal and collective trauma. They promised forms of recognition, participation, and authority from which my interlocutors, both as Kurds and as women, had mostly been excluded.[1]

The voice constitutes a powerful trope promising empowerment and recognition not only in Kurdistan, of course. In many parts of the world, marginalized, disadvantaged, and dispossessed subjects are regularly encouraged to "raise their voice" as a means of asserting their identity, engaging in public discourse, and participating in political decision-making. Many feminist, development, and human rights activists are deeply invested in measures that seek to give voice to the ostensibly silenced so as to bolster their agency and ensure their participation in social and political life. Mental health practitioners and transitional justice activists encourage the voicing of personal experiences of trauma, hardship, and suffering as a path toward personal healing and societal reconciliation (Schlichter 2014; Slotta 2015). In documentary films, we encounter the voices of the disenfranchised as a token of their belonging to a common humanity (Rangan 2017b), while the foundations of representative democracies tell us that decision-making should rely on us citizens voicing our opinions and sentiments in the public sphere (Habermas 1990).

Tying political and personal agency, recognition, and participation to "having a voice," liberal discourse and practice invest the voice with immense emancipatory promise, political value, and ethical weight. *Voices That Matter* sets out to examine some of the consequences of this contemporary valorization of the voice as a route to empowerment and agency. Following Daniel Fisher (2016), I approach representational politics as a framework that powerfully incites minoritarian subjects to raise their voices, noting that such politics render the voice at once an object of desire and aspiration for the marginalized, a linchpin of subaltern resistance, and a site of moral anxiety, governmental intervention, and bureaucratic management. Based on an ethnographic account of Kurdish women's struggle for voice in contemporary Turkey, I argue that "raising one's voice" is not always or necessarily empowering but constitutes an endeavor that is equally shaped by risk, dilemma, and contradiction. What is more, an equation of voice with agency and empowerment fails to adequately capture the effects of the hailing to voice that I observe. These effects reach beyond the question of whether and how voices empower those who enunciate them, or represent the subaltern who speaks. They also inhere in the ways that contemporary politics of voice shape the contour and flow of vocal sound and thereby determine how voices affect those they encounter.

Like the voices of so many other women of the Middle East, those of Kurdish women, too, have long constituted an object of speculation, suspicion, and intervention. From a Western perspective, Kurdish women form part of that broad category of the "muslimwoman" so astutely described by miriam cooke (2007), whose alleged silence and invisibility function as markers of her ostensible suppression by her own culture. Within Turkey,

Kurdish women have similarly been portrayed as silenced and oppressed by the "backward" forces of Kurdish tribalism, mobilizing generations of Turkish state feminists to come to their rescue over the course of the last century. When Kurdish women have disrupted these tropes of silencing and oppression, they have been met with responses ranging from surprise and admiration to violence and exposure. Following the massive capture of territory by the so-called Islamic State across Iraq and Syria in 2014, for instance, Kurdish women gained much international attention and praise for fighting against and eventually defeating the Islamist group in northern Syria, displaying a resolve many would not have expected.[2] In Turkey, on the other hand, Kurdish women who use their voices to speak out against discrimination and injustice are regularly disciplined for their "excessive" agency through a variety of legal and extralegal means (Üstündağ 2019b).

Whether the audibility of Kurdish women's voices is celebrated as proof of their bearers' emancipation from restrictive custom and tradition or condemned as evidence of their transgressive agency, implicit in such evaluations stands the assumption that voices inherently represent the will and identity of those who enunciate them. It is this assumption that allows us to see in the circumscription of Middle Eastern women's voices an act of suppression, and in their becoming audible a sign of empowerment. As I have come to realize over the course of researching and writing this book, however, voices do not in any inherent or universal way represent the interiority of those who pronounce them. In the Kurdish contexts where I conducted research, voices often became detached from the subjects who uttered them, expressing not the emotions of the self but those of others, for example, or featuring like a service that could be commissioned and exchanged rather than being tied to a singular individual and their intimate experiences. How, this prompts me to ask, has the voice evolved from a vehicle that is in principle detachable from its bearer into one that is read as the direct expression of the self and as proof of their agency? And what are the consequences of this positioning?

When highlighting that in Kurdish contexts voices occasionally mean or do things that are not easily captured by dominant frameworks that understand voice primarily as an index of the self and its identity, my aim is not to map out a space of anthropological difference or radical alterity. Doing so would risk casting as inauthentic the desires for voice that women like Gazîn and Zehra so vividly expressed, brushing them aside as mere mimicry of Euro-American ideologies of voice, self, and agency. Yet these desires were all too real, as were the consequences my interlocutors faced when they set out to pursue them. The task I set myself in this book, therefore, is to acknowledge and honor my interlocutors' insistent desires for voice, without either dismissing them as inauthentic or naturalizing the equation of voice with agency that they rely upon. Instead of taking this equation for granted, I ask what social, historical, and political forces have turned voices into the objects of women's desire and aspiration—and into sites of moral anxiety and violent disciplining. In this way, I seek not only to understand the hopes and expectations with which women like Gazîn and Zehra embarked upon the struggle to raise their voices, but also to critically interrogate why it is that their hopes were so routinely disappointed.

It is important to underline that women like Gazîn, Zehra, and others you will meet over the course of this book are not in any way representative of Kurdish women in general. Kurdish women harbor a range of different desires and aspirations, and a good number of the women I encountered showed little interest in making their voices heard in public. Nevertheless, I believe that the women who did can shed important light on the emergence of new imaginations of voice and self in a context where "having a voice" has become ever more crucial for social and political recognition. As such, they have much to teach us not only about the promises and opportunities that the voice holds in the contemporary world, but also about the conflicts and disappointments it can engender.

Vocal Form, Sound, and Mediation

Gazîn's and Zehra's passionate investment in Kurdish women's voices as a means of empowerment and liberation revolved in many ways around the capacity of those voices to represent the interiority, will, and agency of their bearers. Where voices stand for the innermost self of those who pronounce them, silencing or circumscribing voices easily becomes tantamount to suppressing subjects and their desires, while ensuring voices' free circulation secures social progress and liberal advancement. The vocal practices that actually unfolded in the rooms of the association for women singers that Gazîn had founded, however, suggested that voices did a whole range of other things apart from (or in addition to) functioning as indicators of their enunciators' will and agency and as a benchmark of their emancipation and empowerment. As I spent many hours during my fieldwork listening to the voices of dengbêjs singing about experiences of hardship, pain, and tragedy at the association and beyond, I observed how voices had the power not just to *represent* women's agency or Kurdish culture and history but also to viscerally *affect* their audiences because of how the voices of these performers reverberated, trembled, wailed. These were voices capable of moving listeners to tears, making them shiver, or, as local idioms put it, "burning their hearts," thanks to the trembling of a vowel or the weight of a poetic image. They provided a means to express not only one's own sorrows but also those of others, making pain travel between bodies and beyond the boundaries of individual subjects. If I was to understand the power of Kurdish women's voices, it became clear, it would not suffice to frame them solely as indicators of women's resistance against patriarchal restraint and political repression or as a means of therapeutic healing from traumatic experience. I would also have to take into account the social labor they carry out in Kurdish everyday life because of how they sound, move, and circulate. And I would have to understand how these two aspects relate to each other: how do voices' sonic contours and aesthetic qualities render them more (or less) amenable to representing the interiority and self of those who pronounce them, allowing them to become powerful metaphors for personal agency and political authority?

To develop a conceptual grip on the ways in which voices become socially consequential not just because of what they represent or signify but because of how they sound and circulate, I draw on the work of anthropologists who have sought to destabilize the familiar idea of the voice as a natural and universal index of agency and empowerment. As anthropologist Amanda Weidman (2014a, 39) has argued, this idea stands at the heart of a distinctly modern ideology of voice that relies on two implicit assumptions. The first is that the voice constitutes a direct and authentic expression of the interior self, assuring self-presence and truth. As Miyako Inoue writes, this is an understanding of "I speak, therefore I am," where the act of speaking is equated with the expression of human agency and where "the speaker's voice guarantees her full presence 'here and now'" (2003, 180). The sovereignty of the subject is thus founded on the resonance of her voice, such that "having a voice" becomes an index of personal will, intention, and authority. The second, linked assumption holds that the voice functions as a transparent channel of communication whose acoustic form is inconsequential to the content transmitted. Only once vocal form is effaced in this way does it become possible to read the voice as a direct emanation of the individual self, its will, and its agency.

Historical and anthropological scholarship on voice has shown that these assumptions are intimately tied to contexts of (post)colonial modernity and their characteristic understanding of the self as endowed with a bounded, private interiority and the privileged seat of agency. While according to the philosopher Adriana Cavarero (2005) the privileging of vocal content over form has marked much of Western philosophy since Plato, it was during the European Enlightenment that the privileging of signifying speech over sonic vocality solidified. As Leigh Eric Schmidt (2000) demonstrates, during this period a concerted reeducation of the senses turned voices from highly affective, spiritual, and sensual objects into tame and technical vehicles of communication. Since then, the primacy of meaningful content over vocal sound has become foundational to power relations in the (post)colonial world (Bauman and Briggs 2003). The result has been lasting hierarchies between "civilized" and "barbaric," "cultured" and "carnal" citizens that oppose the "rational" speech of imperial and national elites to the seemingly meaningless or excessive sounds produced by colonized, black, and working-class populations.[3] Women's voices, too, have often been heard as saturated with excessive emotion, playing into long-standing associations of female gender with emotionality, hysteria, and even madness, in opposition to male reason.[4] Under contemporary conditions of neoliberalism, moreover, voices feature no longer just as vehicles of individual will and rational self-expression as they do in classic liberal formulations, but in a context that prizes transparency and immediacy they have become increasingly potent signs of personal sincerity and authenticity.[5]

If the eclipse of vocal form is what sustains modern ideas about the voice as an expression of self and agency, this eclipse is also what founds the kinds of representational politics that routinely hail minoritarian subjects—including Kurdish women—to voice. Within these political regimes, the voice can promise political agency and authority, social recognition and personal fulfillment, only because it is seen as a direct emanation of the individual self, while its sonic contours, lyrical density, or aesthetic elaboration matters little. What this also means is that if we are to critically interrogate such regimes and their consequences, we need to return to *voice as form*—precisely what this book sets out to do. Attending to voice as form means holding at bay powerful notions of voice as a representational trope, indicative of agency, will, and presence. It means shifting attention from vocal content (what voices say) and symbolism (what voices represent) to vocal form (how they do so) in order to give prominence to the social labor that voices routinely carry out as they travel and circulate, echo and reverberate, chant and tremble. And it means interrogating how vocal form sustains and nourishes particular kinds of subjects and communities and the political formations they inhabit.

To understand how vocal form relates to the making of subjects, politics, and communities, I have found it helpful to think about the voice as a "thick event" (Eidsheim 2019) that is at once a material, vibrational sound object and "a key representational trope for social position and power" (Feld and Fox 1994, 26; see also Feld et al. 2004, 341).[6] What the anthropological literature teaches us is that the relationship between these dimensions is culturally and historically malleable. This means that we cannot take for granted that voices always indicate the self and authority of those who pronounce them.

Quite to the contrary, the voice as a sonic, material object or force may relate to speakers, their selves, and bodies in a multiplicity of ways. Take spirit possession, for example, where a possessed person finds that their voice is no longer their own but has been usurped by a spirit speaking through them. In those instances, voice and self become radically detached from one another, often enabling the voicing of issues that defy public scripts or entail uncomfortable truths.[7] Linguistic features may have similar effects. Wolof speakers in Senegal, for instance, employ several different speech registers that vary in tempo, pitch, and intonation depending on the social status of the person they interact with (Irvine 1990). Rather than expressing themselves through a singular and immutable voice, Wolof speakers thus strategically handle a variety of different voices, indicating less a stable identity than fluid positionings of the self. Some even renounce speaking altogether and instead employ griots (storytellers) to communicate for them. In Kurdish contexts, too, musicians regularly become the mouthpiece through which wedding guests utter praise for the party's hosts (Çakır 2019, 197–236), and can be drawn on to carry out arguments on behalf of their patrons (Christensen 2002, 747–748)—constellations of bodies, speech, and intention that can be described as forms of "delegated voice" (Keane 1991). Delegation is also at work in South Indian Tamil cinema, where the voices of actors seen on screen have historically been animated by playback singers, engaging in "a play of matching and mismatching" sonic voices with onscreen bodies that disrupts Euro-American ideals of voice-body unity (Weidman 2021, 2).

Following Erving Goffman (1979), we may understand these various instances of voice delegation as moments when the performer or animator of a speech act does not concur with its author. As Goffman notes, Western folk models of speech presume these roles to converge in a single speaker, which is what underwrites understandings of voice as an immediate expression of the self. In the instances above, by contrast, the voice emerges as a resource open to inhabitation and use by others, highlighting that, as Webb Keane writes with reference to Mikhail Bakhtin's work (1981a), "there is no single and singular distribution of 'voices' over bodies" (1997b, 229).

Such ethnographic material is useful for unhinging the easy association between voice and self that modern ideologies of voice propose and that we tend to take for granted. It helps denaturalize the idea that voices inherently represent their bearers. And it underlines that changing vocal practices can engender transformations in subjectivity. When Christian missionaries in the Philippines forbade the profuse, indirect articulations of Ilongot oratory in favor of speech forms considered to be more sincere, for example, Ilongot men began to see themselves less as subjects motivated by external passions than as submissive to divine and state law (Rosaldo 1984). Similarly, the rise in popularity of music reality TV shows in South India where singers' bodies are now visible as the source of their own voice hints at new imaginations of subjectivity that increasingly center around ideas about sincere expression and authentic representation (Weidman 2021). In Sri Lanka, on the other hand, mental health practitioners encouraging women to unambiguously articulate their experiences of the civil war have unwittingly produced vocal subjects whose unprecedented outspokenness has risked upsetting strategies of evasive speech that previously helped contain violence (Argenti-Pillen 2003). And when people in India and Ghana converse and engage with hallucinatory voices rather than trying to suppress them as psychopathological disturbances, as is often the case in North American contexts, the potential of these voices to unsettle a person's sense of self radically diminishes (Luhrmann et al. 2015).

Drawing on these insights, this book is based on the premise that vocal form and practice—how voices sound, how they circulate, and how they are employed—are crucial to the fashioning of different kinds of selves and of the worlds they inhabit. In making this argument, I take my cues from literature that has argued for the power of aesthetic form to shape subjects and their senses, generate embodied habits, and structure experience.[8] As Jacques Rancière (2010) asserts, the aesthetic needs to be recognized as a politically consequential site of struggle over what he calls the "distribution of the sensible," organizing forms of perception by regulating what becomes available to the senses and how. In this vein, scholarship in sound, music, and voice studies has convincingly demonstrated that sound is not simply a passive surface on which meaning becomes inscribed, but that its acoustic qualities actively shape cultural practice and political formations.[9] Charles Hirschkind (2006), for instance, has argued that soundscapes are crucial for sustaining political regimes like secularism by forming the kinds of subjects that these formations demand and rely upon (see also Furani 2012). As Hirschkind demonstrates, in Egypt sound consequently becomes a site of political struggle, as communities seeking to challenge the state's official secularism invest in curating sonic environments they see as more conducive to forms of Islamic ethics and subjectivity. In South Korea, on the other hand, Evangelical Christians painstakingly cultivate the "clean"-sounding voice of Western classical music in the attempt to embody and foster the nation's progress and prosperity (Harkness 2013), while in South Africa the sound of hybrid local genres like *kwaito* contributes to shaping the national community as one that lacks any racial or ethnic essence that could durably define it (Steingo 2017).

In coming to an understanding of the social potency and political significance of vocal sound, I am particularly indebted to feminist scholars who have demonstrated that voices play a crucial role in the making of gendered, racialized, and classed subjects.[10] Think, for instance, about the catcalls and whistles that routinely penetrate the aural space of women and nonnormatively gendered people when they move in public and how these sounds leave a lasting impact on self-awareness and bodily comportment (Lentjes 2016). Or consider digital assistants like Amazon's Alexa or Apple's Siri and the way in which their female voices nurture and fortify ideas about women's inherent submissiveness (UNESCO and EQUALS Skills Coalition 2019). Voices also play an active role in perpetuating and naturalizing ideas about race. For example, black opera singers in the US produce what is considered a black timbre or tone of voice not because this is in any way inherent to their voices, but because it is expected and even actively encouraged by teachers and audiences (Eidsheim 2019). Vocal sound thus both reflects and, at every instance of performance, (re)produces gendered and racialized hierarchies. This (re)production of social difference relies on the sonic and material qualities of voices congealing into recognizable vocal types—what linguistic anthropologists call registers of voice—which then become mapped onto specific bodies or social positions (Agha 2005; Harkness 2013). Given that the voice is a product of the body, different vocal registers easily appear to be grounded within a seemingly unchanging biology and in this way contribute to making racial, gendered, and classed differences seem natural and inevitable.

The insights produced by scholarship in sound and media studies, finally, remind us that the productive quality of vocal form is inseparable from the specifics of its mediation.[11] As different media direct and transmit vibrations in different ways, they create landscapes of differential vocal affordance, allowing voices to have certain effects while foreclosing others. Scholars have thus shown how sound technologies like the gramophone have contributed to the formation of modernity's private, self-contained individual thanks to the isolated listening practices they enable (Sterne 2003), how the radio's capacity of mass broadcasting has sustained and shaped how communities are imagined and experienced (e.g., Spitulnik 1997; Moorman 2019), and how amplification technologies like the microphone have fostered new forms of public intimacy by allowing for voices to be heard with an unprecedented degree of proximity (Stokes 2009).

Voices That Matter draws on these insights in its interrogation of contemporary politics that promise empowerment and agency to those who raise their voices. It asks not simply whether such politics successfully grant voice to the marginalized but interrogates how they foster specific kinds of subjects and communities because of the vocal form they encourage and demand. The question, in other words, is not simply whether the subaltern can speak

(Spivak 1988), but how subaltern voices sound when they do so and what kinds of social labor they are consequently able to carry out. The promises that representational politics hold out to those who raise their voices rely on the assumption that those voices represent the desires, ideas, and opinions of those who utter them. But if, as the anthropological record teaches us, voices are not naturally or universally representational vehicles of the self, what does it take to make them so? And what happens when disadvantaged subjects like Kurdish women seek to access the promises promoted by representational politics through actually raising their voices? Laying claim to voices as representational vehicles, this book demonstrates, lastingly influences how voices sound and circulate, how they impact bodies and affect listeners. If voices are socially and politically consequential because of their aesthetic form and sonic materiality, then such changes to vocal form are significant, heralding new ways of imagining self, other, and community.

In taking such an approach, this book brings a radically new perspective to the study of oral genres and performances in the Middle East, a rich and long-standing field of scholarly inquiry. Scholars in this field have long emphasized the social significance of oral repertoires. Orally performed poetry, epic narratives, and historiography, they have shown, play a crucial role in constructing and upholding social and political authority, in shaping moral values, and in fostering gendered subjectivities.[12] While scholars have paid much attention to the dynamic nature of oral genres in the face of social, technological, and political change, they have approached these genres primarily with a focus on their language and content as well as their social and performance contexts.[13] By contrast, the focus on voice as I propose it here—one that recognizes the voice as both a sonic-material object and as a metaphor dense with value and meaning—allows me to situate oral genres and the transformations they are undergoing within the broader contours of contemporary politics of representation and the ways in which these politics valorize, discipline, and elicit voice. In this way, I am able to approach oral genres as sites where selves are imagined, hopes nurtured, and anxieties registered, recognizing them to be "*productive* of particular subjects or subject positions, rather than merely *reflective* of social structures or *expressive* of identities" (Weidman 2006, 12; original emphasis).

Female Vocality in the Middle East

As I set out to chronicle, understand, and interrogate Kurdish women's struggle for voice, I am approaching a highly charged, if not overdetermined subject matter. The voices of women in the Middle East have long constituted an object of fascination, suspicion, and anxiety not only in academic scholarship but also in public and political debate. The image of the silenced Muslim woman, her voice curtailed by religious doctrine, retrogressive tradition, and male authority, is a pervasive one. It informs mainstream discourse in many Euro-American contexts and has long echoed through the narratives of secular-liberal elites in the Middle East. It works to delineate progress from tradition, modern from backward, agency from suppression—often in ways that sustain persistent class and racial divides. And because of the way in which it upholds the voice as an index of agency, empowerment, and progress, it has also played a key role in making the voice a central site of intervention for various political, activist, and scholarly projects. "Saving" Muslim women in this way becomes a question of giving them voice and encouraging them to speak up.[14]

But these ideas have of course not gone unchallenged. Feminist scholars, in particular, have invested much energy in confronting simplistic ideas about passive and submissive Muslim women by providing evidence for the depth and complexity of Muslim women's lives and the active roles they take in their communities. Much of this pushback has been framed as an attempt at restoring women's voices, with "voice" featuring in such accounts often as a largely unreflected placeholder for women's ideas, opinions, and desires. Perhaps most influential within this body of scholarship has been Lila Abu-Lughod's seminal ethnography, *Veiled Sentiments* (1986), which demonstrated that even though women of the Bedouin tribe of the Awlad 'Ali in Egypt might appear subdued or silent to an outsider, they actually participate in a highly elaborate culture of oral poetry. In her analysis of this poetic discourse, Abu-Lughod looks in great detail at how and to what effect Awlad 'Ali women use their voices, focusing in particular on how their poetry expresses sentiments that defy the dominant moral codes of the community. Cihan Ahmetbeyzade (2007) has approached the voices of displaced Kurdish women living in Istanbul in a similar vein, interpreting their speech, including the silences that permeate it, as moments of resistance against the patriarchal regimes of both family and state. As much as women's actual voices stand at the forefront of analysis in such works, they gain analytical traction primarily as oppositional discourse, indicative of women's capacity to resist hegemonic frameworks. Once their voices are approached as such, it becomes possible to look for the metaphorical voice of Muslim women even where no actual voices are at stake. Documenting the considerable influence Muslim women have on the social life of their communities in ways that are not always visible or audible in public—for instance, thanks to the roles they take up in domestic and all-female spaces—has consequently been a key scholarly arena for projects seeking to restore Muslim women's "voices" and provide evidence of their agency.[15] The impulse to restore women's voices has not, of course, been limited to the field of Middle Eastern anthropology alone, but has driven much of feminist anthropology more generally. That the journal of the Association for Feminist Anthropology used to be called *Voices* is telling in this regard.

As critics have pointed out, however, there is a risk inherent in attempts aimed at excavating the voices of the marginalized, including those of women, both within and without the academy. Indian historian Mrinalini Sinha finds that such undertakings easily reify subaltern subjects, assuming a singular voice to match a singular subject as if that voice "was always there, simply waiting to be expressed" (1996, 483). Instead, she proposes focusing on how subject positions are created at the intersection of axes like gender, race, class/caste, nation, and sexuality and how these intersections allow subjects to take up voice in specific ways. Gayatri Chakravorty Spivak's influential essay "Can the Subaltern Speak?" (1988) leveled a similar critique against scholars of the Subaltern Studies Project who she thought risked essentializing colonized Indian subjects in the attempt to recover their voices from within the British colonial archives. The search for an authentically defiant voice of the colonized, Spivak argued, only ends up silencing the subaltern subject twice over by fixing it in its very subalternity. As historian Luise White put it in the context of African historiography, "the idea that a pure voice can be distilled and disembedded from the struggles of colonial experiences is itself problematic" because it assumes "that colonial African language and thought and imagination were not sullied by the categories and constructs of the oppressors" (2000, 280), when in fact, as her work goes on to show, realities were much more complex.[16]

These critiques have been immensely helpful for grasping how well-meaning projects that set out to "give voice" to the marginalized may end up further delimiting marginalized lives, sacrificing complexity in the search for unsullied authenticity. As Amanda Weidman (2003, 195–196) notes, however, while this critical literature has done crucial work in order to deconstruct ideas about the subaltern subject as a stable and fixed entity, it has stopped short of submitting the voice to equal scrutiny. In the accounts of both those who seek to recover women's voices and those who warn against doing so, the voice itself remains unexamined, largely taken for granted as a shorthand for the political will and personal agency of the subject who bears it. Annette Schlichter (2011) describes this refusal to acknowledge the voice beyond its semantic content and metaphorical positioning as a form of "phonophobia," which she traces back to a poststructuralist discomfort with the oral as a false guarantor of presence, truth, and sincerity, perhaps most famously articulated by Jacques Derrida (1998b). The result, Schlichter argues, is a side-lining of the material, sonic voice in poststructuralist literature that reduces voice to a metaphorical placeholder. Yet as linguistic anthropologist Susan Gal (1989) noted over three decades ago, it is only once we investigate women's actual speech practices alongside voice in a metaphorical sense that we can begin to move away from the idea of an undifferentiated, homogeneous "woman's voice" toward the acknowledgment of women's ambiguous, even contradictory speech practices that challenge dichotomies of voice versus silence, resistance versus oppression. Such an approach is useful because it allows us to submit the relation between metaphorical and sonic aspects of voice to analytical scrutiny, raising questions about how both vocal meaning and form are historically, politically, and culturally constructed.

Voices That Matter follows these leads. Rather than restoring voice to Kurdish women in an attempt to provide proof of their agency, I thus ask how Kurdish women's voices have come to stand for the will and agency of their bearers in the first place. While much critical literature has distrusted the voice for its failure to represent the full complexities of subjectivity, I ask how voices contribute to shaping subjects and the lifeworlds they inhabit. By bringing into view how voices may have social effects not just because of how they represent the will and interiority of those who utter them but because of how their sounds and reverberations fashion subjects and communities, this book hopes to move beyond discussions about whether or not Kurdish women have agency (or "voice"). Instead, it inquires how narratives that celebrate voice as an expression of agency and empowerment have invested Kurdish voices with political value and ethical weight, turned them into objects of aspiration as much as debate, and shaped their acoustic qualities and circulatory paths.

What this also means is that I do not cast aside ideals like agency, empowerment, and liberation as somehow alien to the lifeworlds of my interlocutors. Saba Mahmood's (2005) work on pious women's groups in Egypt has perhaps been most influential in pointing to the historical situatedness of these concepts, arguing that we cannot assume that desires for liberation and empowerment are shared by all women. In contrast to Mahmood, however, I find that my interlocutors do not embrace an alternative ethical domain, where freedom or empowerment would constitute irrelevant ideals. My interlocutors also did not seek to remain anonymous as did the Bedouin women Lila Abu-Lughod (1986) worked with, for whom the formulaic expressions of oral poetry provided a welcome screen to hide their identities. Women like Gazîn and Zehra, by contrast, had little intention to remain hidden. To them, public audibility held liberatory potential and promised social progress. Their investments in these promises cannot simply be brushed aside as inauthentic or self-deceptive. As Shahrzad Mojab (2021, 10–11) has argued, the experience of Kurdish women cannot be delinked from histories of patriarchy, nationalism, capitalism, and imperialism and the aspirations they have engendered, which is what approaches that cast Muslim lifeworlds as a radical alternative to Western liberal modernity risk doing (Savcı 2021, 3–5).

In this book I take my interlocutors' desires for voice seriously by asking what forces have nourished and nurtured them, inquiring how they are lived and expressed, and interrogating how they foster new dilemmas and vulnerabilities.[17] Such a perspective allows me to grasp contemporary contestations around Kurdish women's voices—including the disciplining and violence experienced by many of my interlocutors—not in terms of cultural or religious difference, but as a consequence of how novel aspirations toward public voice, fostered by representational politics and ideas about voice as empowerment, challenge long-standing patriarchal concerns about female exposure in heterosocial spaces.

While subsequent chapters will explore these aspirations and hopes, anxieties and contestations, in some detail, at this point it will be useful to briefly sketch some of the cultural-historical parameters within which women's voices sound and acquire meaning in Kurdish contexts. The anthropological record suggests that how voice is valued and allocated in Kurdish communities is often tied to social status, with gender playing one role among other social markers such as age, marital status, political authority, and economic standing. All-male social gatherings in rural contexts, for instance, often follow "a strict order of speech governed by people's respective statuses" (Çakır 2019, 125), meaning that younger men of lower status would typically choose not to raise their voices in front of men occupying more powerful positions. In the past, newly married women similarly refrained from raising their voices in front of superiors in the household, including their fathers-in-law and other male in-laws, availing themselves of children as mouthpieces when necessary (Grabolle-Çeliker 2013, 195). Only as women gained in age and standing, especially by bearing children, did they also gain in voice, becoming entitled to speak up in front of male family members. Restrictions on voice thus mirror patriarchal hierarchies that accord precedence to seniority and male gender, although it is important to acknowledge that these priorities continually shift as they are challenged, reinforced, and reinvented.[18]

The audibility and circulation of voices are also related to patterns of gendered socializing. Kurdish women's voices circulate with more ease within all-female spheres than they do in gender-mixed contexts, where women may choose to stay silent or speak with subdued voice to protect their modesty and social standing (Grabolle-Çeliker 2013, 202–203). In fact, the more a context is marked by forms of male stranger sociality, the more the audibility of women's voices is likely to provoke moral anxieties, which would typically be expressed through a vocabulary of (im)modesty or shame ('eyb, şerm). Importantly, judgments about the moral dangers incurred by women's voices tend to be less concerned with what those voices pronounce than with the fact of audibility as such. This highlights that what is at stake in circumscribing the audibility of women's voices is less a form of silencing personal will and interiority than the maintenance of a hierarchical social order. Here, voices become circumscribed not necessarily because they are an instrument of personal self-expression, but because they function as an indicator of social status. From this perspective, the restriction of Kurdish women's voices to domestic or all-female realms represents less an attempt at subduing women's individual selves than a means to maintain and reinforce patriarchal hierarchies of gendered sociality.

And yet, in northern Kurdistan today, circumscriptions on women's voices *are* increasingly understood as repressing personal will and individual selves. These more recent understandings of voice are intimately connected to how processes of nation-state building and modernization have unfolded in the region over roughly the last century, and how they have radically shifted patterns of gendered sociality. Before the nineteenth century, much of everyday life in the Ottoman Empire and neighboring countries like Qajar Iran occurred in homosocial contexts.[19] This meant that women's bodies would become visible—and their voices audible—mostly in all-female spaces. When women ventured into gender-mixed realms, particularly in urban contexts, they typically veiled their bodies and restrained their vocality so as not to compromise patriarchal standards of female respectability.[20] But under the influence of aggressive European encroachment and homegrown nationalisms starting in the nineteenth century, homosociality was increasingly perceived as a sign of backwardness, while modernity came to be associated with gender-mixed socializing. As a result, the public exposure of women's bodies—including their voices—has become a central terrain on which debates about modernity and tradition, progress and backwardness, are carried out across the Middle East.[21]

In Turkey, the Kemalist regime that took over the country following the disintegration of the Ottoman Empire after World War I swiftly set about according women a visible position in public life, prohibiting the wearing of the veil in public institutions, promoting gender-mixed forms of socializing, and encouraging women to enter education and the labor market. At the same time, however, women remained associated with domestic homemaking and motherhood, while patriarchal norms about women's sexual modesty remained in place.[22] While efforts at making women's bodies visible in new ways have been recognized as central to the making of Turkey's gendered modernity— coming to the fore perhaps most clearly in discussions about the veil[23]—less attention has been paid to how the audibility of women's voices has been equally central for delineating modernity from tradition, progress from ret- rogression. The modern woman of Turkey's urban middle classes has thus distinguished herself from her "backward" sisters in the countryside not only because she is not veiled but also because she is ostensibly not silenced. Importantly, these distinctions have from the outset been highly racialized. "Traditional" gender relations in Kurdish communities—including Kurdish women's assumed lack of voice—have long served as evidence of an alleged Kurdish incompatibility with the terms of Turkish modernity, legitimizing state policies ranging from violent disciplining and discrimination to denial and assimilation.[24] Turkish state feminism's mission to emancipate Kurdish and other rural, "uncivilized" women in this way became "one means of sub- ordinating [them] to the nation-state" (Mojab 2001, 4).

More recently, the task of bringing Kurdish women to voice has been taken on by a burgeoning sphere of civil society organizations, many generously funded by EU and other Western bodies, who call upon Kurdish women to be vocal in the name of mental health and trauma programs, gender main- streaming efforts, and civil society initiatives (Clark 2015; Yıldırım 2021). At the same time, over the last four decades the Kurdish women's movement has worked tirelessly to transform gender relations in Kurdish communities and accord women a central place in public and political life based on left-wing, socialist principles. In this context, too, the audibility of women's voices has featured as a central index of female self-assertion and emancipation, but here paired with a radical critique of both familial and state patriarchy and in the service of collective political structures, rather than individual well-being.[25]

Turkish state feminism, civil society initiatives, and left-wing Kurdish politics may considerably diverge in their ideological convictions and pre- ferred practices when it comes to "the woman question" in northern Kurdis- tan. Yet they are heirs to a shared historical legacy that heralds the audibility of women's voices as a sign of progress, emancipation, and modernity and that considers the gender-mixed public as the central arena where voice-as- agency is affirmed. It is this legacy that powerfully animates the struggles for voice that Kurdish women like Gazîn and her friends wage today and whose consequences this book sets out to explore. By sustaining a focus on vocal form as much as vocal meaning, the chapters that follow seek to document at once the hopes, desires, and aspirations that the voice has come to hold for

Kurdish women, and understand how the promises tied to it are so routinely disappointed. Assuming voice in public, I argue, is less straightforwardly liberating than fraught with vulnerabilities and failure. In this way, *Voices That Matter* provides an ethnographically nuanced critique of assumptions that equate voice with agency and sheds new light on both the thrills and the pitfalls of gaining voice in the contemporary world.

Governing the Kurdish Voice in Turkey

The Kurdish contexts where this book is set have been shaped by a long and rich legacy of expressive orality. In past centuries, written texts often remained on the margins of Kurdish everyday life while oral genres—ranging from epic and heroic narratives to wedding and work songs to jokes and riddles—existed in "superabundance," to invoke early twentieth-century Russian Kurdologist Oleg Vilchevsky (in Allison 2010, 129). But as the social, economic, and political structures of Kurdish communities have massively changed over the last century, such genres have been lastingly transformed.[26] These changes are inextricably linked to the rule that Kurdish communities have been subjected to by the nation-states they find themselves in today—chiefly Turkey, Iran, Iraq, and Syria—and how these states have variously sought to eradicate, exclude, and assimilate Kurdish difference. But they are also, at least in Turkey, related to the more recent revalorization of Kurdish voices within the context of a pluralist politics of representation. In what follows, I briefly outline the historical legacies that have shaped how Kurdish voices become audible in Turkey today. While persecution and oppression are central to this history, maintaining a focus on vocal sound and reverberation allows me to bring into view how Kurdish voices have always contributed to the shaping of subjects and communities, despite the pressures they have been exposed to. As Nancy Rose Hunt has noted in her work on the Belgian Congo, paying attention to the acoustic "releas[es] colonial subjects from being slotted in as the downtrodden, as prey" (2016, 20). This is not to romanticize sound as a domain of unfettered freedom or resistance. Rather, it is an attempt to shed light on the sensory, embodied, and affective contours of belonging and citizenship in the Turkish republic beyond stark dichotomies of voice versus silence (Stokes 2010, 2015).

When Turkish elites set out to craft a national citizenry after the disintegration of the Ottoman Empire following World War I, streamlining the acoustic worlds of the diverse populations that inhabited the territories of the new nation became a central plank in their efforts.[27] The modern Turkish nation was to prove its unity through the homogenization of its citizens' various tongues, rendering the sounds of Turkish a key element in the project of cultivating national citizens and sculpting their affections and loyalties (Jamison 2015). The early history of republican Turkey is, as a result, littered with attempts at containing and subduing Kurdish voices. After the 1915 Armenian genocide and the 1923 Greek-Turkish population exchange, Kurds became the largest non-Turkish community within the country, a fact that exposed their voices to intense governmental scrutiny. Turkish state authorities clearly perceived Kurdish voices as a potent threat to national sovereignty and swiftly moved to contain them, applying a variety of measures from the broader colonial toolbox with which Turkey has ruled over its Kurdish-inhabited eastern provinces (Yarkın 2019).[28]

While outright bans of Kurdish were discussed by Turkish elites as early as 1925 (Hassanpour 1992, 133; Yüksel 2011, 5–10), assimilation soon became a central policy objective. A classified circular issued by the Ministry of Interior in 1930 asserted, for example, that Turkification of languages and customs was considered "an important national duty of all Turks" (Coşkun, Derince, and Uçarlar 2011, 28). Governors were instructed to make sure "Turks speaking foreign dialects" ("Kurds" was a word that did not exist in official Turkish vocabulary) would acquire Turkish as a mother tongue, suggesting as adequate policy measures, among others, the resettlement of Kurdish communities, the Turkification of personal names, the encouragement of interethnic marriage, and the disparagement of local costumes, songs, and dances. In eastern Turkey, some People's Houses (Halk Evleri) associated with the ruling Republican People's Party (Cumhuriyet Halk Partisi, CHP) took to organizing Turkish-speaking competitions that offered oxen as prizes, while others sought to make Turkish literacy classes attractive by handing out gifts and showing films. In the hope that perpetuating Turkish sounds across Kurdish landscapes would increase the uptake of the language, particularly among children, administrators also suggested distributing radios to villagers (Aslan 2015, 66–67).[29]

The voices of Kurdish singers and storytellers—whose repertoires brimmed with accounts of Kurdish autonomous rule and of fierce resistance put up against Ottoman and Turkish forces—were a particular annoyance to Turkish authorities. Folk songs were deemed a dangerous source of Kurdish nationalist sentiment, leading in at least one documented case to their singers' arrest following a clash between Turkish military and Kurdish tribal forces in the 1930s.[30] Accounts from the period even suggest that Turkish soldiers forced dengbêjs to drink kerosene in order to eradicate the threat that their voices posed (Elend 2021, 127). The threat was so potent that it prompted the authorities to extend their reach beyond Turkey's national borders. In 1936, for instance, Turkey's ambassador to the Levant requested that French authorities in Beirut ban gramophone records by the Kurdish dengbêj Said Axayê Cizrawî that had been released in Aleppo and eulogized the 1925 Sheikh Said uprising in Turkey's Diyarbekir (also Amed, Tk. Diyarbakır) region (Yüksel 2011, 92–93). Turkish authorities also carefully monitored Kurdish radio broadcasts abroad, including those by stations in Armenia, Egypt, Iran, and Iraq, and exerted pressure on foreign governments to halt their public broadcasters' Kurdish programs (Elend 2021, 84–85).

The attempt to forge a homogeneous soundscape also entailed a concerted state effort aimed at Turkifying musical repertoires. From the 1920s onward, state institutions began collecting thousands of Greek, Armenian, and Kurdish folk songs from the Anatolian countryside only to Turkify their lyrics and then broadcast them back to the people as their national (read: Turkish) heritage.[31] Decoupled from their original communities, these disembodied tunes became a powerful tool for cultivating a transcendental attachment to the abstract nation (Ahıska 2010, 86). This was a nation where not only the people, but also the land was to sound Turkish. Starting in 1957, non-Turkish toponyms—including the names of villages, rivers, mountains, and other landmarks—were systematically replaced by Turkish versions. By 1978 government commissions had changed more than one-third of all village names in Turkey, a figure that reached up to 91 percent in the Kurdish-inhabited eastern and southeastern provinces (Öktem 2008).

State attempts at containing Kurdish voices only intensified with the military coup d'état of 1980 and the beginning of the PKK's armed insurgency in 1984. The coup brought to power a military junta that systematically eradicated any leftist dissent in the country, jailing and forcing into exile thousands, many of them Kurdish. The 1982 constitution for the first time explicitly prohibited "the expression and dissemination of thought" in any language other than Turkish. The military junta also stipulated that "the mother tongue of all Turkish citizens is Turkish" (Zeydanlıoğlu 2012, 110). Following such legislation, the 1980s saw the systematic destruction of vast amounts of Kurdish printed and recorded material at the hands of state security forces. This was a time when Kurdish music tapes came to circulate clandestinely in the country, smuggled across borders from Iraq, Syria, or Iran to be listened to secretly in blacked-out homes or under the cover of night. It was also a time when many Kurdish families took to burying their collections of Kurdish audiotapes in their backyards for fear of imminent house searches—some to be salvaged later on, others to remain buried forever. In turn, contributing to the circulation of Kurdish voices by purchasing recording equipment, hiding tapes from state authorities, or gifting them to friends or strangers came to be regarded as sacrificial acts (*bedel*) in the service of the Kurdish community (Kuruoğlu and Ger 2015, 223).

Although the language ban was repealed in 1991, the anti-terror legislation that was passed on the same day has effectively continued the ban via other means, further entrenching Kurdish voices in a logic of state security paradigms. Kurdish politicians, singers, and artists are regularly subjected to fines and prison sentences on the grounds that their speaking or performing in Kurdish undermines national unity and connotes support for Kurdish separatism. While Turkish is accepted as a neutral and transparent code of communication, Kurdish indexes identitarian difference, marking speakers as potentially disloyal to the national project (Jamison 2015, 218–219). In Turkey today, Kurdish complexly signifies rurality and social conservatism, while modernity, progress, and urbanity, with all the allure and aspirations these notions evoke, sound categorically Turkish. This has meant, not least, that proficiency in Kurdish keeps declining.[32]

More recently, however, in a seeming reversal of previous policies, Kurdish voices have become an object of systematic bureaucratic elicitation and even state-orchestrated display. Fueled by the EU accession process, in the early 2000s and 2010s Turkey witnessed the opening of private Kurdish-language schools, the founding of Kurdish-language departments at state universities, the establishment of a Kurdish-language public TV channel, and the introduction of Kurdish as an elective at public schools. Kurdish voices were not the only ones that came to enjoy previously unknown presence in public spheres. The years 2008, 2009, and 2010 saw the ruling Justice and Development Party (Adalet ve Kalkınma Partisi, AKP) launch a series of so-called democratic initiatives aimed at improving civil liberties, which led to what some have described as a veritable "memory boom" (Kaya 2015). Books, plays, conferences, museums, documentation projects, and heritage tours devoted to topics including the Armenian genocide, the Greek-Turkish population exchange, and the Kurdish conflict (among others) brought histories and experiences to public attention that had until then been discussed only in hushed tones and through veiled allusions.[33]

Critics have argued, however, that the Turkish government's overtures have largely remained confined to symbolic gesturing while leaving untouched deep-seated structures of inequality and histories of injustice.[34] As Banu Karaca suggests, the state has been soliciting ethnic and religious difference in the attempt to shore up an "aestheticized notion of multiculturalism" (2013, 167) that remains largely devoid of real political commitment to changing underlying power relations (Ayata and Hakyemez 2013). Even though Alevi ritual, for instance, is now publicly permissible, it can be performed only as long as it is framed as a matter of cultural tradition rather than as politically consequential religious difference (Tambar 2010, 2014). And while Kurdish singers might be celebrated on public television as evidence of Turkey's cultural diversity, state authorities still refuse to recognize Kurdish—native tongue to millions of Turkish citizens—as a language of public conduct and education. This lack of commitment has become abundantly clear as Turkey has seen the rise of an increasingly authoritarian regime intent on repressing all political dissent over the course of the last decade. Such repression has only accelerated following the collapse of the Kurdish peace process in 2015—which had seen Turkish state authorities negotiate with the leaders of the PKK over an end to the nearly four-decade-long armed conflict—with Turkey today increasingly engaged in warfare not only at home but also beyond its borders.

The critiques of scholars writing about the limits of the state-orchestrated tolerance that Turkey witnessed in the 2000s and 2010s strongly resonate with scholarship on the governance of difference elsewhere. Critics of pluralist politics in a variety of contexts have argued that such politics routinely fail to grant minoritarian subjects the recognition they promise by making political participation conditional upon the outright erasure of difference, or by reducing such difference to the status of inconsequential folklore, private custom, or marketable commodity.[35] This body of critical literature helpfully underlines how regimes that purport to "give voice" to the disenfranchised often end up stripping these voices of their critical potential, and thereby only entrench existing inequalities. Nick Couldry (2010), for instance, has argued that neoliberalism constitutes a "crisis of voice" because it undermines people's ability to give a unique and distinct account of themselves, by placing market logics above all else. Ultimately, however, Couldry and others leave unquestioned the assumption that voice by default indicates its speakers' agency, self, and presence and that this is its prime value. This failure to recognize voice as historically, culturally, and ideologically constructed means that such critiques are unable to grasp that contemporary politics of representation have effects not just because of how they grant or deny voice, but because of how they construct and value voice as a certain kind of thing. More specifically, such politics recognize voices as politically consequential only insofar as they reliably represent the will and agency of their speakers. This means that they eschew or diminish other ways in which voices may have social effects—for instance, with regard to their sonic qualities and affective charge—and that they require subjects to relate to and make use of their voices in specific ways.

It is only by bringing into view how liberal politics shape, elicit, and frame voices both sonically and metaphorically, I contend, that we will be able to better understand these politics and their effects. *Voices That Matter* embarks on this undertaking by investigating what happens when subaltern subjects actually raise their voices in the hope of attaining the promises held out to them (Fisher 2016; Kunreuther 2018). How do voices need to sound in order to count within political regimes that place prime value on "having a voice"? What makes some voices more amenable to delivering promises of agency and empowerment than others? And how do the requirements that liberal politics of representation impose on vocal sound determine how voices become socially and politically potent? By tracing how Turkey's "pluralist moment" has fostered actual soundscapes as it has incited the marginalized to raise their voices, this book sets out to move beyond critiques of liberal pluralism that would evaluate such regimes only with regard to whether they successfully give voice to the disenfranchised. I suggest that one of the crucial yet often overlooked effects of representational politics is that they powerfully shape vocal sound and meaning precisely because they demand that voices ought to represent their bearers if they are going to carry political weight. As the following chapters will outline in detail, in the Kurdish context these demands have been transforming how people employ and understand their voices, and how voices consequently sound, how they travel, and what impact they have on listeners. As a result, voices have come to carry out new forms of social labor that revolve more and more around questions of representation rather than, say, the affective and embodied impact of vocal sound. On the one hand, this has brought within reach forms of authority, recognition, and even financial profit to which Kurdish women have long been denied access. It has allowed women to lay new claim to voices imbued with increasing political value and moral weight. On the other hand, it has also fostered new conflicts and debates, and rendered women vulnerable in new ways. When Kurdish subjects raise their voices in contemporary Turkey, I therefore argue, this is not simply an act of liberation or empowerment. Rather, it is an act that implicates those who bear voice in the complex legacies of state governance and in the promises—as well as pitfalls—extended by pluralist representation.

Researching Kurdish Voices

My investigation is based on a total of twenty months of ethnographic fieldwork with Kurdish female singers, dengbêjs, and women's rights activists, the bulk of which took place in 2011–2012, with several shorter visits in 2015, 2018, 2019, and 2020. During this time, I was based in Wan, a regional hub and growing urban sprawl in northern Kurdistan, present-day eastern Turkey, with approximately 500,000 inhabitants. Located close to the Iranian border—the nearest crossing is just over an hour's drive away by car—the region of Wan bears a topography that Anoush Suni (2019) describes as a palimpsest of state violence. Ruined churches and overgrown Christian tombstones attest to the Armenian communities who inhabited the region side by side with Kurdish pastoralists until the genocide in 1915,[36] while frequent military checkpoints and abandoned villages speak of the ongoing armed conflict between the PKK and the Turkish army. A regional trade hub with a small but growing urban elite, and a center of Armenian religious life during Ottoman times, under the republic Wan was reduced to a minor provincial town. Nonetheless, Turkish governments saw it as an important site for the consolidation of Turkish rule in the region. As prime minister İsmet İnönü wrote in 1935, "the town of Van will be an important foundation for the Republic in the east. Such a foundation is essential in every respect with regard to Turkish hegemony (*hâkimiyet*)" (Ağçakaya 2019, 91). To fortify this hegemony, successive governments designed policies that have seen Turkish populations from Turkey's Black Sea coast, the Caucasus, Russia, Iran, and even Kyrgyzstan being settled among Wan's Sunni Kurdish communities, often on formerly Armenian land (Ağçakaya 2019). Wan's urban center, too, was partially repopulated by ethnic Turks following the expulsion of its Armenian residents (Bilik 2019). It was only with the forced evacuation of thousands of Kurdish families from their villages at the height of the armed conflict in the 1990s—when many of the internally displaced sought refuge in Wan—that the city took on a marked Kurdish character, turning into what is today one of the centers of Kurdish oppositional politics in Turkey (Yükseker and Kurban 2009). By the time I arrived to do my fieldwork, Wan had, moreover, developed into a hub for civil society initiatives operating in town and the wider region, variously financed by Turkish state authorities, European or other foreign donors, or the pro-Kurdish municipality that had been voted into office in 2009.

It is in this context of a growing and diversifying NGO-sector, one heavily tilted toward questions of women's and minority rights, that Gazîn's association—which soon became the hub of my field research and which I will refer to as the Women Dengbêjs Association in what follows—has to be situated. It was with the women involved in running the association that I developed the most trusting and intimate relationships, and it was in its offices that I spent many days simply "hanging out": drinking tea, observing the comings and goings, and overhearing many a conversation, all of which proved incredibly useful for honing my Kurdish language skills. Because I was a young, unmarried woman with no local ties, the women soon took me under their wings, taking care that I was looked after and helping me find my way around town and navigate local networks. I had previously lived for several years in Istanbul, which meant that I was fluent in Turkish and familiar with the national context. This fluency in Turkish proved both a boon and a bane. While it allowed me to find my way in Wan with relative ease, it also meant that I ended up speaking much more Turkish than I would have liked to. As a result, attaining fluency in Kurdish took longer than I would have wished. My "data," including interviews, field notes, and recordings, reflect this, with the two languages continuously mingling and mixing. This situation is, however, also very much a reflection of daily life in the region, where linguistic purity has always been more of a fantasy than actual reality.

The fortunes of the Women Dengbêjs Association waxed and waned throughout my stay in the field. Gazîn was undoubtedly its driving force. Officially the association had over thirty members, though the women who regularly frequented the office never numbered more than ten. Many of the female members had extended families to take care of and little disposable income to spend, which made it hard for some of them to even afford the bus ride to come to the city center from the neighborhoods where they lived. Older women, with less caring responsibilities and more authority in their households, found making time to attend the association generally easier than younger women. Men, many themselves knowledgeable in dengbêjs' repertoires, would also often stop by for tea and a chat, even though Gazîn tried to keep the association first and foremost a place for women. Apart from simply providing a safe space where women would be able to raise their voices, the association aimed at organizing concerts and performances for its female members and provided music classes for girls. The main problem, though, was that the association was chronically short of money, since it did not have any stable income. Paying rent and bills at the end of the month was always a struggle. Gazîn did her best trying to approach various private and public donors, but both her own and her collaborators' lack of familiarity with the civil society sector (not even to mention the lack of alphabetic literacy) proved a real handicap over time. I tried to help out as best as I could, familiarizing myself with different funding schemes, submitting project applications, and trying to mobilize my own networks to arrange concerts and create publicity, though my success was overall rather limited. Lack of funds meant that the association moved its offices several times while I stayed in Wan. It was forced to finally shut down in 2018.

Outside the singers' association, I forged close relations with women's rights activists engaged at several other civil society organizations in Wan. With them, I attended workshops and conferences, marched at women's rights rallies, participated in family visits, sat in on counseling services, visited government offices, and had numerous informal conversations over endless rounds of tea. It is thanks to these multiple engagements that I came to realize that the aspirations and longings, frustrations and disappointments, of Kurdish women in contemporary Turkey exceed the neat boundaries of categories like oppression and resistance, voice and silence. This book is the outcome of my attempts to make sense of these observations—one that I hope does justice to the complexity of Kurdish women's lives, taking seriously my interlocutors without always sharing their interpretations.

During fieldwork I visited many a friend's mother, grandmother, aunt, or cousin who was knowledgeable in dengbêjs' repertoires. These inquiries took me across Kurdish geographies to towns and villages in the provinces of Agirî (Tk. Ağrı), Bidlîs (Bitlis), Diyarbekir, Hekarî (also Colemêrg, Tk. Hakkâri), Îdir (Tk. Iğdır), Mûş (Tk. Muş), Wan, and Qers (Tk. Kars), leading to semiformal interviews with close to thirty women. While some of these women were more than happy to talk to me, many others were reluctant if not outright suspicious. In a context where women raising their (singing) voices easily offended sensibilities of gendered propriety, and where decades of political violence have wreaked havoc with local relations of trust and intimacy, speaking to an unknown foreigner and perhaps even having their voices recorded carried substantial risks. Building trust took time and would have been impossible without friends who helped me reach out and establish contacts. Gazîn herself became, in fact, one of my closest collaborators, as it turned out that she was extremely keen to undertake what she, too, referred to as research. She was convinced that women proficient in dengbêjs' repertoires held invaluable knowledge about Kurdish culture and history and that this knowledge urgently needed to be documented—a task she hoped we could at least begin to accomplish by traveling the countryside and finding hitherto unknown women singers. Embarking on this undertaking with Gazîn and eventually living with her family considerably directed the course of my ethnographic ventures. I benefited immensely from our collective endeavor, not only because of the access Gazîn provided through her various networks but also because I became intimately acquainted with the social life of the Kurdish voice. For Gazîn, on the other hand, I and my research funding constituted important resources that not only covered our expenses but also gave her access to technologies like photography and video recording, computers, and the internet, as well as simply to writing—all of which Gazîn felt were indispensable to the kind of research she was eager to carry out. We hence came to constitute a kind of research team where it often was not clear who acted as whose assistant, both of us being embedded in networks the other sought access to and equipped with skills the other lacked yet required. While this form of cooperation did not always unfold smoothly, it evolved into a lasting friendship. It was therefore with all the more pain that I received news of Gazîn's untimely death in the summer of 2018, just days before I was set to visit. I dedicate this book to her.

In retrospect, the period during which I conducted the bulk of my field-work—from the summer of 2011 to the winter of 2012—was in many ways exceptional. From 2009 to 2015, the Turkish government was involved in ne-gotiations with the PKK leadership that sought to bring an end to the armed conflict.[37] The process was marked by contradictory and ambiguous political developments. Periods of ceasefire and plans for disarmament were followed by periods of renewed heavy fighting; the introduction of new freedoms, nota-bly with regard to Kurdish voices, was accompanied by large-scale legal pros-ecution of members of the Kurdish political movement. And yet, despite all the setbacks and disappointments, this was a period of genuine hope, with the prospect of a peace agreement on the horizon and, as I describe above, a fledgling pluralist framework taking hold. These hopes have in the meantime been cruelly dashed. With the resumption of full-scale warfare in Turkey's southeast since July 2015, which has inflicted massive destruction on Kurd-ish livelihoods, killing nearly 3,000 and displacing up to 400,000,[38] the bru-tal crackdown on oppositional politics following the failed military coup in 2016, as well as Turkey's 2018 and 2019 invasions into Kurdish-held territories in northern Syria, Kurdish rights are increasingly imperiled. In Turkey today Kurdish voices have once again become an object of intense governmental surveillance and nationalist agitation. The sounds of Kurdish reliably call forth tired accusations of separatism and treason, with Kurds repeatedly being at-tacked in public, even lynched and murdered, merely for speaking Kurdish.[39]

And yet, despite the increasing curtailment of voices that had gained public presence during the peace process, the brief period during which these voices circulated with relative ease has unleashed expectations that cannot easily be contained. If nothing else, the peace process has entrenched the voices of Kurdish women as a barometer of political emancipation and empowerment, further cementing their position as an overdetermined object exerting con-siderable allure and fascination and holding substantial moral, political, and affective value. This book excavates the forces that have led Kurdish women's voices to occupy this position and inquires how their reverberations, cadences, and echoes shape Kurdish imaginations, struggles, and hopes.

What Follows

The chapters that follow seek to unsettle common understandings of voice as a natural vehicle of individual will, self, and agency by shedding light on what voices do in Kurdish contexts apart from representing those who enunciate them, and how their sonic and aesthetic qualities are central for this labor. Later chapters then move on to consider how voices have increasingly come to stand for their bearers in northern Kurdistan, and discuss the manifold consequences that ensue.

Chapter 1 sets out to show how Kurdish women's voices are anchored in a cultural poetics where voices function less as a means of expressing personal interiority than as a mobile force capable of making sensations of pain, suffering, and tragedy circulate among listeners. The social potency of voices lies here, in other words, in the affects they are able to transport and solicit. Genre, I argue, is key for imbuing voices with affective charge, as it ties sonic and textual elements to specific emotions, creating tightly knit webs of connotation and association. Outlining the textual, poetic, and melodic characteristics that render women's voices socially and affectively potent, the chapter makes a case for viewing vocal form as crucial for the kinds of social labor voices are able to carry out.

Based on the observation that women singers often "lend" their voices to others, making their own voice the vehicle for another's pain, chapter 2 further develops the idea of the voice as a mobile affective technology (rather than an instrument for the expression of the personal self). The chapter argues that in a context where voices are not inextricably tied to their enunciators' selves, audio technologies—elsewhere often associated with an unsettling separation between voice and self—have readily been taken up to extend and amplify the reach of affectively charged voices. At the same time, I show how technologies like cassette tapes and the radio have also fostered new experiences of intimacy with disembodied voices and thereby opened up novel avenues for imagining voice as the expression of individual interiority and collective identity.

Long-standing Kurdish oral repertoires corroborate the idea that in Kurdish contexts, female voices often constitute a vehicle to express not the pain of the self but that of another. In many epic accounts, for example, women's voices figure as a means to tell of the tragic fate of courageous brothers, brave husbands, wounded fiancés. Chapter 3 discusses how the constellations of voice, self, and pain that come to the fore in these repertoires are undergoing important transformations. Focusing on the work of two modern women singers, Gazîn and Eyşe Şan, I trace the emergence of a novel vocal aesthetics in which the voice increasingly becomes the means to express women's own, personal suffering. These changes in vocal form, I argue, pave the way for a politics in which voices represent ever more directly those who enunciate them. Yet it would be wrong to read these transformations simply as empowering; as the chapter shows, they open up new challenges, fears, and anxieties that women must face.

Once voices come to represent speakers and their selves, how to lay lasting claim to them becomes increasingly important. Chapter 4 explores the struggles that ensue as a result. I situate the fact that women singers spent much time worrying about "stolen" songs and repertoires in the context of a Turkish politics of pluralism that has not only imparted new value to Kurdish voices, but also reconfigured them as ownable property—as something, in other words, one can (and must) "have." Yet Kurdish oral repertoires are steeped in genealogical logics that make it difficult to claim ownership in any straightforward way. Pieces need to be wrought from the expanding genealogies to which they are tied in order to make them unequivocally belong. Doing so has allowed women to challenge the patrilineal logics underlying oral genealogies and reclaim Kurdish oral traditions as a distinctly female domain. But in a context where the public exposure of women's voices retains patriarchal discomfort, it is not always easy for women to live up to the representational imperative of having a voice.

As representational politics make audibility a key benchmark for political participation, inclusion, and recognition, they render the public voice an object of intense desire and aspiration, particularly for marginalized subjects. Yet the hopes attached to "gaining a voice" are all too often disappointed. Chapter 5 examines this dilemma by focusing on two concerts, one in Istanbul and one in Wan, at which the voices of Kurdish women were celebrated for how they symbolized female assertiveness and Kurdish heritage. Even though the two occasions were animated by very different feminist ideologies, they similarly framed the singers' voices as metaphorical figures rather than as sound objects in their own right. Such framing, however, risked curtailing voices' affective impact and social force, rendering them but tame symbols of cultural tradition and women's empowerment. Gaining public voice, the chapter shows, is therefore not always empowering, but may expose the bearers of voice to new forms of discipline.

In the conclusion to this book, I return to the voice as a site where complex issues of agency, subjectivity, and representation crystallize. Based on my involvement in an exchange project between Kurdish and Armenian female singers, I reflect upon the limits of ideologies of voice that champion the (female) voice as a universal medium capable of transcending linguistic, ethnic, and national divisions. Revisiting the voice's capacity to forge intersubjective resonance and attunement, I ask how this capacity is refracted by (neo)liberal discourses that construct the voice as an icon of transparent communication, and point to the limits of that construction.

Tracing how Kurdish women's voices reverberate in a multiplicity of sites, this book tracks the shifting configurations, meanings, and ideologies that become attached to these voices as an overdetermined site of governmental intervention, subaltern aspiration, and feminist activism. It explores what happens when liberal forms of government interpellate minoritarian subjects to raise their voices, including the dilemmas and vulnerabilities that unfold, as well as the hopes and dreams that make such interpellation successful. Ultimately, my aim is to shed light on how contemporary politics of representation, as they incite the marginalized to voice, are implicated in generating new hopes, anxieties, and contestations.

FIGURE 1 **Sociality**. The Women Dengbêjs Association in Wan. (Photo by author)

1

The Potency of Vocal Form

When there is a funeral (*taziye*), when somebody dies, I go and sing. I sing and they cry. The pain becomes one, because people's hearts are injured, they are aching. Look, that's what being a dengbêj is: for example, if a relative of yours passes away, then you turn the pain of your heart into a *kilam* [sung narrative] about that person. You use your voice. Or, for example, if your son dies, then again, your pain, you . . . Or if your son disappears, you also make a kilam, because you are in pain. Actually, it's not just a kilam. You keep yourself together. You bring that pain from the inside of your mind in front of your eyes, and you become a dengbêj. In that sense everyone knows dengbêjî.[1] For example, if a boy and a girl fall in love with each other, each will sing a song for the other. They become dengbêjs out of their love. Others become dengbêjs out of the pain in their heart, out of their suffering. When somebody is killed, for example, they make a kilam about them, about that pain of the killing.

Esma laid out an intricate map of sentiments and emotions, of voices and ears, of pain and affection for me, as we were sitting in her living room, surrounded by the photographs of the loved ones that life had taken away from her. In her account, affectionate relations and their rupture held the potential to make people raise their voices. Once personal sentiment became transformed into sonic presence, she maintained, it would be able to draw others into its fold, allowing for pain to become one and for romance to turn contagious. While Esma conceded that dengbêjs might be born out of love, for her it was pain that made her raise her low-pitched, grainy voice.

"The dengbêjî that I sing, I sing it for my pain, for the suffering that I have experienced. I sing kilams out of my pain, the pain tormenting my heart. For example, when I remember my son, I sing a kilam. I bring the pain in front of my eyes and [. . .] I tell that pain." Esma's pain was intimately linked to the ways in which life unfolds for many Kurdish women of her generation in Turkey. In her early fifties when I met her in 2012, Esma lived with her husband, daughter-in-law, and two small grandchildren in a modest, single-story house in Bazîd (Tk. Doğubayazıt), a small Kurdish town situated at the eastern edge of the Turkish nation-state, a mere thirty kilometers from the Iranian border. Bazîd is marginal to the Turkish national frame not only in geographical terms. The town is situated in one of the poorest regions of the country, and its population relies as much on smuggling goods over the adjacent border as it does on the war economy.[2] Bazîd is surrounded by some of the highest mountains in Turkey, including the iconic Mount Ararat whose majestic peak overlooks the plain on which the settlement is situated. Yet in this geography mountains signify less rugged natural beauty or touristic potential than the harsh realities of state violence and guerrilla warfare. The mountains around Bazîd have long been strongholds for Kurdish guerrilla forces, rendering the region a center for recurrent military operations. In town, small shops selling military equipment and souvenirs line the central pedestrian street, catering to the hundreds of conscripts stationed in the many barracks situated in and around town. While Bazîd's merchants may make their living thanks to the cash brought in by these soldiers, the surrounding countryside (like elsewhere in Turkey's Kurdish regions) has borne the brunt of the army's counterinsurgency warfare. As thousands of villages have been emptied and highland pastures sealed off over the last forty years, as villagers have been forced from their land or recruited as paramilitaries, the social fabric of rural Kurdish communities and the local economies supporting them have been left in ruins.[3]

The pain and suffering that made Esma raise her voice was intimately connected to these dynamics of chronic underdevelopment, poverty, and state violence. Esma's family had moved from the village into town just before she got married at the age of fifteen. She thus escaped becoming a direct witness to some of the most brutal military clashes that took place in Bazîd's mountains in the 1990s. Nevertheless, Esma's childhood was short. She gave birth to her first child a year after being married and from then onward, she says, "I have seen misery (*derd*)." Of her five children, none is with her today. One of her sons died while still a child; another was killed in a traffic accident. Her third son joined the guerrilla forces of the PKK several years before I met her—a life trajectory that boded yet another violent death[4]—while his brother, whose wife and children were living with Esma, was serving a prison sentence of over ten years for his support of the Kurdish armed struggle. Finally, Esma's youngest daughter had, like thousands of other young Kurds, left home to look for more prosperous futures farther west, leaving behind only the photographs of a smiling young woman on the television cabinet in the living room.

Esma regularly employed her voice to turn the pain that life had lodged in her heart into melodized words or kilams, a genre that blurs the boundaries between speech and song, combining sections of rapid speech with more markedly melodized sections in which the voice clings to and extends single syllables, descending from a higher pitch to a lower base tone in trembling, quavering movements (Amy de la Bretèque 2012). She was therefore locally known as a dengbêj. Dengbêjs are performers of oral genres who are often described as Kurdish bards or oral historians, given that the kilams they sing provide nonfictional accounts of both past and contemporary events, ranging from histories of tribal conflict and Kurdish uprisings to personal experiences of tragic love, hardship, and pain. In a society that has relied for the transmission of its cultural repertoires primarily on the spoken word, dengbêjs enjoy the social prestige that comes with the telling of communal history and the mastery of poetic skill and vocal modulation. Historically their vocal art is closely tied to the precapitalist social order that prevailed in parts of Kurdistan until well into the twentieth century (Hassanpour 2020a, 8–32). Some dengbêjs stood in the service of wealthy patrons, including political leaders and landlords, while many others performed within local networks of kin and tribal relationships. Though both women and men have long been knowledgeable in the oral repertoires associated with dengbêjs, it is men's voices that have historically enjoyed public audibility and the social recognition associated with it. Women, by contrast, have begun to publicly claim the term *dengbêj* and perform in this function only recently.

Etymologically, the term *dengbêj* is a compound that derives from *-bêj*, literally "sayer or teller," and *deng*, "news, word, or repute." In that sense, the dengbêj may be understood as one who tells of news, keeps information in circulation, and spreads (as well as determines) fame and renown (Doxan n.d.). Much has been made of the fact that in Kurdish *deng* also means "voice," which would render the dengbêj literally a teller or pronouncer of the voice. Kurdish novelist Mehmed Uzun (1991, 2008), for instance, has written at length about how dengbêjs "tell" and give shape to the voice, how they transform sound into meaning, and as such stand as the originary creators of Kurdish memory, history, and identity. While from a linguistic and etymological point of view, casting the dengbêj as a "voice-teller" seems doubtful,[5] the persistence of this trope tells us much about the appeal that the voice holds as an index of self, identity, and authenticity in northern Kurdistan today. This book sets out to investigate this appeal, tracing how voices have come to take on value and meaning as representational vehicles, how this has rendered them objects of desire and aspiration—particularly for women— but how it has also engendered new forms of anxiety and contestation.

To lay the groundwork for this investigation, this chapter begins to explore how voices in northern Kurdistan are grounded in a cultural poetics that refuses stable associations between voice, self, and identity. Women like Esma may have used their voices in response to experiences of pain and suffering, but, as I shall argue, their voices were not necessarily direct expressions of their personal selves or interior lives. Voices rather featured as potent forces that would pick up on, transmit, and augment affective currencies saturating a place or a situation, carrying out the crucial work of what Kathleen Stewart (2011) describes as the attunement necessary to create an atmosphere. As Esma put it, "every time your heart is burning, your songs (*kilam*) will also be heart-burning. If, on the other hand, you go to a place filled with love, you will feel that love and sing songs (*kilam*) of love. And if your heart is aching, if you find yourself in a place of pain, then you will share that pain." Rather than expressing a private, inner self, in the vocal aesthetics to which Esma introduces us here, voices carry out different kinds of social labor as they share and augment prevailing sentiments, as they burn hearts and induce love. But if dengbêjs' voices, as this suggests, do not naturally or universally represent self and identity, this raises questions about how they have come to be understood as such, questions that later chapters will explore in more detail.

In this and the following chapter, I set myself the task to account for the forms of social labor that voices carry out in Kurdish contexts apart from representing their bearers. Doing so means taking a step back from all-too-common assumptions about the voice as a channel that humans deploy, first and foremost, to communicate specific content, while not mattering much in its own right. Here, by contrast, I want to think about how the form of a voice might matter for the kinds of effects it is able to have in the world. Form, as I use it here, is a capacious concept that refers to the way a voice sounds, the poetics that shape its articulation, the material infrastructures through which it is transmitted. It refers to vocal style and aesthetic, to timbral and acoustic qualities, to lyrical elaboration and restraint. It is thus akin to what linguist Roman Jakobson (1960, 356–357), in his attempt to draw attention to how language gains significance not just for the content it transmits but for the form in which it does so, has described as language's "poetic function."

Dengbêjs are masters at deploying vocal form—as are many practitioners of oral and musical traditions across the world. After all, it is precisely once speech is melodized that voice becomes more than signifying language and form is stylized and elaborated (Duncan 2004). Central to dengbêjs' mastery

of vocal form is the genre of the kilam, a type of sung narrative or what Estelle
Amy de la Bretèque (2012) describes as "melodized speech." Deriving from
the Arabic kalām, meaning "speech, word, or utterance," the kilam comprises
a broad field of vocal expression held together less by a finite set of formal
characteristics than by its affective charge. As a genre of tragedy, pain, and
suffering, the slow-paced kilam stands opposed to lighter, rhythmic, and
danceable genres that evoke joyfulness and exuberance. As such, the kilam
forms part of a broader cultural sphere that stretches across Turkey and the
Middle East, where musical and poetic arts represent culturally elaborated
and socially valued means for exploring suffering and dwelling in pain (Gill
2017; Racy 2004). The way in which the genre thrives on the mobilization
of sad and painful emotion also sets it in proximity to genres like American
blues (Keil 1966) and country music (Fox 2004), Spanish flamenco (Hirschkind 2021), and Portuguese fado (Gray 2013), which similarly derive their appeal and popularity from artfully elaborating tragic suffering.

In what follows, I set out to explore this wide and fluid genre of vocal expression as a means of developing a conceptual grip on the social efficacy of
vocal form. I seek to understand, in other words, how the voices of women like
Esma were—as local idioms insist—able to move others to tears, burn their
hearts, or ignite their livers. This ability, I argue, is tightly linked to the specific
acoustic and poetic form that the voice takes on when it pronounces a kilam.
As we shall see, these characteristics of vocal form also work to detach voices
from the subjects pronouncing them. Aspects like reported speech, (self)quo-
tation, rich metaphorical embellishment, and the conventionality of vocal
form—well known to scholars studying formal speech and political oratory[6]—
all contribute to removing the kilam from the individual self. By highlighting how the form of the kilam works to detach this vocal artifact from those
who pronounce it, this chapter thus takes a first step toward destabilizing ideas
about the voice as a direct expression of personal will and interiority. Contrary
to the thrust of representational politics, I argue that voices do not always already represent those who pronounce them. That voices should do so is not
naturally given, but requires social, sonic, and imaginary labor and investment.

Genre, Affect, and Aesthetic Sensibility

When it comes to describing and conceptualizing the significance of form in
cultural production, genre has long been a key category. Genre provides a way
of thinking about style and standards, about aesthetic conventions and the
formal properties of cultural artifacts. Categorizations of genre allow sorting
discourse and artifacts into distinct groups, establishing hierarchies, legacies,

and genealogies in the process. When I was doing my fieldwork in 2011–2012, questions of genre were on the mind of many of the dengbêjs and singers I encountered, as well as (or perhaps even more so) the Kurdish writers, scholars, and cultural workers with whom I spoke. This was a moment when political relaxations led to a veritable explosion in performances of and discourse about Kurdish oral culture after decades of censorship and repression. There was a general consensus that Kurdish language and culture were at imminent risk and that urgent measures were necessary in order to safeguard their survival in the future. In this context, dengbêjs came to be heralded as key figures whose oral repertoires constituted invaluable treasures chronicling Kurdish history, culture, and language. In the attempt to salvage the knowledge of these mostly elderly men and women, much energy went into trying to map, archive, describe, and classify the oral repertoires they knew.

Doing so required imposing order on a field of cultural production where classificatory systems regarding oral repertoires vary immensely between regions. As Christine Allison (2001, 62) has noted, "even the most commonly found Kurdish generic terms are rarely understood without ambiguity throughout the entire Kurmanji-speaking area," referring to the variety of Kurdish that is spoken by most Kurds in Turkey and northern Syria as well as by Kurdish populations in northern Iraq, Iran, and the Caucasus. A longstanding history of decentralized rule in Kurdish geographies, the twentieth-century division of Kurdish populations across four different nation-states, and the censorship these states have enacted have all played their part in perpetuating a landscape of cultural production where regional variation thrives. The kilam is no exception. The term is most commonly used in the region of Serhed, the mountainous highlands north of the Diyarbekir plain that extend toward the Caucasian massif and in which Wan is centrally located. Inhabitants of the Kurdish areas farther south, on the other hand, often employ different terms to describe similar forms of oral tradition. The Badînî-speaking[7] Yezidis in northern Iraq, for instance, use the term *stran* to refer to the kind of melodized speech Serhedîs know as *kilam* (Allison 2001, 65–69), while in the Mêrdîn (Tk. Mardin) area in southeastern Turkey this kind of oral tradition would be known as *şer* (Çakır 2019, 119–121), which in eastern Kurdistan (Iran), in turn, would be referred to as *beyt* (Blum, Christensen, and Shiloah 2001).[8] And while those pronouncing kilams are commonly referred to as *dengbêj*s in the Serhed region, elsewhere such performers are designated as *stranbêj*s or *beytbêj*s, as *mitirb* if the performers are professional, or simply as *şaîr*, literally meaning "poet" (Blum, Christensen, and Shiloah 2001).

Over the last decades, the expansion of a mass-mediated Kurdish public sphere has, however, contributed to a certain streamlining of oral repertoires and the terms used to describe them (Çakır 2020). In today's Turkey, one can thus hear the term *kilam* being used both within and outside the Serhed region to refer to a whole range of oral traditions that rely on melodizing speech. *Dengbêj* has similarly turned into an umbrella term for various performers of Kurdish oral genres. As I will explore in further detail in chapter 4, this generalization of formerly regional terms simultaneously reflects and produces a novel imagination of an overarching "Kurdish voice," one that belongs to the Kurdish people as a collective subject and represents its history and identity.

Scholars and writers have spent enormous effort trying to impose order and classification on the unruly variability and fluidity of Kurdish oral genres. With regard to the genre of the kilam alone, much discussion has gone into defining its various subcategories. Scholars concur that one can roughly divide kilams into, on the one hand, tales about war, battle, and other instances of manly courage and bravery and, on the other hand, narratives about romantic love and infatuation (incidentally, both types tend to end in tragedy and loss). But a variety of further classifications abound.[9] To give just one example, a recent compilation of kilams sung by famous Serhedî dengbêj Reso (1902–1983) divides his repertoire into kilams about rebellions (*serhildan*), love (*evînî*), war and internal tribal conflicts (*şer û pevçûnên navxweyî-eşîrî*), and finally kilams about nature, thought, and life (*xweza, raman, jiyan*) (Güneş and Şahin 2018). Time and again, though, such classificatory enterprises run up against the difficulty of trying to define fixed categories where actual vocal practices are highly fluid, variable according to performance context, and hard to classify unambiguously (a kilam about a rebellion may well contain a love story at the same time). Importantly, moreover, the attempt to capture oral traditions through formal categorization typically ends up prioritizing genres that are publicly performed and carry social prestige—genres, in other words, that are more readily associated with the male voice. Women's oral practices, on the other hand, often simply fall out of dominant genre classifications altogether. As Samuel Liebhaber (2018) argues in his work on Mahri poetry of the Arabian Peninsula, rather than objective representations of oral-poetic discourse, genre classifications might therefore more usefully be thought of as specific points of intersection that are culturally marked thanks to the frequency with which they occur and the prestige they carry.

In trying to pin down how voices become socially potent, I have therefore found it helpful to think of genre less as a set of classificatory standards than as a "dynamic pattern" (Berlant 2008, 20) through which formal aspects of speech, song, and poetry become sites of affective investment and social meaning. Lila Ellen Gray (2013), for instance, has shown how the Portuguese fado gains social significance because of the way in which it ties the specificities of melody, timbre, and vocal elaboration to certain affects and emotions, thereby creating tightly knit webs of connotation and association that prime audiences toward certain responses and imbue the genre with historical and political meaning. From this perspective, genre constitutes first and foremost an "orienting framework for the production and reception of discourse" (Briggs and Bauman 1992, 142–143). As stories are countless times retold, performances attended, and songs rehearsed, predictable generic conventions shape listeners' dispositions and expectations and forge their aesthetic sensibilities. As Karin Barber writes, "a genre is simultaneously a memory and a promise," constituting "both an assemblage of conventions drawn from past instantiations, and a set of parameters within which new creation can take place" (2007, 211).

In my attempt to account for the social life of vocal form, I take inspiration from scholars like Barber and Gray to survey the kilam not in terms of fixed boundaries and formal categories, but in terms of the affects it commands and the emotions it calls forth. Doing so allows me to bring into view broader patterns regarding the social potency of vocal form beyond the narrow politics of naming and classification. While drawing primarily on ethnographic material from the Serhed region where the terms *kilam* and *dengbêj* prevail, I thus hope to illuminate more general tendencies of how voices come to have social effects thanks to their affective charge. Such an approach might upset some who will find me drawing too wide a boundary around the kilam, ready to include pieces that lack the poetic sophistication or melodic elaboration to merit this prestigious label—pieces, perhaps, that do not seem manly enough in their exposure of sentiment and vulnerability. Others may find my account wanting for attributing too much meaning to a regionally specific term. Approaching genre with a focus on how it ties form and affect together, however, serves me well here simply because I observed this tie to be at the center of the social labor that voices like those of Esma carried out. Audiences valued voices for how they were able to induce and transmit powerful sentiments and emotions, particularly those related to pain and suffering. A skilled dengbêj, I was often told, is one who will make you cry. And performers, in turn, took pride in being able to move their listeners to tears.

Contours of Speech, Song, and Melody

But how would a kilam be able to make someone cry? To gauge the social meaning and potency of the genre, one useful starting point is to outline how the kilam gains its specific affective charge through the ways in which it is situated in relation to other genres of oral expression.[10] Thus—despite its etymological roots designating it simply as words or utterances—the genre distinguishes itself from ordinary speech by singing or melodizing words. Singers tend to recite the narrative of a kilam within a narrow range of notes, sometimes quite rapidly, without a fixed rhythm or meter, before drawing out and embellishing the last vowel or syllable of each phrase as the voice descends in a series of quavering, trembling progressions. Musicological terminology would describe these embellishments as involving melismas (the singing of a single syllable over a succession of different tones) and vibrato (a regular, pulsating change of pitch).[11] Usually, the narrative is organized into blocks of varying length—what we can think of as verses or stanzas—with particularly heavy embellishments at the beginning and end of each unit. It is these extensive, melismatic elaborations of the descending voice that centrally contribute to the plaintive, tragic feel of the *kilam* as a genre. This is in no small part because these embellishments bear close resemblance to funerary lamentations and to the shape the voice takes on when actually sobbing or wailing.

Yet, although speech in kilams is invariably melodized, the genre is set apart from other forms of melodic singing that are more akin to music in a Western sense (Amy de la Bretèque 2010, 2012). Known in the Serhed region as *stran*,[12] these more fast-paced repertoires communicate joy and cheerfulness with their regular, upbeat rhythms, simple melodic lines, and clear rhyme patterns, and are typically performed at weddings and other festivities, often sung in groups with a call-response pattern. While strans encourage listeners to dance, the kilam is a much heavier genre to which audiences listen attentively, often while seated, during intimate moments of exchange or larger public performances.[13] Strans are, moreover, often performed with the accompaniment of musical instruments equally associated with exuberance and celebration, like the *dahol* drum and the high-pitched *zirne*, a type of oboe, while kilams are performed either without musical accompaniment altogether, relying on the power of the a capella voice alone, or in accompaniment of a single instrument like the *duduk* (a woodwind instrument similar to the oboe, popular in the Serhed region and Caucasus), the *tembûr* (a longnecked lute often used for accompaniment farther to the south around Riha [Tk. Urfa], Maraş, and Efrîn [Afrin] in northern Syria), or the *kemaçe* (also *kemançe*, a spike fiddle common in the southeast, particularly in the Mêrdîn, Sêrt [Tk. Siirt], and Qamişlo areas).

Another aspect of the "words" of kilams that distinguishes them from ordinary conversation is their poetic register, situating the genre in proximity to genres of Kurdish (oral) literature like myths (*efsane*), legends (*destan*), and fairy tales/folktales (*çîrok*), as well as poetry proper (*helbest, şiîr*). With these genres, kilams share not only a common pool of poetic motifs and metaphors, but also narrative themes and characters (Allison 2001, 13). What sets the kilam apart from these different literary genres, however, is its decidedly nonfictional character. Its melodized speech is firmly believed to relate historical experience, either as witnessed by the performer herself or as transmitted by others. Many of the most widely shared and enjoyed kilams are pieces that recount historical events of the late nineteenth and early twentieth centuries, including Kurdish resistance to the encroachment of Ottoman and Turkish authorities and the upheavals brought about by the collapse of the Ottoman Empire and the violence that accompanied it. As such, they can be (and have been) mined for the historical information they contain.[14] More recently, this claim to historicity has paved the way for an appreciation of the genre as a (if not *the*) central form of Kurdish historiography.

Even if kilams are cast as nonfictional accounts, however, these are not neutral or objective narratives of lived experience, but deeply saturated with affects related to loss, grief, and pain. I have already mentioned that this affective charge partly derives from how kilams share some of their acoustic characteristics—including the descending lines, the melismatic elongations, the quavering voice—with funerary lamentations. Esma's account at the beginning of this chapter, too, spoke of the ease with which kilams may function as funerary lamentations and laments parade as kilams. Many of my interlocutors explained this proximity between the two genres in genealogical terms, claiming that the genre of the kilam had developed out of funerary lamentations somewhere in the distant past.[15] And indeed, the narratives of many classical kilams are set up as situations of bereavement, in which a female relative of the kilam's male protagonist recounts her son's, brother's, or lover's heroic exploits, relating a dramatic course of events that ends in the protagonist's tragic death, which the female narrator then amply laments in the kilam. The elaboration of male strength and bravery, of courage and perseverance, becomes entangled here with the lamentation of loss and the expression of grief. On the other hand, kilams also show proximity to lullabies, a genre that serves mothers across the Middle East to express their sorrows and longings, including the estrangement newly married women often experience in their in-laws' household (Bilal and Amy de la Bretèque 2013).[16] Lullabies share with both laments and kilams an association with a semantic field of sorrow, grief, and loss, which finds sonic shape in a shared melodic structure of descending lines that often end in the melismatic elongation of single vowels or syllables and is expressed poetically through recourse to a common pool of imagery and metaphor. Laments, kilams, and lullabies, then, partake in a broad field of aesthetic expression and cultural elaboration to which sentiments of pain and loss are central.

Importantly, this field of aesthetic sensibility is thoroughly gendered. Both laments and lullabies are explicitly female genres that men do not perform, reflecting culturally sanctioned associations between female gender and the expression of sentiments related to suffering, pain, and mourning.[17] These genres are traditionally also held in lower esteem (Allison 2001, 176; Hamelink 2016, 79). As a result, the greater the resemblance between dengbêjs' repertoires and the musical and poetic aspects of lamentations and lullabies, the more they will be associated with the female voice. It follows that male dengbêjs generally prefer to intonate repertoires where epic sentiments prevail over expressions of emotional vulnerability, as in the long, narrative kilams that celebrate masculine virtues of heroic perseverance and courage while recounting the histories of tribal feuds and Kurdish uprisings. While women can and do perform these repertoires, when they do so their voices are often characterized (and praised) as manly. These are also the pieces that carry most social prestige and are most readily associated with public performances in all-male or mixed-gender settings. Repertoires that betray their ancestral heritage of lamentation more readily, on the other hand, tend to be more closely associated with the female voice. These include kilams that women assemble extemporaneously as a means to share their sorrows and afflictions.[18] Nevertheless, even the most epic and heroic stretches of the genre continue to carry the reverberations of the female voice, not only because of the affective charge that suffuses the genre as a whole but also because a considerable number of these "classical" kilams are recounted through the voices of women lamenting the losses wrought by violent conflict and tragic fate. Intonating those kilams, men thus find themselves regularly ventriloquizing female voices and the sentiments of grief and bereavement they express, upsetting any expectations we may have of how voice, self, and gender ought to overlap.

Crafting Vocal Potency

The kilam's situation within a web of oral discourse and melodic expression, the above goes to show, is what gives the genre its particular affective "feel" and gendered associations. But how does this affective charge translate into social potency or what the philosopher Walter Benjamin, in his essay "The Storyteller," refers to as the "germinative power" (2007a, 90) of oral narrative? How, in other words, would a kilam be able to burn hearts and proliferate love in the way Esma had suggested (rather than simply representing or expressing a person's emotions and experiences)? To get a grip on this social labor of the voice, I turn to a kilam that was performed for me by Asya, a Kurdish woman in her forties, on a hot summer afternoon in 2012 when I came to visit her at the modest mud-brick house where she was staying together with her brother and his family over the summer. They had been hired as seasonal laborers by one of the affluent farming families in this village close to Wan to work in the fields, tend livestock, and process the fresh milk into different dairy products, including cheese and yogurt. Asya's life, like those of so many women of her generation, was marked by hardship and poverty. Following the forced evacuation of her village by the Turkish army in the 1990s, she had spent much of her life as a seasonal laborer, working in the orange fields of Edene (Tk. Adana) hundreds of kilometers to the southwest. Her husband's death had left her to fend for herself and her three young children and made her dependent on the goodwill of her brother and his family. And on top of all that, her elderly mother was serving a long prison sentence for her involvement with the Kurdish political movement.

As became clear during our conversation that day, being able to translate the hardship that life had meted out to her into sorrowful kilams was for Asya a crucial means of coming to terms with these experiences. Yet Asya made use of her vocal skills not only to express her own sorrows. That hot summer afternoon, she told me at length about Hozan Feraşîn, a young Kurdish man from her neighborhood in Wan who had disappeared several years ago and whose dead body had been found weeks later in a small stream close to the city, so disfigured that his mother did not recognize him. The death of this fervent youth activist, Asya was certain, must have happened at the hands of Turkish security forces, another in the many extrajudicial killings of Kurdish activists and politicians over the years.[19] At the time, Asya had spontaneously made a kilam about the event during the young man's funeral (*taziye*), where it probably functioned much like a funerary lamentation. But the kilam—whose transcript follows below—did not remain confined to this performance context. It kept circulating after the event, as Asya performed it in spaces as diverse as cultural centers, festival stages, and relatives' living rooms, channeling its emotional weight and political charge as far as the village house where we were drinking tea that day.

Wey lê dayê, wey dayê o, wey lê dayê, wey dayê o	Oh mother, oh mother, oh mother, oh mother oh
Seat bû çarê sibê o, serê xwe rake ji xewê o	It was four o'clock in the morning oh, wake up from sleep

Keçê dînê ma nizanî, Hozan Feraşîn ket avê o	You foolish girl, don't you know, Hozan Feraşîn has fallen into the water, oh
Wey la dayê, tu dêranê, here berê xwe bide çemanê	Oh mother, miserable you, go and have a look at the rivers
Gazî ke keç û xortanê, bêje Hozan Feraşînê'm kanê?	Call the girls and boys, ask them, where is my Hozan Feraşîn?
Wey la dayê negirîne, tu dilê xwe nehelîne	Oh mother, don't cry, don't let your heart melt away
Rondika çava nebarîne, rondika çava nebarîne	Don't shed tears, don't shed tears
Wey dayikê, te li me çi kir, binê avê gola sar kir	Oh mother, what have you done to us, put [him] beneath the cold water of the lake
Hozan Feraşîn reng degîş kir, dayê rebenê te nas nekir	Hozan Feraşîn changed color, poor mother, you did not recognize him
Hey la dayê tu dêranê, gazî ke keç û xortanê	Oh mother, miserable you, call the girls and boys
Bêjê wezê li bextê we me, bextê Xwedê hûn ê cenazê Hozan Feraşînê min o bîne Wanê	Tell them, I beg you, for God's sake, bring the body of my Hozan Feraşîn, oh, to Wan

As Asya recited the kilam in her somber, plaintive voice, her sister-in-law, who had joined us for tea, began to cry in silence, tears rolling down her cheeks. Asya's voice had thus achieved what a skilled dengbêj was supposed to do: she had made her audience cry. Her voice was, like Esma's, able to burn her listeners' hearts, imbuing factual information with an affective charge that touched those listening, drawing them into the scene of pain and suffering described. This effect, I believe, was linked not only to what Asya was recounting in her kilam, but equally to the qualities of her voice, what I refer to in this book as vocal form. Three aspects of vocal form, in particular, seem to me crucial in explaining how Asya's voice and those of (women) dengbêjs more broadly acquire their social potency: first the polyvocal structure of kilams, second their poetic elaboration, and third their patterns of melodization. As we shall see, at the same time as these characteristics render voices socially potent, they also systematically contribute to detaching voices from the subjects pronouncing them. This observation should caution us against overly quick interpretations of women's engagement in singing sorrowful kilams as a therapeutic exercise, an act of resistance against long-standing attempts at subduing Kurdish culture and history, or a refusal to accept patriarchal restrictions on women's voices. After all, it calls into doubt the implicit

assumption undergirding such interpretations: namely, that the voice constitutes a natural and universal expression of personal self, will, and interiority.

MULTIPLE VOICES

The first aspect of vocal form that I identify as contributing to a kilam's social
potency concerns the way in which it refracts the events it recounts through a
multitude of different perspectives. Kilams do not usually provide a disinter-
ested third-person account of an event or experience. Instead, the narrative
is told from the perspective of different actors involved in the event, whose
voices the dengbêj quotes throughout her performance. In the kilam about
Hozan Feraşîn, we thus hear Asya giving voice to the lamenting speech of the
bereaved mother herself, awoken early in the morning by her anguish (e.g.,
"where is my Hozan Feraşîn"; "bring the body of my Hozan Feraşîn, oh, to
Wan"), but she also reports the voices of what appear to be bystanders, friends
and relatives who are counseling and instructing the bereaved mother (e.g.,
"don't cry"; "don't shed tears"). This multiplication of voices is a typical feature
of kilams, which tend to amply report the direct speech of the different characters involved in the narrative that is being recounted (Sharifi and Barwari
2020). In reciting a kilam, the dengbêj thus becomes what Erving Goffman
(1979, 17) would call an animator, someone who reports the voices of others
rather than someone who pronounces their own words and sentiments.

At times, this multivocality can take the form of a dialogue, often found
in love songs, where the voices of lover and beloved are reported in alternating order, pleading or accusing, defending or praising each other. In other
kilams, an event or occurrence is told through the direct speech of multiple
figures, drawing listeners right into the dramatic course of action. In the famous kilam "Filîtê Quto," for example, we have a total of three voices recount
the tragic events of a tribal battle of the early twentieth century that left not
only the protagonist, Filît, dead, but also took the lives of fifty-two of his
tribesmen. In the following version recorded by Salih Kevirbirî from Dengbêj Cahîdo, Filît's mother, Şemê, can be heard lamenting her son's decision
to challenge Mamê Emê, leader of the Etmank tribe, for crossing his lands.
Mamê Emê is known to be a relentless warrior, and Şemê anticipates nothing
but misfortune from the encounter. We then hear Filît confronting Mamê
Emê, who condescendingly tells Filît off, instructing him to content himself
with several mules as a way toll, instead of the sparkling new rifle that Filît
had set his heart on. To illustrate the change of speaker position in the narrative, I have set the reported speech verbs that introduce each speaker's voice
in bold.[20]

Şemê go Filîto lo lawo bes e! Ji êvar da min hêvî kir, çiqas min bi te da hêvî kir

Min dî Filîtê min ê Quto rabû, bazbend girê da hemayîl ji bîr kir

Berê xwe dabû Pozê Qirê Kevanê, li Delana Paşo li Pira Batmanê

Xwedê dizane qesta Emê Beranê kejê qemerê serbirêşî kir

Filît çû pêşiya Emê, go Emê lawo, dilê min dibêye sed carî dilê min dibêye

Lawo, ez hatime pêşiya we ji we distînim, bac û xeraca serê rê ye

Emê go Filîto lawo, hestirekî ji qola dawiyê, yekî ji qola ortê, yekî ji qola paşiyê bigire ji xwe re bike, lawo, bac û xeraca serê rê ye

Ergê tu ji malê dinyayê feqîr î, lawo, bajo bajara hevraz ji zariyê xwe re bike xerc û mesrefa malê ye

Şemê said, Filît oh son, it's enough! No matter how much I have implored you since last night

I saw that my Filîtê Quto got up, tied his brassard, but forgot the amulet

He set out toward Pozê Qirê Kevan, toward Delana Paşo at the Batman bridge

God knows he headed to the dark brown tassel-head Emê Beran

Filît cut into Emê's path and said, hey Emê, lad, my heart says a hundred times

Hey, I am approaching you to collect from you the toll for the road

Emê said, Filît, oh son, take one mule from the end, one from the middle and one from the beginning row [of the caravan] and take it as your toll for the road

And, oh son, should you be in need, head down into town and use this to cover your expenses for your home and children

Kilams like the above are populated by a multiplicity of voices uttered from different speaker positions, which become engaged in lively dialogue as the narrative proceeds (Sharifi and Barwari 2020, 144–146). As such, the genre displays something of the polyphonic structure that Mikhail Bakhtin identifies in Dostoevsky's prose, where various "independent and unmerged voices . . . are not only objects of authorial discourse but also subjects of their own" (1984, 6–7). In Kurdish kilams, the dengbêj similarly animates voices that she does not fully own or control, providing a stage for these voices to engage with each other on their own terms rather than delivering an authoritative, bird's-eye account of the event in question. This kind of narrative structure where singers, storytellers, or lamenters become the animators of the multiple characters populating their narratives is in fact widespread in oral traditions across the world. Similar polyvocal dynamics have been observed by anthropologists in contexts as diverse as China (Mueggler 2014), South India (Trawick 2017, 112–137), and sub-Saharan Africa (Barber 2007)—to name but a few—challenging common ideas about the voice as a natural vehicle for expressing the intimate interiority of a single, bounded individual.

By contrast, across all these contexts we see how performers routinely utter words of which they are not the authors, hinting at selves that are as composite as the voices they pronounce.

This impression is further solidified if we consider how even kilams that represent the single viewpoint of an individual, typically in intimate accounts of personal experience, often employ reported speech such that the personal voice appears multiplied and displaced. In these cases, singers do not recount their thoughts and sentiments in a straightforward first-person narrative, but instead quote themselves by introducing their own speech with reporting verbs like "I say" or "I said." Erving Goffman (1979, 21–22) refers to this kind of speech as "embedded animation," whereby a speaker's voice no longer animates her current self (as would be the case in direct speech) but what appears like an earlier incarnation of herself. The effect is a distance between self and narrative, unhinging, in a sense, the account from the subject enunciating it. As Amy de la Bretèque (2012, 144–145) argues, this may make it easier for singers to give expression to painful sentiments and experiences because the emotional weight of an utterance becomes detached from the subjectivity of the individual singer. Consider, for example, the following kilam from Amy de la Bretèque's own material, voiced by Altûn, a fifty-one-year-old Yezidi widow from Armenia who lost not only her husband but also her brother and her only son, Şalik, father to her grandson Romîk. Note how she systematically quotes her own thoughts and utterances throughout.[21]

Ax **mi go**, bira wêrana Ûkraînê nekuştana lawê min	Ah **I said**, if only that cursed Ukraine had not killed my son
Bira neşewitiya qîza birê min	If only my brother's daughter had not burnt to death
Bira înfartê lênexista birê min	If only that infarct had not struck my brother
Bira xwe gullenekira Romîkê bavê min	If only the father of my Romîk had not been shot
Eman, eman	Mercy, mercy
[…]	[…]
Mi go, Şaliko lao, were vê yekê minra neke	**I said**, Şalik, my son, don't do this to me
Terka wêrana Ûkraînê bike	Leave that cursed Ukraine
Dayka te guneye	Have pity on your mother
Neke p'izka serê rya	Don't enter that dirty world of the street
Neke hêsîra ber derya	Don't become an orphan
[…]	[…]
Ay **mi go**, tune kurê min	Ay **I said**, I have no son
Guman hebû birê min,	I had hoped that my brother

Çaxê bimrama, wê biketana bin çar- dara min	Would carry my coffin when I die
Romîkê bavê min we destê bida ser çevê min	The father of my Romîk would have put his hands over my eyes
Ew hemû kulê dinê derxista ji dilê min	He would have dislodged all the sorrows of this world from my heart
Ay li minê, ay li minê, ay li minê	Oh woe is me, woe is me, woe is me

We see Altûn here plaintively reflecting on how life might have unfolded otherwise, beseeching her deceased son to leave the country that has seen his demise, and imagining how her own funeral would transpire were her brother and son still alive. She spins a narrative of subjunctives, imagining both past and future in a mode of counterfactual conditionality. This effect is heightened by the way in which Altûn makes use of reported speech, introducing each utterance with an "I said" in the past tense. As a result, her speech and the sentiments it expresses appear as if they belonged not to her current but to a previous, different self. Reporting painful thoughts and emotion as if they belonged to another place and time, to a space divorced from the speaking self in the here and now, might have made it easier for Altûn to give voice to her emotions. At the same time, we may presume that this detachment also enables those listening to identify more readily with what is being recounted. Once detached from the enunciating subject through forms of (self-)citation, the experience recounted in the kilam no longer strictly belongs to the performer herself. Instead, it is now able to circulate: it may be shared and appropriated, further reported and reiterated. Loosened from the singer, the kilam in this way becomes "a text that transcends the speaker" (Barber 2007, 133) on which listeners can project their own experiences of grief and suffering. Amy de la Bretèque (2010, 144) describes the resulting effect as an "autonomization" of the utterance that creates a "suspended universe" into which listeners may enter and let themselves be affected by what is being recounted. The detachment of the vocal artifact from the speaker in this way enhances the impact it may have on listeners, contributing to the kilam's remarkable capacity to make hearts burn and tears flow.

POETIC IMAGERY

A second aspect of vocal form that augments the affective and emotional force of a kilam concerns the poetic elaboration of its lyrics and the expressive speech particles permeating its narrative. Key to the impact these elements have on listeners is how the repeated use of the same formulas renders them powerful indices of particular affective states. Kilams draw upon a pool of poetic images and vocal motifs that can be found in countless other pieces. These images function like a recurring pattern, a "residue of past social interaction" (Silverstein and Urban 1996, 5) that infuses each new kilam with the affective charge of already circulating pieces and directs future perception and impact (Stokes 2010, 6n11). These stock formulas are not limited to the genre of the kilam alone. The same expressions occur as markers of pain and affliction in adjacent Kurdish literary genres and oral traditions, including laments and lullabies as well as legends, folktales, and poetry. But they also flow in and out of everyday speech, cited in moments of recollection, cried out during scenes of loss, or even parodied by youth intent on mocking the traditional world of their parents. Whether kilams are about love or war, whether they are newly assembled or have been in circulation for generations, a common pool of lyrical expressions and metaphors, of sonic images and vocal formulas—a pool that transcends and knits together different genres and historical periods—allows dengbêjs to evoke a broad universe of pain and affliction by pronouncing just a few words (Allison 2001, 181, 185).

The poetic motifs that are part of this pool firmly anchor emotion in different parts of the body and the material environment. As Lila Abu-Lughod suggests, this "phenomenology of emotion" (2000, 99) is very different from modern understandings that vest emotionality in the interiority of the individual self. Here, by contrast, sentiments become manifest on the surface of body parts, plants, and weather formations. As in other parts of the Middle East, within this phenomenology the heart (dil) stands out as "the subject of emotional experience" (Good 1977, 37). It is the prime organ for registering sorrow and grief, though the liver (ceger, kezeb), lungs (kezeb), and internal organs (hundir, hinav) can do so, too. Pain works upon these organs like fire, igniting, burning, and melting.[22] In kilams, hearts are routinely said to be burnt or burning (şewitî, dişewite) or set on fire (agir ketiye dilê min). They may also be broken (şikestî) or in mourning (şîn e); they may ache (diêşe), be filled with sorrow (bi keder e, tijî derd û kul e) or fear (tirs ketiye dilê min), or be injured (dilbirîn). Hearts can also act: they can shed tears and cry out, they often speak, and they can rejoice. Similarly, the internal organs, lungs, and liver can be filled with sorrow and misery (derd, kul), or, indeed, with blood, and like the heart they can be burnt, burning, or melting from the intensity of pain. Unlike the heart, however, the liver and lungs register only grief and melancholy, not joy. Eyes, on the other hand, come to the fore when they shed tears, imagined like rain falling from somber skies. "Do not let your eyes rain tears," Asya thus exhorted Hozan Feraşin's mother. Pain may also keep subjects awake, literally preventing their eyes from catching sleep (xew nakeve çavê min), or it can render subjects deaf and dizzy (ker û gêj) as a force that numbs the senses, dislocates, and upsets. In addition, sorrow and misfortune may become concrete through imagery of nature, as when a "black and dark cloud" (*ewrekî reş û tarî*) looming on the horizon suggests that disaster is about to strike, or when plants whither and wilt. In a kilam about the unrequited love of a young woman called Kinê, the protagonist likens herself to basil and clover plants, both metaphors of female beauty, shedding their leaves.[23]

Noticeable, too, is the frequent reference to the mother as a figure who is either herself in pain or to whom a suffering person cries out, for example, through common expressions like "oh mother" (*lê dayê*) and "oh miserable mother" (*dayê rebenê* or *dayê dêranê*). Often, these figures of speech are not in any obvious way tied to a kilam's narrative. They rather figure as evocative images through which suffering is expressed, suggesting how pain is imagined as an inherently gendered force firmly tied up with the experience of motherhood (more about which in chapter 3).

Apart from lyrical imagery, kilams also feature a great number of expressions with no or minimal semantic meaning that nevertheless function as powerful elements for evoking situations of pain and suffering, including "ax," "ay," and "oh," "wey" and "hey," as well as "lê" and "lo." The first three onomatopoetically evoke the sound of a sorrowful, deep sigh or the way one would cry out when in pain. They often figure at the end of lines, where they are elongated with a quivering voice, transforming into what Greg Urban calls "icons of crying" (1988, 389–391). "Wey" (or sometimes "hey"), on the other hand, is a particle common in everyday speech, where it functions as an interjection when confronted with bad news, suggesting astonishment as much as sympathy. In kilams, these particles often get combined with short expressions into lyrical formulas. In Asya's kilam, for instance, we find "wey" (and "hey") combined with "mother, what have you done to us" (*wey dayikê, te li me çi kir*), as well as with "mother, miserable you" (*hey la dayê tu dêranê*). Another typical such expression that we saw appear in Altûn's kilam is "*ay li minê*" or "woe is me." The expression literally translates to "ah upon me," offering an image of pain as a heavy burden, or perhaps of fate weighing down the subject. Finally, "lê" and "lo" are gendered vocatives, used to call out to or address, respectively, a female or male person. They are commonly used in everyday speech and appear in both upbeat strans and sorrowful kilams, depending on who the piece is addressed to. Of the elements listed above, these vocatives carry the least inherent emotional baggage, but become affectively charged as the vibrating voice clings to their final vowels, extending and embellishing them within a kilam.

These formulas and expressions are typically found at the beginning or end of lines or stanzas, framing, as it were, the narrative and providing it with a mode of address. Particularly when situated at the end of lines they regularly become the basis for the melismatic elaboration so typical of kilams, with the voice stretching out the individual vowels, quavering along a descending path that sends ripples through many a listener. Amy de la Bretèque describes these formulas as "triggers (*déclencheurs*) of emotion" (2010, 139), since they can have powerful effects on listeners. The middle-aged Yezidi women with whom Amy de la Bretèque worked explained, for instance, how upon hearing others utter particles like "ax" and "wey" they remembered their own experiences of loss and misery. As the tears shed by Asya's sister-in-law suggest, this memory is thoroughly embodied. Sound and poetry have the capacity to stir not only the mind but also the body and the senses in this context, and are capable of reawakening the past and the injuries it has inflicted.

Citation of poetic imagery within and between genres, as well as iteration of expressions and metaphors over successive performances, thus contributes to consolidating the kilam as a genre with a specific emotional tone, one firmly embedded in a broader aesthetic world saturated with sentiments of pain and suffering. While the boundaries of this genre are fluid—allowing for great variation of narrative content, ranging from heroic drama to historical events to personal sentiment and experience—these cross-citations hold together the genre through the affective charge they carry and create. At the same time, a recurring set of motifs and phrases, used over and over again in a wide variety of kilams, also renders poetic expression relatively homogeneous. As widely varying dramatic events and experiences are recounted through a limited pool of lyrical imagery, idiosyncratic expression becomes subdued in favor of collectively known and experienced sentiment. The conventionality of poetic expression in this way contributes to detaching the kilam from the individual singer and her personal views and opinions. As much as this allows listeners to appropriate the content for themselves, letting themselves be impacted by the familiar aesthetics of poetic expression, it casts further doubt on interpretations that would read these vocal artifacts as uniquely personal expressions of loss and affliction.

MELODIC MOLDS

Finally, the affective impact of a kilam is also determined by the way in which the words are melodized, turning from ordinary speech into sung tune. Different from the upbeat stran, however, the kilam does not evolve within a fixed melodic structure and does not follow a regular meter or rhyme. The overall move of the melody is usually descending, sometimes following an initial ascent, such that melodic lines end on a base tone, which gives occasion for heavy melismatic, trembling elaboration of a line's final word or syllable. The ascending and descending movements of the voice occur within a relatively narrow range, typically not exceeding one octave, and singers often try to sing in as high a pitch as they are able to (Christensen 1975, 3). As Amy de la Bretèque (2013, 76–81) outlines, a kilam can contain several melodic lines or motives, each of which usually coincides with a phrase or subclause of the lyrics and incorporates the same base tone present throughout the kilam. These melodic lines are repeated as the narrative progresses, giving the kilam a sense of acoustic unity. Within a line, the performer will typically declaim chunks of the narrative in rapid recitation or *parlando*, almost creating a sort of suspense that is then counterbalanced by the much slower, trembling and quavering ornamentations that accompany the descent of the melody toward the final, base note. The melody may continue to descend when the actual narrative has already expired, in which case onomatopes or expressions of pain and affliction come into place (such as *ax*, *wey*, or *lê/lo*), which then become the vehicle for the gliding descent of the voice (compare Saygun 1976). My interlocutors identified these melismatic embellishments as the most challenging aspect of performing kilams, which they explained required a skillful manipulation of the larynx (*qirik*, *gırtlak*).

Performers have considerable liberty in curtailing or expanding certain sections of the narrative and they can emphasize passages by delaying or prolonging the melodic line. Because melodic lines are repeated and tend to end on the same melismatically elongated vowels, there is a regularity to the performance even though a strict rhyme or meter is absent. The form of melodization leaves plenty of space for the incorporation of "icons of crying," that is, forms of vocal modulation that imitate actual crying and function as potent sonic indicators for sadness and bereavement (Urban 1988, 389–391; see also Beeman 2005). In kilams, Amy de la Bretèque locates such imitations of crying in the choppy succession of recitative stretches that create an effect reminiscent of sobbing, in the use of *glissando* effects that evoke forms of moaning, and in the vibrato present in the final melismas that resembles the trembling of the crying voice (2013, 79–81).

As a free-metered genre that combines recitative sections with heavy vocal embellishments the kilam bears strong similarities to other forms of sung narrative practiced in the wider region, including the Turkish genre of *uzun hava* (lit. long tune) or the Arabic *mawwal*.[24] Notably, such genres associate similar musical characteristics—including vocal ornamentation of final vowels and syllables and descending melodic patterns—with a similar emotional range of sorrow and tragedy, hinting at a broader cultural sensibility that is highly attuned toward the aesthetic elaboration of pain and suffering and that crosscuts ethnic, linguistic, and religious divides.

Among my interlocutors, the melodic patterning of kilams did not form the object of an explicit musical discourse, and the terminology used to describe the characteristics of melodization was relatively limited. When I asked for clarification, my interlocutors often lacked the words to explain how melodization worked, and would prefer to illustrate by performing an example instead. One term they did often employ to refer to the melody of their pieces, however, was *maqam* (from Arabic *maqām*), evoking a key aspect of musical theory prevalent across the Middle East. In the classical music traditions developed over centuries in Ottoman, Persian, and Arabic courts and urban centers, *maqam*s serve as melody types, each *maqam* corresponding to a scale and defining the melodic development of a piece of music. While *maqam* theory is highly elaborate and stringently codified in these urban traditions, my interlocutors would use the term very loosely to describe the melodic pattern of a kilam without in any systematic way categorizing or naming these different patterns. In order to distinguish between different melody types, they would often simply refer to a well-known kilam or performer as an example of what they sought to describe (e.g., "This is the same *maqam* as in Şakiro's 'Dewrane' ").

Despite the absence of an elaborate terminology to describe melody types, they were considered important for giving a kilam its particular emotional tone or mood, reflecting a long-standing appreciation of melody modes as incubators and catalyzers of affect and emotion across the Middle East.[25] According to my interlocutors, the form of melodization should ideally reflect the content of a kilam, its pattern, pitch, and tempo illustrating and amplifying the emotional content and moral message of the piece. One young Kurdish woman, a passionate listener of dengbêjs and herself an aspiring singer, explained this relation to me by noting that the *maqam* of a love song between a Kurdish boy and an Armenian girl would be "softer" than that of a kilam about conflict and war, which would be "hard." "It depends on the kilam's meaning," Asmîn noted. A love song, she continued, would be sung softly (*bi nerma nermo*), because it tells a story of affection. A song like "Filîtê Quto," on the other hand—the kilam in which Şemê laments her son Filît's youthful audacity and tragic fate in tribal conflict—would have a "harder" *maqam* because it is a war song, where the dramatic narrative of the events would be recounted in rapid citation. Lacking the words to express what she was trying to say, Asmîn intonated several lines from the kilam about Xalit Begê Cibirî for me, a much-celebrated Kurdish nationalist leader who was hanged by the

Turkish regime in 1925. "This," Asmîn announced, "is a political kilam." Now her voice stretched single syllables into entire melodic passages, slowly moving through the text with a sense of weightiness and heavily ornamenting line endings through quavering trebles, as if on the verge of breaking into a lament. "So the *maqam* of a political kilam is different from that of a kilam about war, which is different from that of a kilam about love," she summed up. "Depending on the kilam's meaning, the *maqam* will also vary."

But as much as melodic patterns might vary from kilam to kilam, amplifying and enhancing each piece's affective impact among audiences, ultimately their range and variability remain relatively limited. Compared to everyday speech, where speakers make use of broad variations in pitch and accent to emphasize the semantic dimensions of what is being said and to convey nuances of individual sentiment and emotion, the melodization prevalent in kilams significantly reduces these variations. As Amy de la Bretèque (2012, 139–142) writes, kilams rely on a monotone voice that moves between a much narrower range of tones than would be the case in ordinary speech. In addition, both modulations of pitch and loudness are severely constrained, creating overall a more structured and formalized form of speech compared to what one may encounter in an everyday conversation (Amy de la Bretèque et al. 2017). Effectively, the melodic lines that appear in kilams thus mold a wide range of emotional states and personal utterances into a limited number of conventional musical motives, removing these utterances from a speaker's idiosyncratic speech patterns. The result is one that is similar to the recurring poetic formulas discussed above, in that voices become molded into predictable, standardized forms that give precedence to conventional patterns over personalized or original expression. As much as the melodic elaboration of kilams thus contributes to underlining and accentuating their emotional content, it also plays a role in further detaching these vocal artifacts from the singer's personal self, reinforcing the effects already achieved by both reported speech and poetic conventionality.

Conclusion

Summing up, we may note that the kilam constitutes a genre that provides Kurdish women and men with a preset vocal mold through which to relate personal experience and bear witness to historical events. We may think of it as a ready-made yet flexible framework for relating unique content through a set of conventional textual, poetic, and melodic patterns. The elements that it musters include a preference for multiple narrator positions, rhetorical features like reported speech, a pool of frequently recurring poetic formulas, a number of conventional melodic types, reduced acoustic variability, and a heavy reliance on vocal ornamentation. Once personal experience is expressed through this particular vocal form, it becomes inserted into a long-standing aesthetic tradition of elaborating trauma and tragedy. As each kilam cites countless previous performances, it draws on a collectively accumulated affective charge that renders voices powerful vectors of pain and suffering. It thus functions as what Sara Ahmed (2004, 10–11) calls a "sticky object": an object to which affects, emotions, and sentiments become attached and which, as it circulates, makes this affective baggage travel.

The kilam is of course not unique in functioning in this way. From Andalusi *nubas* (Glasser 2016) to Portuguese fado (Gray 2013), from the Awlad ʿAli's *ghinnāwa* (Abu-Lughod 1986) to Kaluli laments (Feld 1982), musical genres thrive on the sedimentation of affect into aesthetic form. They function, as Lila Ellen Gray writes, as "a ground upon which affect and memory accrue and are figured, one performance stacked upon another, one listening overlapping with a previous listening" (2013, 17). The ability of dengbêjs' voices to make affect iterable[26]—that is, their capacity to elicit in repeated and recognizable ways particular affective responses among their listeners—relies precisely on this cumulative effect of performance and listening practices. Genre is in that sense, as Gray (2013, 8) astutely observes, not just a structure *of* feeling but also a structure *for* feeling.

But if the conventionality of genre explains part of the kilam's affective force and social potency, it also works to remove personal experience from the idiosyncrasies of the individual self. By enveloping individual testimony in a cloak of well-known, recurring aesthetic forms, the kilam mutes unique, personal experience in favor of broader socio-affective patterns. The conventionality of poetic imagery and melodic patterns as well as the ample use of reported speech all work to detach the stylized voice from its bearer while simultaneously rendering it available to others. In that sense, the kilam shows similarities to genres of expression well known to anthropologists, including ritual speech and oratory, where formalization has been identified as key to distancing a speech act from an individual speaker.[27] It turns the speaker into the "mere" animator of an utterance authored by other agents (Goffman 1979), in this way imparting to speech the authority of the ancestors, tradition, the divine.

This insight gains particular relevance in a context where the voices of female dengbêjs are all too easily read as symbols for female resistance against patriarchal tradition or as a therapeutic coming-to-terms with traumatic experiences of pain and suffering. As I have tried to demonstrate, in the cultural poetics of voice that is at stake here, however, the voice does not in any straightforward way represent the interiority, will, or agency of those who pronounce it. As a genre in which multiple perspectives routinely intermingle and where personal experience comes to be expressed through preset aesthetic formulas, the *kilam* is rather geared toward detaching the voice from the individual self. As we shall see in the next chapter, this detachment allows women to strategically employ their voices as potent tools capable of provoking, augmenting, and distributing affect. Yet, what will also become clear is that representational logics increasingly demand that voices should map onto clearly defined subjects, opening up novel sites and avenues for voices to carry out social labor.

FIGURE 2 **Connection**. Voices traveling via mobile phone network. (Film still by Braxton Hood)

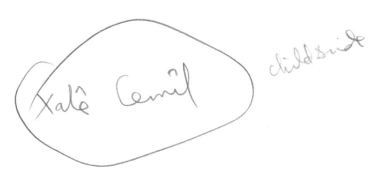

Vocal Services

One summer evening, an amicable group had assembled around the table on Gazîn's porch. It was after dinner, the time when neighbors and friends visit each other for tea, fruits, and heaps of sunflower seeds, making their rounds to exchange the latest neighborhood news and gossip, nurture friendships, and catch up with relatives. That night, at Gazîn's family we were joined by friends living in the neighborhood who had brought along their guests: a young teacher from the Kurdish town of Êlih (Tk. Batman) several hundred kilometers farther south—let me call him Adnan—and his fiancée. The conversation soon turned toward dengbêjs and how their art had flourished in the past, the pleasures and trials of life in the village, particularly for women, and the seemingly inevitable decline of Kurdish oral traditions today. Gazîn clearly enjoyed standing at the heart of attention that evening. She recounted in detail the difficulties she experienced trying to enter the world of professional music-making as a Kurdish woman, teased her husband about his flirtations in the village when they were young, and demonstrated her vocal skills by reciting kilams old and new, wedding songs and other upbeat strans.

At some point during the evening, Adnan's cell phone rang. At the other end of the line was his mother calling from Êlih. Upon hearing that her son was having tea with Dengbêj Gazîn—whose name she recognized as the singer of "Xalê Cemîl" (Uncle Cemîl), a kilam whose recording had secured Gazîn a certain fame among Kurdish audiences in Turkey—the mother seized the opportunity to ask Gazîn to sing the piece for her through the phone line. "Xalê Cemîl" is a widely known, long-established kilam about a fourteen-year-old girl who is to be married to a man the age of her father. The kilam foregrounds the perspective of the girl, who we hear recounting her misfortune of being promised to an old man whom she despises, but also features the voice

of Uncle Cemîl, praising the girl's beauty and telling her not to pay attention
to village gossip about their age difference. That night, Gazîn gladly agreed
to Adnan's mother's wish and soon began to intonate the sad story of a young
woman contrived into a marriage she abhors. Adnan had handed Gazîn his
phone with his mother on the line, and, now singing, Gazîn held it carefully
in front of her mouth like a microphone, eyes closed, making sure her lamenting, deploring voice would reach Adnan's mother, who was avidly listening hundreds of kilometers away. Once the last notes had dispersed, Gazîn
laughed that she had just given a concert for free and, taking the phone to
her ear, teased the woman at the other end of the line for not knowing how to
sing kilams herself. While the details of the ensuing conversation escaped the
rest of us gathered on the porch, it was clear that Adnan's mother—apparently
taking great pleasure in this unexpected form of live broadcasting—had
asked Gazîn to sing yet another kilam, a wish that Gazîn fulfilled with great
pleasure.

I begin this chapter with this scene of amicable sociality on a warm summer night for how it sheds light on the ways in which the (female) voice
shapes the fabric of everyday life in northern Kurdistan, suffusing it with the
sounds of gendered patterns of injury, conjuring loss, and speaking of longing, but also giving opportunity for pleasurable exchange, drawing people
together around tables and over phone lines. It thus serves here as a fitting
entry point for my inquiry into the kinds of social labor that the voices of
Kurdish women routinely carry out thanks to their sonic form and poetic
elaboration—forms of labor that, as this chapter will further develop, cannot
in any straightforward way be equated with the assertion of personal will
or the expression of private interiority. In the previous chapter we saw how
Kurdish women's voices gain social potency because of the ways in which
the genre of the kilam imbues them with affective charge. The aesthetic form
of the kilam, I proposed, plays a crucial role in turning voices into vehicles
capable of inducing sentiments of suffering, pain, and loss among their listeners. Building on this groundwork, this chapter asks how Kurdish women
make use of the affective charge that their voices carry to achieve specific social effects. It sets out to show how Kurdish women's voices have—thanks to
their social potency—contributed to animating Kurdish sociality in the face
of colonial and gendered violence, repression, and denial.

To bring into view the social labor that Kurdish female voices, once clad
in the plaintive tones of the kilam, so routinely carry out, I suggest thinking
about the voice as a *technology of affect*.[1] Technology is a useful term here because it suggests a sense of productiveness: it draws attention to the voice as
something that can be put to use in order to harness specific effects. In Michel
Foucault's work, the notion of technology heralds a move away from assump-

tions about power's alleged repressive essence toward an understanding of power as a productive force that shapes bodies and forms subjects (Behrent 2013; Foucault 1998). In this chapter, technology similarly allows me to steer clear of an understanding of voice as humanist essence, which would locate in the voice the ground of personal identity and authentic presence (Derrida 1998b). Conceptualizing voice as a technology allows me to focus instead on what voices afford those who emit, handle, and receive them. Akin to how Tia DeNora has conceptualized music as a "prosthetic technology" that "affords capacity, motivation, co-ordination, energy and endurance" (2000, 102–103), I approach voices here as forces that extend bodies and capacitate subjects.

By foregrounding affordance (what voices *do*) rather than essence (what they *are*), this approach is able to level the ground between seemingly natural, authentic voices and those mediated by modern sound technologies. In the hands (or rather mouths) of Kurdish women who knew how to wield them, voices featured as pliable and potent instruments—as technologies—whether they were mediated by not much more than the air separating a singer and her audience, or by more complex assemblages of wires, amplifiers, and receivers.[2] As the vignette above makes clear, the affective charge that rendered Kurdish women's voices so potent traveled as easily via phone networks as it would animate a live performance. This is not to say that different media did not make a difference for how voices were able to impact their listeners. As we will see in what follows, different forms of mediation endow voices with different affordances because of the specific ways in which they make vocal sound travel, circulate, and expand. But rather than positing a sharp divide between "natural" a capella voices and those that are emitted from speakers and machines, the notion of technology highlights the fact that all voices are always already mediated. Another way of saying this is that ideas about authentic or immediate voices are less objective indicators of an absence of mediation, than themselves socially, historically, and technologically produced.

Finally, the notion of technology is useful because it does not presume a specific relationship between voices and their bearers. As such, it allows me to further develop the idea that voices are not always or inherently tied to those who enunciate them in the Kurdish contexts at stake here. As we saw in the previous chapter, while the kilam is a genre of heightened emotional expression, textual and musical features frequently end up detaching it from those who pronounce it, in this way upsetting ideas we may hold about the voice as a natural vehicle for the communication of personal interiority and selfhood. This chapter further pursues this line of investigation. It provides evidence of the ways in which voices that are intensely saturated with personal sentiment can nonetheless be commissioned, gifted, and exchanged, unhinging emotional expression from the intimacy of the individual self. It also points to the ways in which disembodied voices resounding from tape decks and radio receivers construe new forms of intimacy, dispelling ideas that would cast "natural" voices as more immediate than those allegedly alienated by technologies of sound recording and reproduction.

The material put forward in what follows thus further supports the idea that voices do not always or necessarily represent those who pronounce them. It underlines this book's overall argument that voices need to be worked on to represent the will, intentionality, and interiority of their bearers; they do not do so in and of themselves. At the same time, this chapter also chronicles how sound recording and reproduction technologies like the cassette tape and the radio have raised novel questions about how the voices that these technologies bring into unprecedented circulation should relate to those emitting them. Representational logics, I propose, have provided convenient answers to these questions, contributing to the increasing ease with which voices stand for individual selves and collective identity.

Delivering Vocal Services

How might one think of voices as affective technologies? Let me return to the warm summer night on Gazîn's terrace to outline what I mean here. Picking up the reasoning advanced in the previous chapter, it becomes clear that the capacity of Gazîn's voice to have an effect that night had much to do with how the kilam as genre was able to endow her voice with affective potency. The grievances of a young girl lamenting the fate of an early, unwanted marriage found expression in the way in which Gazîn's voice softly moved through the lyrics, enveloping the story line in plaintive, descending tones, stretching the final vowel of each line in long, trembling melismas. Quavering "ax"s and "lo"s at the beginning and end of lines gave a sonic body to the sorrow and misery permeating the song, while the reiterations of Xalê Cemîl's name at the beginning and end of each stanza provided an address for the song's mournful yet accusatory tones. Thanks to this vocal stylization, Gazîn's performance tapped into a culturally highly elaborated aesthetic of suffering, in this way not only transmitting information about patriarchal privilege but also giving a sonic body to the injuries that such privilege inflicts, and thereby rendering them emotionally tangible.

It was precisely this affective impact of Gazîn's voice—the way in which it was able to call forth embodied sentiments and perhaps evoke certain memories—that we may presume rendered it such a sought-after object. Adnan's mother asked for "Xalê Cemîl" not because she sought to find out about the historical particularities of this unfortunate relationship, but because of the sensations the kilam evoked in her. In according her request, Gazîn, in turn, made instrumental use of her voice: she thus sang about the miseries of a young Kurdish woman without finding herself in that same misery at that particular moment. Doing so, her voice became the means for the establishment of a relation between two women who had never met but who shared linguistic repertoires and aesthetic sensibilities that modern sound technologies allowed them to explore. Turkey's telecommunication network thus enabled the affective charge of Gazîn's voice to reach Adnan's mother, who was receptive to this charge because of how technologies like audiocassettes, radio, and television had already shaped her sensibilities and familiarized her with Gazîn's interpretation of "Xalê Cemîl." Even though most female singers I met were not nearly as well known as Gazîn, their voices were no less prone to be relayed via sound technologies, even if at different scales and via different media. Cell phones, for instance, were always close at hand when a woman performed a kilam, allowing for live transmission and exchange as well as more durable recordings. Nieces and nephews, children and grandchildren, moreover, were eager enough to capture such performances, which by the 2000s had become widely perceived as valuable cultural heritage, and share their recordings via Facebook walls and WhatsApp groups. Yet kilams were shared and performed, captured and transmitted, not only as symbols of heritage and tradition, or for the purposes of pleasure and entertainment. Having access to their affective charge could also constitute a more pressing personal or social need, rendering those able to cater to it akin to the providers of a vocal service. It is in those instances that the quality of voice as technology—as an implement that may be employed for the effects it promises—comes to the fore most readily.

One of the women who provided such vocal services was Fadime, a feisty and quick-witted, middle-aged woman who was one of the founding members of the Women Dengbêjs Association. Her aptitude in giving vocal form to experiences of pain and suffering was in high demand among those who were struck by misfortune yet lacked the skills to give their experiences vocal expression. This included Eray, a young man in his early twenties and talented player of the ney, a long-necked flute. During the Newroz celebrations the previous year he had fallen in love with a young woman, and the two had begun seeing each other. Yet the romance was disrupted by the girl's unmarried aunt, who—envious of her niece's love affair—prevented the two from uniting. Heartbroken over this failed love, Eray confided his experience to Fadime and asked her to make a kilam that would give expression to his pain. After having listened to the details of Eray's account, she did so right on the spot, assembling what she described to me as "a very beautiful love song,"

which she left at Eray's disposal by recording it on his cell phone. At the same time, she also kept a copy for herself, recorded on an audiocassette at home, so that she would be able to work on the piece further in the future.

While Fadime supplied this kilam to Eray, whom she liked and cared for, as a favor, she was also ready to supply her vocal services to less close acquaintances for monetary remuneration. A few years back, an elderly man similarly troubled by unrequited love had thus commissioned Fadime to make a kilam about his heartache, having been directed to Fadime by acquaintances who knew of her skills. Happy to provide him with the relief he was looking for, Fadime first had him recount the intricacies of a complicated romance full of anticipations, hopes, and disappointments. She then proceeded to transform this information into a kilam, choosing the classic format of a dialogue between lover and beloved, which first gave voice to his feelings of resentment in the face of her repeated rejections and then had the woman reply to his assertions. Rendering the dialogue between the two lovers in direct speech in her kilam, Fadime composed the kind of multivocal account that we saw is typical of this genre, in which the characters are able to take on a life of their own while the dengbêj primarily features as an animator of their speech (Bakhtin 1981a). Lending her voice to her client's thoughts, opinions, and emotions, Fadime thus allowed his pain to pass through her, giving it a home in her voice (Das 1997). As with Eray, Fadime provided her client with a recording of her kilam, which she proudly told me he had made the ringtone of his cell phone, so keen was he to have this vocal artifact reverberate in his daily life.

But the range of sorrows that women tended to was not limited to the pains of star-crossed lovers. The affective potency of their voices also promised a way of engaging with the scars that a situation of protracted conflict and cycles of state violence have left on Kurdish intimate relations and everyday lives. Not long before I arrived in Wan, for instance, the Women Dengbêjs Association had been visited by a woman searching for someone to make a kilam about her sorrows as the mother of two sons who had "gone to the mountains" to join the ranks of the PKK, of whom one had fallen. Meanwhile, the woman's third son was doing his compulsory military service in the Turkish army, with more violent loss thus looming over the family. The advent of yet another instance of violent disruption, however, meant that this attempt at externalizing personal pain through the voice of another never came to fruition: after Wan was struck by a heavy earthquake in October 2011, the woman in question never returned to the association.

While the kilams that Fadime provided for friends and clients may have been brimming with sentiment, heartbreak, and romantic longing, she approached her craft from a decidedly prosaic perspective. When she told me about how she had made the kilam for Eray, for instance, she explained that making kilams was similar to cooking: "When you prepare a meal, you know what you need: potatoes, salt, water, peppers, tomato paste. You bring these together and make your meal. In the same way, the moment I get to know something, I know what to do. When I hear of someone's sorrow (*derd*), I do the necessary. I find out about their worries and make a kilam about it." During another conversation, she similarly suggested that making kilams was a process akin to the making of tea, involving a defined set of ingredients—water, tea, a teapot, and sugar—that needed to be assembled in the correct fashion in order to achieve the desired outcome. Drawing her metaphors from the lifeworld of the kitchen and household, Fadime's words not only lent the process of making kilams a prosaic matter-of-factness, but also characterized this craftsmanship as a thoroughly gendered one. Like preparing food and making tea, she suggested, kilams form part of a distinctly female sphere of labor that is key to the nourishing of social and kinship relations. As such, women may be seen as providing a vocal service complementary to that which male dengbêjs would have historically provided when offering their vocal skills to wealthy patrons seeking to spread their fame and renown or to prominent families asking to have the deeds of a deceased relative commemorated through a kilam (Çakır 2019, 120).

The way in which women's voices featured here as a vocal service to their community also closely resembles the practice of funerary lamentations—a genre that, as we saw in the previous chapter, shares aspects of musical and poetic form as well as affective charge with the kilam. Although there exists some variation across Kurdish contexts, generally lamentations are performed spontaneously by the close female kin of the deceased during the funeral proceedings (*taziye*). But women known in a community for their vocal skills—even if they are not related to the deceased—can also be invited to join or lead the lamentations.[3] As we saw in the previous chapter, Esma was one such woman who would lend her vocal skills to the bereaved community, assisting mourners in expressing and managing their grief with the help of the lamentations she would extemporaneously compose at a funeral. Fadime similarly told me that when her older sister passed away, her family asked her to make a kilam so that they would be able to cry and "feel at ease" (*içimiz rahat olsun*), suggesting that Fadime's voice provided a crucial resource for her relatives to channel their painful and potentially overwhelming emotions.[4]

What unites these examples of laments, praise songs, and love-themed kilams is how the voice functions at a remove from the interiority of the enunciating subject, taking on an instrumental quality as an object or service that can be gifted, commissioned, even purchased. Thus a specialist in lamentation like Esma did not have to be in a situation of bereavement herself in order to make the attendees of a funeral cry. Neither did Fadime have to experience the throes of rejected love or feel the pain of a mother mourning for her deceased child in order to fulfill her clients' requests for kilams that would give expression to these sentiments. And a dengbêj would not have to feel personal admiration in order to compose an effective eulogy for a patron. Rather than a singer's personal emotional state, it was the poetic formulas and vocal modulations, the multiplicity of reported voices and the echoes of intertextual connections—what I call voice as form—that allowed my interlocutors to produce sonic objects capable of having social effects. It is precisely because the potency of the voice was here rooted in its form, I suggest, that these vocal objects could not only be gifted and shared with such ease but also circulated so effortlessly via sound technologies like cassette tapes and cell phone recordings. Since their potency did not depend on the direct emotional involvement of the performer, the traction of these kilams was not threatened once they circulated apart from their original bearers, emerging in disembodied form from headphones and loudspeakers.

That the voice may function as a tool at the strategic disposal of those adept at modulating it rather than the natural expression of a person's inner self is by no means unique to the Kurdish context. The anthropological record provides ample evidence that voices are routinely separated from the interiority of those emitting them. Among Sudanese Dinka, for example, where personal songs constitute a form of individual property, those who lack the skills to compose their own can commission one from a more skilled singer in exchange for a fee (Impey 2013). In Romania professional Roma musicians employ their voices (and instruments) at family festivities like baptisms, weddings, and funerals to articulate their clients' emotional state rather than their own (Bonini Baraldi 2013; Stoichita 2008). And in Egypt, poets act as official mouthpieces for the public praise that notable guests direct at the patrons of a wedding (Reynolds 1995, 110), a role that wedding musicians take on in Kurdish contexts where this practice of public praise-giving is known as şabaş and, as in Egypt, monetarily remunerated (Çakır 2019, 197–236). Across these different contexts, we see how vocal objects are capable of expressing, arousing, and transmitting powerful sentiments without necessarily representing the intimate self and interiority of the enunciating person, rendering these vocal objects free to be gifted, shared, and exchanged.

By arguing that the voice can be strategically deployed in Kurdish lifeworlds (and elsewhere) as a vocal service catering to the social and emotional needs of others, I do not mean to suggest that performers are insincere, nor that the resulting emotions on the part of listeners are artificial. Such questions of sincerity and authenticity have long occupied the anthropological scholarship on emotions and their culturally variant forms of expression.

How can highly stylized and conventional cultural forms, like lamentations, become a means for the expression of genuine emotion, anthropologists have asked themselves. Marcel Mauss (1921), for instance, sought to reconcile what he saw as the "social, obligatory" nature of Aboriginal ritual wailing with its "violent and natural" side, concluding that the conventionalized expression of emotion is essentially the fulfillment of a social obligation rather than a spontaneous manifestation of genuine sentiment. Opposing "obligatory" to "natural," "conventional" to "sincere," expressions of emotion, however, relies on a specific (and arguably modern) notion of the subject, which distinguishes between interior essence and exterior surface. From this perspective, voice and other forms of cultural expression serve individuals as a means to bring interiority to the surface, and if they do so genuinely, a subject's expression becomes sincere (Keane 2002). What this model assumes is that the means of expressing interior emotion—voice, language, literature, song—are themselves inconsequential, serving as transparent channels that make it possible to authentically represent the interiority of the self toward the outside (Cavarero 2005; Keane 1997a, 683–684).

The notion of technology as I suggest it here, by contrast, draws attention precisely to the consequentiality of the means of expression by focusing on how vocal form matters for rendering a kilam (or a lamentation) an "efficacious sonorous object" (Stoichita 2008, 74). From this perspective, whether an expression of sentiment is sincere comes to matter less than what effects that expression is able to bring about. It thus opens up the potential to think of aesthetic form as an incubator of affects that are not in any way less authentic for being induced by concerted stimulation, challenging dominant Euro-American ideas about the primacy of content over form, of emotional interiority over embodied expression. By highlighting the consequentiality of sensory and aesthetic engagement in shaping subjective experience and collective relations, thinking of voice as an affective technology "moves us away from the mentalist understanding that locates experience in a silent interior toward one that places it in a body practically engaged with the world" (Hirschkind 2006, 29).

Voices on the Move

The vocal aesthetics I describe here, then, is one where voices were able to move, touch, jolt, because of their acoustic qualities and poetic form, and not because they necessarily represented a particular self and its interior world of opinion and feeling. As the above also makes clear, the social potency of voices was not limited to scenes of face-to-face interaction but thrived in contexts of mediation brought about by modern sound technologies. In what follows, I want to investigate the effects of such mediation in more depth. If audio technologies like cassette tapes and radio receivers allowed Kurdish voices to circulate across increasingly vast distances, how did listeners encounter these potent yet disembodied voices? What did modern sound recording and reproduction technologies afford those wielding them, and what effect did they have on understandings of self and other?

Studies by cultural historians and anthropologists on the use and uptake of modern sound technologies have shown that these technologies, because of the way in which they enable a separation of the voice from the body emitting it, raise acute questions about the status and efficacy of the voice as sound object (Chion 1982; Schafer 1977).[5] In Euro-American contexts, apparatuses like the phonograph and its successors were often perceived as uncanny or outright frightening when they were first invented, since they emitted human voices without visualizing their embodied source (Gitelman 1999; Sterne 2003). Arguably, however, such anxieties are premised on an ideology of voice that regards voices as the stable indicators of equally stable selves. As we have seen, this relation cannot be taken for granted in Kurdish contexts, where voices are routinely detached from the selves enunciating them. In such a context, sound technologies do not carry the same threat of alienating "natural" voices from their bearers, because voices are already free to roam independently of their source. This, then, might be one reason why technologies of sound recording, reproduction, and amplification were taken up with such enthusiasm by many of my interlocutors, who were unencumbered by fears that these technologies would diminish the affective impact of their voices.[6] Nonetheless, by enabling the circulation of disembodied voices on unprecedented scales, technologies like the cassette tape and the radio have also raised new questions about the relation between such disembodied voices and their bearers—and, as we shall see, representational logics have provided powerful new answers.

Fadime, we already heard, made frequent use of the recording function of cell phones and tape recorders when lending her voice to the pain of others. But she also had recourse to sound technologies to make her own suffering and hardships circulate, letting her voice do its affective labor among addressees physically far removed from herself. In the 1970s, when she was twelve years old, Fadime's father decided to marry her as a second wife to a man his own age. She was horrified at the decision, and physically resisted being taken to her husband's village on the day of the marriage, though to no avail. Situated on the other side of a high mountain pass, her in-laws' village was not far away in terms of distance, but the rugged terrain made it difficult for her to visit her family, where she might have found solace, comfort, and respite from the hard work young brides are expected to shoulder in their new households. She did, however, occasionally meet her brother while herding sheep on the high mountain pastures, which became an occasion for Fadime to send cassette tapes to her family on which she recorded her own voice. One of those tapes contained a kilam that Fadime intended as a message to her father that would tell him about her suffering and resentment. Of the originally thirty stanzas Fadime remembered only a couple over three decades later, long after she had moved to the city, her husband had passed away, and most of her own children had gotten married. These stanzas were, in her own words, "all sorrow" (*hep keder*).

Were min go wez keçek bûm, ax la bi dil şikestim, lo bi dil şikestim, ax-ey	I said, I was a girl, oh with a broken heart, oh with a broken heart, oh
Were min go bîst û şeşan, ax la wez dixwestim, lo wez dixwestim, ax-ey	I said, twenty-six people came to ask for my hand, oh they came to ask for my hand, oh
Xwedê ji bavê min ra qebûl neke, ez nedame xortekî çardeh salî, ez dame kalekî hevalê xwe, bîst û çar saetan ez digirîm, ax la ez diwestim, ax la ez diwestim, ax-ey	May God not forgive my father, he did not give me to a boy of fourteen years but to an old man his own age, I cry for twenty-four hours, oh I get tired, oh I get tired, oh
Were min go ez piçûk bûm, ax la min nezanî, lo min nezanî, ax-ey	I said, I was young, oh I did not know, oh I did not know, oh
Ez nemayê ez niza ne bi xêrê du hezar panot pere anîn nîşaniya, ax la min jî danî, la min jî danî, ax-ey	Wretched me, they paid two thousand ominous notes, oh, for my bride price, oh for my bride price, oh
Wele qezeba çilekana destê zorê ewan ez hildam anîm dame li ser heft nevisiyan, li ber derê mêrê kal da, ax la bi jin anî, ax la bi jin anî, ax-ey	Oh [. . .] they took me by force and made me the custodian of seven stepchildren at the gate of the old man's house, oh they married me, oh they married me, oh
Were min go derê mala babê ax la min hirmî ye, lo min hirmî ye, ax-ey	I said, in front of my father's house, oh there is a pear tree, oh there is a pear tree, oh
E nê keriyê pezê kekê min ê were mozelanê ku wî girtî ax la berx û mî ye, lo berx û mî ye, ax-ey	My brother's flock of sheep is like a honeycomb full of lambs and ewes, oh
Wey Xwedêyo min çi kiribî te qedera min nivîsiye, serê evî kalê ax la êl-wilî ye, wey, ax la êlwilî ye, ax-ey	Oh God what have I done that you have written this fate for me and given me to this old man, oh this ominous person
Wele min go nê sibe ye, ax la sibe sar tê, lo sibe sar tê, ax-ey	I said, it is morning, oh, the morning is cold, oh the morning is cold, oh

E nê serê Sîpanê Xelatê qebeqeba ax
la kewê lal tê, lo kewê lal tê, ax-ey

Bê lome be ecêb sed ecêb ha Marlina,
çawa xewa qîzka can cahil paxila
ax la mêrê kal tê, ax la mêrê kal tê,
ax-ey
Wele mi go bihara min tu ji halê ax
la xwe nezanî, lo xwe nezanî ax-ey
Nê min ê xîma Birca Belek ax eman
taze danî, lo taze danî ax-ey
Kuro kalê Miksî, te xortîniya xwe
berdabû, çima te cahiltiya min
pirreşê ax la ser xwe danî, ax la ser
xwe danî

From the top of Sîpanê Xelatê[7] comes
the chirping of the mute partridges,
oh the mute partridges, oh
God forsake, Marlene, it remains a
wonder, a big wonder, how could the
young girl go to sleep in the bosom
of the old man, oh of the old man, oh
I said, my springtime never got to blossom, oh it never got to blossom, oh
I had just laid the foundation of the
Tower of Belek,[8] just laid it, oh
Oh old man of Miks, you had already
lost your youth, why did you turn
my innocence into misfortune too,
oh misfortune

Fadime emphasized that when she sent the tape with those plaintive notes
and reproachful lines to her paternal village via her brother, her intent was
to communicate to her father the misery he had brought upon her: "I said
[to him], look, this is how you imprisoned my life, you plainly threw me into
fire." The tape was thus not only a means of sharing information between
separated family members, but also a moral reprimand. It reminded listeners
of how out of all the suitors that had come to ask for Fadime's hand, her father
decided to give her to an old man, just because he was able to pay up—an act
that, she insists, should not be forgiven. At the height of her youth, she ended
up tied to her husband's house, obliged to look after his seven children, while
her paternal family lived in abundance and prosperity in a house surrounded
by fruit trees and with herds rich like honeycombs. The springtime of her life,
she laments, was taken away from her when she was pushed into a cold world
where even the birds were rendered mute.

Told in the first person, this was clearly a song about Fadime's personal
misery, one that was meant to speak of her unique situation. And yet, by quot-
ing her own thoughts and emotions using the reporting verb *I said*—a common practice in many intimate and personal kilams composed by women, as
we saw in the previous chapter—Fadime effectively recounted her experience
at a remove from herself. This may not only have made it easier for Fadime to
tell of her pain and hardship, but it also opened up the account to the projec-
tions of others. Together with familiar lyrical motifs of broken hearts, mute
partridges, and the passing of spring, this distancing of the account from the
speaker rendered it one in which others—other women in particular—could
see their own hardships mirrored. Adding to that, the interspersed "ax"s and

"lo"s and the quivering descent of Fadime's voice at the end of lines all rendered this kilam an emotionally highly charged sonic object.

As such, this was a vocal artifact capable of unfolding considerable social effects. As Fadime told me, once the kilam reached her paternal village, it soon began to circulate among households, and many villagers were moved by the misery it recounted. Some even decided to take Fadime's father to account for having wrongfully treated his daughter, which, as Fadime gleefully recalled, considerably eroded his status in the village. Her voice, this goes to show, constituted a powerful instrument capable of leaving a mark on social relations, calling forth emotions that we may imagine ranged from anger to pity, which in turn contributed to altering relations of authority and perceptions of social status in the village. Importantly, these effects did not require Fadime to be physically present. Thanks to the tape recorder turning her voice into a physical, tangible object that could be exchanged and transported, played and replayed, Fadime was able to extend the reach of her voice across the rugged terrain that separated her from her paternal family, inserting herself into social relations that would have otherwise lain beyond her reach.

But the interpenetration of voice and machine did not only extend the established affective potential of voices across space. It also meant that this potential encountered its addressees in different ways. Sound-recording technologies capture sighs, tremors, and vibrations that we typically associate with physical copresence, which means that they are able to project a sense of physical proximity despite the absence of the human source that lies at the origin of the recorded sounds (Chion 1982). As such, these technologies create an almost uncanny kind of intimacy given that the voices they emit imply, as John Durham Peters (2004) notes, "a body without touch yet with acoustic traces of breath, saliva, warmth, pronunciation."[9] The indiscriminate recording of ambient and bodily sounds by the cassette recorder foregrounds the voice as an acoustic object, emphasizing embodied presence despite bodily absence. As such, the tape recorder appears to be capturing and then reproducing a comprehensive, acoustic image of "reality," where that very notion emerges as the aftereffect of the process of technological mediation (Kittler 1999). The auditory excess of sound technologies in this way produces the double fantasy of, on the one hand, an originary, "real" voice that seems to precede its own mediation and, on the other hand, sound technologies as the means that provide immediate access to that voice (Kunreuther 2006). A fantasy of immediacy is thus sustained by the very features of mediation itself, including its "unintended spillages" (Campbell 2012; see also Eisenlohr 2018; Mazzarella 2004).

It is partly as a result of the cassette recorder's capacity to produce such an impression of immediacy and copresence that, we may presume, Fadime's voice recording was able to have the effect it did. As the tape with her plaintive, accusatory voice circulated from house to house, Fadime and her worries, suffering, and anger rematerialized each time the play button was pushed, resounding from afar and yet from so close. Hissing and crackling, her recorded voice pointed to a reality of misery and hardship, not only transmitting an account of personal experience dressed in the familiar sonic aesthetics of the kilam, but also indexing a sensing, suffering body located beyond the reach of those listening. The crackling sound of the magnetic tape, deteriorating with each consecutive round of listening, may also have reminded listeners of how fragile this connection with Fadime based on circulating audiocassettes actually was (Bohlman and McMurray 2017). While the tape with her kilam rendered Fadime's suffering intimately present in acoustic terms, at the same time it also poignantly highlighted her absence, underlining that—as a newly wed bride in a community with a patrilocal settlement pattern—part of her misery lay in being at a distance from her own kin and family, structurally the main source of support for a young married woman in this setting. The mediation by cassette tape thus conferred upon Fadime's voice novel qualities, endowing her accusatory lament with an additional sense of intimate presence and immediate urgency. In this way, technological mediation augmented this young woman's capacity to interpellate her listeners, impelling them to take a stance vis-à-vis the account of her suffering and the quest for accountability it implied.

What this account indicates, then, is how for Kurdish women like Fadime sound technologies constituted useful tools to distribute and amplify the affective potential of their voices, in the process creating new forms of intimacy at the intersection of voice and machine. As such, they played an important role in sustaining and nourishing kinship relations and, at the same time, in remaking them. For Fadime, sound technology worked as a prosthetic extension of family relations, allowing her to stay in touch with her natal family despite the rugged terrain that separated them. Yet it also opened these relations up to scrutiny and critique. At the same time, the sense of intimate presence that the tape recorder was able to bestow upon Fadime's voice raised fresh questions about how her disembodied voice was going to relate to its origin. Even if the sense of immediacy projected by a tape recording like Fadime's might have been an effect of the technology itself, it nonetheless suggested that the voice resounding from this tape could provide direct access to the person emitting it. The recording in this way allowed imagining Fadime's voice to be the direct expression of her personal, interior self—an association that, as I have so far argued, the genre of the kilam and the vocal aesthetics in which it is embedded doggedly resist. But by creating new experiences of intimacy with disembodied voices, modern sound technologies like the cassette tape open up new ways of thinking about the voice as a direct and immediate emanation of those who pronounce it, simultaneously drawing on and feeding into representational logics that stand at the heart of modern politics.

A Kurdish Soundscape

In addition to cassette tapes, the radio is another technology that brings into circulation voices separated from the bodies emitting them. As such, it similarly raises questions about how to conceptualize the relation between disembodied voices and their points of origin. But if, as I have suggested, audiocassettes encourage new imaginations of the voice as a privileged channel of access to the individual self, then the radio might be thought of as a medium that enrolls voices in the making of collective forms of representation. Key to this effect is how radio technology allows transmitting sound signals from one broadcasting center to a multiplicity of receivers simultaneously, in this way creating contemporaneous soundscapes across vast geographies. This is why the radio has historically played such a crucial role in interpellating listeners as members of the "imagined communities" (Anderson 2006) of nations and empires, of transnational diasporas and marginalized populations.[10] As scholarship on radio broadcasting has pointed out, however, the radio does not simply speak on behalf of communities that already exist, but rather contributes to their making. Important for my argument here is how this process of constructing a collective subject that can appear as the source and bearer of voices emitted by the radio crucially relies on representational logics inclined to read voices as standing in for selves and their identity, both individual and collective.

As with any other technology, however, it is important to bear in mind that the cultural meanings and social effects of the radio are not inherent to its mechanics (Bessire and Fisher 2012a). In colonial Africa alone, radio "was simultaneously a dubious tool of colonial assault; a new, fascinating communication and recreational technology; a prized, symbolically powerful piece of property; and a weapon that enabled the colonized to engage the colonist" (Chikowero 2014). Tracing how the radio has historically been "seized upon" (Spitulnik 1997, 181) by Kurdish-speaking radio makers and listeners, here I am interested in the role that mediatized voices have played in constructing and upholding Kurdish forms of sociality in spite of systematic state attempts at curbing them; what Daniel Fisher (2016), in his study of Aboriginal radio production in Australia, refers to as the imperative of "linking up." The radio, I suggest, needs to be recognized as a politically consequential technology not

only for how it has historically contributed to the formation of what Stephen
Blum and Amir Hassanpour (1996) call, with reference to Anderson, Kurdish "listening publics,"[11] but also for how, in the process, it has enlisted the
socially potent voices we have encountered over the previous pages into the
representational logics of nations and communities, thereby suggesting new
pathways for imagining how Kurdish voices may relate to their bearers and
renegotiating the space in which these voices come to carry out their social
labor.

To outline these arguments, in what follows I turn to the history of one
of the most influential Kurdish-language broadcasting services, that of the
Public Radio of Armenia. Also known as Radio Yerevan, this was the station
that most directly shaped the listening habits and vocal sensibilities of my interlocutors in the Serhed region. Radio Yerevan's influence was certainly not
uniform across Kurdistan; farther to the south and across the border in Iran,
Iraq, and Syria, other Kurdish-language programs, such as those broadcast by
Radio Baghdad, were equally if not more prominent.[12] Nonetheless, I believe
that the story of Yerevan's Kurdish-language broadcasting points to broader
dynamics in how voices may become socially and politically powerful in an
age of mass mediation.

While in Turkey Kurdish voices became the target of prohibition and denial soon after the foundation of the republic in 1923, the authorities of the
neighboring Armenian Soviet Socialist Republic followed a markedly different path toward their Kurmanji-speaking population, which constitutes the
country's largest minority. The vast majority of these Kurdish speakers are
members of the Yezidi faith who escaped the genocidal violence against non-
Muslim communities that took place in the Ottoman Empire during the late
nineteenth and early twentieth centuries. While Armenia's Yezidis are primarily a rural community, Soviet policies focusing on literacy as a central
instrument to modernize the working masses, pursue social progress, and
shape communist subjects soon fostered the emergence of a Yezidi intelligentsia (Maisel 2018, 168–169). At a time when Kurdish sociopolitical and cultural
engagement was strictly suppressed in countries with sizable Kurdish populations, including chiefly Turkey, Iraq, Iran, and Syria, Armenia's Kurdish-
speaking Yezidis came to play a central role in sustaining and developing
Kurdish literary and cultural life. Armenia thus saw the production of the
first Kurdish film, "Zarê," in 1926, and the publication of the first Kurdish
novel in 1935. Kurmanji Kurdish was made part of the national curriculum at
Yezidi schools as early as the 1920s, while the first Kurdology conference, with
over ninety participants from all over the Caucasus, took place in Yerevan in
1934. The Armenian capital is also where a Kurdish newspaper, *Riya Taze*, has
been published since 1930 (Elend 2021, 55–67).

The opening of a Kurdish section at Armenia's public radio station in 1955 has to be seen in this context. Following a visit by Iraq's Kurdish leader Mele Mustafa Barzani to Moscow, it was first launched for a test period of two years, which was eventually extended (Ağcakulu 2012, 57). Approved by and under the strict surveillance of the communist leadership in Moscow and Yerevan, the Kurdish-language broadcasting service was part of a broader effort at establishing and diffusing Soviet modernity inside and outside the Soviet Union, an effort to which mass media like the radio were central (Lovell 2015). While spreading the socialist message constituted the central impetus for the founding and continued operation of the Kurdish-language service, it soon engendered effects far beyond the party cadres' intentions. Technologies are after all, as Brian Larkin (2008, 3) writes, "unstable things." As its airwaves began to traverse national boundaries following the installation of a powerful shortwave signal in 1957 that reached as far as Baghdad, Khorasan, and central Anatolia, Radio Yerevan, as it came to be popularly known among Kurdish speakers, emerged as a central medium through which dispersed Kurdish communities came to relate to each other (Elend 2021).

The transformation of Radio Yerevan from a communist broadcasting service into a central medium for the making of Kurdish sociality was due not least to the efforts of successive generations of Yerevan's Celîl family. When Yezidi writer and intellectual Casimê Celîl was appointed as head of the Kurdish section of Radio Yerevan in 1955, he was far more interested in using the technological infrastructure at his disposal to systematically record, archive, and transmit the rich oral repertoires of Armenia's Yezidi community than in broadcasting news bulletins. Initially, the administration was skeptical about Celîl's plans for broadcasting the repertoires of Kurdish-speaking singers and musicians, whom Celîl began to bring to the studios in Yerevan from the Yezidi villages in the countryside. Once it became apparent that it was precisely those music recordings that drew Armenia's Yezidi villagers to radio receivers, however, the administration agreed to combine news broadcasts with music transmission and gradually increased the time accorded to the Kurdish-language program from fifteen minutes to an hour and a half daily by the 1960s (İnanç 2016, 93–94). Music programming thus quickly became central to Radio Yerevan's Kurdish-language service, appealing to listeners far beyond Armenia's national borders. While Armenia's own Kurdish-speaking population numbered no more than several tens of thousands, across the border in Turkey millions of Kurds—particularly those in the northern regions of Serhed, adjacent to the Armenian border—listened regularly to the station's broadcasts. Assembled clandestinely around radio receivers in towns and villages, they would eagerly wait for the signal "Yerevan is speaking, dear listeners" (*Êrîvan xeber dide, guhdarên ezîz*) to emerge from the crackles and hisses of the ether, heralding the onset of ninety minutes filled with Kurdish words, tunes, and melodies, made all the more precious because in Turkey these were rigorously banned. Turkish state authorities, clearly aware of the political significance of this unfolding acoustic world, responded with their own "sound-wave warfare" (Fanon 1965, 85), which involved not only prohibiting the broadcasts but also seizing radio receivers from Kurdish families (Glastonbury 2018) and reinforcing Turkey's own broadcasting network in the Kurdish regions (Elend 2021, 181–185; Yüksel 2011, 340).

The content of Radio Yerevan's broadcasts was closely controlled by Moscow and the communist cadres in Armenia, and the radio makers needed prior approval for everything that was to be transmitted. This meant that the broadcasts had to adhere strictly to socialist principles and the official party line. If traditional kilams were seen as depicting feudal and tribal relations too explicitly, overseers did not hesitate to censor them. Karapetê Xaço, for instance, a Kurdish-speaking Armenian from the region of Êlih in today's Turkey, who settled in Armenia in the 1940s and became one of the most well-known dengbêjs broadcast by the radio, recalls how the radio makers discouraged him from singing long-established narratives about tribal conflicts and asked him to sing love-themed kilams instead, something he was reluctant to do (Kevirbirî 2002, 54–55). Such pressures, in addition to the communist leadership's potential accusations that the program fostered minority nationalism, reinforced its focus on "nonpolitical" content, including upbeat dance songs, tragic kilams (as long as they were not deemed too politically sensitive), folk tales, and radio plays. This did not make the broadcasts any less valuable to their listeners, however—quite to the contrary.[13] In Turkey, Radio Yerevan's broadcasting rhythm quickly came to structure time for Kurdish speakers. Many of my Serhedî interlocutors recalled the broadcasting hours as cherished moments when households, even entire villages, would assemble around the radio receiver to listen to Yerevan's Kurdish voices. Initially the broadcasts were a cause of great wonder. They coincided with the arrival of the first radios in Turkey's Kurdish regions, and this new technology, which was able to make disembodied voices emerge from metallic boxes, arriving seemingly out of nowhere, stirred fascination. Even as the fascination waned, however, the Kurdish-language broadcasts of Radio Yerevan retained their status as occasions that stood outside the flow of ordinary life. The broadcast's voices commanded a sense of weightiness and solemnity, calling for attention and encouraging forms of comportment that would match their significance.[14] One Yezidi family in Armenia, for example, reported to the radio makers how on Sundays all sisters would take their weekly bath, diligently comb their hair, and put on their best clothes before assembling around the receiver to listen to the ninety minutes of Kurdish broadcast (İnanç 2016, 99).

In curating the radio broadcasts and sound archive, Celîl and his collaborators were keen to capture and preserve "traditional" Yezidi voices they feared were being extinguished by the expansion of modern lifestyles. The authenticity they sought to capture in sound, however, proved an evanescent object. In an interview recounting her memories of her time as the head of the section's music department, a position she took over from her father in 1967, Casimê Celîl's daughter Cemîle, for instance, related her worries that the dengbêjs coming to the radio from the countryside would easily feel insecure in the studio with its microphones, mixing tables, and other technological equipment (Alê n.d., 227–228). According to her sister Zîna, singing into a piece of metal called a microphone had the potential to leave a negative impact on the singers' psyche (pisîxîk) (İnanç 2016, 92); something that Cemîle sought to prevent by instructing visiting dengbêjs to disregard the studio environment and instead imagine themselves in their villages or the mountain pastures while they recorded their pieces. Some singers even refused outright to have their voices recorded. A group of young Yezidi women whom Casimê Celîl had invited to the capital when he first began his systematic recordings in the mid-1950s, for instance, feared that the black box into which they were instructed to sing was going to steal their voices and that they would be left with none of their own. It took Celîl's demonstration of the technology with his own voice in order to persuade the group that they had nothing to fear (İnanç 2016, 26–27). In order to achieve the desired quality of voices that were going to sound as clear and sincere (zelal û helal) as "our mother's milk," in Cemîle's words, the radio makers invested considerable efforts to minimize the audibility of technology-induced anxiety on the recordings (Alê n.d., 228). The authenticity that transpired over Radio Yerevan's airwaves consequently came to rely on effacing as much as possible the technological mediation that rendered its capture possible in the first place.

That the voices of the singers and dengbêjs whom Celîl invited to the studio in Yerevan were not trained like those of the singers who animated the Armenian programs was a further element that ensured, as Casimê Celîl's son Celîlê put it in his memoirs, the authentic (ji eslê xwe ne dûr) and natural (sirûştî) quality of the voice that his father envisioned (İnanç 2016, 29). The resulting sound, however, was by no means universally valued. A number of Armenian radio workers and Kurdish intellectuals found the songs broadcast by Celîl to be less pure and natural than simply "primitive." At some point the radio administration even solicited an Armenian opera singer who was to intonate the Kurdish repertoires collected by Celîl so as to increase their quality—much to Celîl's dismay, who quickly put an end to the initiative (İnanç 2016, 30). What Celîl did allow for, by contrast, was that dengbêjs' repertoires would be performed with musical accompaniment. As Gayane Ghazaryan

(2020, 27–28) reports, it was Yerevan's radio makers who introduced the practice of instrumentalization to Armenia's Yezidi dengbêjs, reasoning that this would make listening to their repertoires more enjoyable for radio audiences. At the same time, Celîl was determined that music makers were to stay true to time-honored tunes and refrain from experimenting with extravagant musical elaboration so as to preserve true Kurdishness (*Kurdîtî*) (İnanç 2016, 67).

The "natural" and "authentic" quality of the voices that Radio Yerevan brought into circulation, then, was less naturally given than the outcome of a process of deliberate decision-making, selection, and contestation. Casimê Celîl's insistence on making central to the Kurdish broadcasting service voices that others perceived as primitive ended up decisively shaping what Kurdishness has come to sound like in an age of technological modernity. This is a sound dominated by the guttural, rough voices of dengbêjs, many of them male, singing of heroic tragedy and irreparable loss, and by the voices of Yezidi women, ranging in timbre from clear and high-pitched to thick and gravelly, as they intonate upbeat wedding and work songs (*stran*s) as well as the occasional kilam. It is also the sound of the instruments that were chosen to accompany these voices, including the deep, resonating sounds of the mey and duduk, closely related double reed instruments often likened to a crying voice; the breathy bilûr flute, evoking melancholy and longing for many Kurdish audiences; and the def, a large frame drum, supporting the upbeat rhythms of dance repertoires.

As the Kurdish section acquired more broadcasting time, grew in staff, and managed to secure more resources over time, the program began to expand beyond the repertoires of Armenia's Yezidi communities. Celîl and his successors, ever keen to chart out the vast expanse of Kurdish vocality, invited musicians and singers from Iran, Iraq, Syria, and the Caucasian countries as well as those from Kurdish communities in Kazakhstan and Kyrgyzstan (exiled during Stalin's reign) to come to Yerevan's studios and record their voices. A particularly rich source of material were Kurdish-speaking Armenians who migrated to Armenia from Syria and Iraq and brought with them the musical traditions of these regions (Elend 2021, 171). Once portable sound-recording technologies became more widely available, radio staff also ventured out to the Kurdish-inhabited regions of neighboring countries, collecting voices and capturing tunes. Following the socialist revolution in Iraq in 1958, the Kurdish sections at the Yerevan and Baghdad radio stations began to exchange sound recordings, which added some of the most famous Kurdish voices of the twentieth century to Radio Yerevan's broadcasts, including those of Mehmed Arif Cizrawî, Kawis Axa, and Eyşe Şan. By 1964, the radio staff had in this way managed to assemble an archive of more than 700 recordings, a number that has increased to over 10,000 today (Ghazaryan 2020, 23; İnanç 2016, 142–143).

While Kurdish voices were persecuted, suppressed, and silenced elsewhere, Radio Yerevan's Kurdish broadcasting service was where a Kurdish acoustic universe came to be mapped out, its frontiers delineated, and its contours elaborated. Here, a vast expanse of Kurdish oral repertoires was gathered, registered, and archived, bringing together varieties of Kurdish language, narrative, and song that had previously had little contact. In the process, the radio contributed to creating the very "Kurdish culture" that Celîl and his successors set out to document. If, as Benedict Anderson writes, "communities are to be distinguished, not by their falsity/genuineness, but by the style in which they are imagined" (2006, 6), Radio Yerevan may indeed be understood as having shaped the style—the aesthetic sensibilities, poetic references, and sonic cadences—through which Kurdish communities have come to imagine themselves.[15] Yet Radio Yerevan was not only a site of arrest: it was also a site that put voices into circulation, gathering them for dispersal. As such, it was a crucial force shaping the repertoires of the dengbêjs I encountered in Wan who came of age in the 1960s and 1970s, at the height of Radio Yerevan's influence. Nearly all my interlocutors mentioned the radio station as pivotal in their formation as dengbêjs, for it was through its broadcasts that they encountered repertoires that went beyond those circulating in the villages and towns they hailed from, introducing them to musical traditions from beyond the regional genealogies they were familiar with.[16]

Most of the female dengbêjs I got to know also underlined that Radio Yerevan was important to them because here they encountered, some for the first time, Kurdish women's voices disseminated through a public medium. While women were by no means silent in the communities where my interlocutors grew up, their singing voices tended to be confined to domestic and all-female contexts. The women's voices transmitted over Radio Yerevan's airwaves, by contrast, came to resound among audiences whose gender composition was unpredictable. Arguably, the fact that radio technology allows broadcasting voices without exposing the bodies of those pronouncing them was crucial for women to enter the recording studios in the first place, since it allowed for a degree of anonymity and was in this way able to temper patriarchal anxieties surrounding the public audibility of women's voices. At first, the radio makers broadcasted the voices of female Yezidis anonymously, without mentioning their names, in order to circumvent opposition by the women's families (Ağcakulu 2012, 91).[17] Over time, however, increasing numbers of women chose to have their voices broadcast without hiding their identities, encouraged, we may presume, not only by Soviet gender policies prevalent in Armenia but also by promises of fame and popularity. As a result, the voices of women like Meyrem Xan, Eyşe Şan, Fatma Îsa, Susika Simo, and Aslîka Qedir have centrally shaped what "Kurdishness" sounds and feels like, in the process fostering aspirations among ordinary Kurdish women that had previously been unthinkable.

The central role that the radio played in the making of Kurdish sociality is also reflected in the many letters the radio makers received from avid listeners as far away as Lebanon, Syria, and Iraq, who thanked the radio for the tunes it broadcasted and often expressed their wishes for a particular song or melody. Many Yezidi Kurds from Armenia, for instance, addressed themselves to the radio in order to reach out to family members who were doing military service or who had migrated for work to other Soviet republics, asking for greetings to be sent through the ether or for a song to be dedicated. Military conscripts often replied in the same way. The radio broadcasts thus became a crucial technology for mediating and sustaining kinship relations severed by the pressures of labor migration and the demands of national regimes of citizenship. As such, they functioned akin to the cassette tapes Fadime exchanged with her family members, which had similarly served as a means to shore up existing kin ties. The radio, however, implicated an infinitely vaster community of listeners in this "work of kinship."[18] As Fisher (2016, 43–79) argues for Aboriginal radio in Australia, kinship emerges here as a self-conscious object of reflection—not just an objective reality to which the radio refers, but a mediatized category with its own performative powers. In the Kurdish context this meant that Radio Yerevan contributed to establishing Kurdish dispersal and disconnection as a central matter of social and political concern, which media like the radio could then be expected to address and alleviate.[19] At the same time, it also subjected existing ties of kinship and association to critical scrutiny, just like Fadime's cassette tapes had done. By challenging the monopoly on knowledge dissemination that Kurdish leadership figures like *agha*s and *sheyh*s had long enjoyed, Radio Yerevan played an important role in undermining the authority of these traditional power holders while opening up entirely new worlds of imagination to local Kurdish communities, particularly to women and children (Elend 2021, 161–168).

But the radio was powerful not only because of the information it transmitted. By broadcasting the affectively dense voices of Kurdish dengbêjs it also provided acoustic and emotional resources for engaging histories of suffering, migration, and flight. One Yezidi listener from Armenia, for instance, wrote to the radio makers to ask for "Hêdî Bajo" (Ride Slowly), a kilam about an injured Kurdish horseman, to be played for her grandparents. Whenever the grandparents heard the song on the radio, she wrote, it reminded them of their native villages now situated across the border in Turkey; villages they remembered as being filled with dead bodies when they fled during the genocidal massacres of World War I. Amid these memories, the letter writer explained, the sounds of "Hêdî Bajo" were an important means for her grandparents to soothe the anguish that filled their hearts (İnanç 2016, 98). For these Yezidi grandparents, this goes to show, the radio mattered because it gave them access to voices as powerful affective forces, capable of eliciting and sharing, soothing and alleviating, sensations related to pain and suffering. What mattered less was whether these voices were tied to specific individuals and their intimate selves.

The way in which Radio Yerevan has come to take on significance for many Kurds in Turkey, on the other hand, is notably different. Following the collapse of the Soviet Union, the radio station lost most of its funding, staff, and equipment and quickly diminished in significance, while across the region audiovisual media like the television became increasingly dominant (Ghazaryan 2020, 24–25). As a result, the station lives on today less as an active acoustic medium than as an object of nostalgic reminiscence and longing, one that the elderly look back on during evenings like those with which I opened this chapter and that engaged youth eagerly consume through books and documentaries. Kurdish intellectuals, cultural producers, and politicians, for their part, routinely hail the station for the role it played in upholding Kurdish language, culture, and heritage against the onslaught of Turkish state policies of prohibition and assimilation. When the former mayor of Diyarbekir, Osman Baydemir, visited the Armenian capital in 2014, for instance, he stated that he considered himself to have two mothers: one his biological mother, the other Radio Yerevan (Ghazaryan 2019). Quite literally cast as an element of Kurdish kinship, the radio becomes here a source of cultural and linguistic nourishment in the face of assimilation and denial back in Turkey. As a morally dense and politically charged site of Kurdish identity, Radio Yerevan has as a result become an important point of reference for anyone seeking to project a Kurdish voice—such as, for instance, the young makers of Podcast Kurdî, established in 2020, who have adopted a version of the station's legendary "Yerevan is speaking, dear listeners!" as their slogan.[20]

What drives this embrace of Radio Yerevan is an appreciation of the voices it curated and broadcast throughout the second half of the twentieth century as being representative of an overarching Kurdish culture and heritage. In casting the radio as "the voice" of the Kurdish people, this appreciation radically differs from how listeners like the Yezidi grandparents asking to listen to "Hêdî Bajo" would have approached the radio broadcasts. Their appreciation focused on the actual contours of vocal form transmitted via the ether, on the specific ways in which the kilam's performer would melodize the narrative, rapidly reciting certain sections, while drawing out others, embellishing them with plaintive melismas. The appreciation by figures like Osman Baydemir, on the other hand, casts the radio as a potent index of Kurdish identity, a metonym for the cultural heritage and history of a people whose very existence was denied for decades. What we see here is a shift in how the voices of dengbêjs and other performers of Kurdish oral repertoires are understood and valued, from sound objects dense with affect and emotion to indices representative of Kurdish culture and tradition. What also becomes clear is that radio technology has played a crucial role in fostering these representational logics. As I have argued, one of Radio Yerevan's key achievements was to expand the reach of Kurdish voices' social potency and affective charge across vast geographies. In the process, these voices provided not only important sonic and emotional services to far-flung audiences; they also encouraged new forms of listening. By bringing into circulation voices without making visible their human source, the radio raised fresh questions about what these voices stood for and how they related to their bearers. Representational logics, I contend, have provided powerful answers that have allowed imagining a collective Kurdish subject to match the voices broadcast over Radio Yerevan's airwaves, opening up new avenues for understanding the station and its voices as representative vehicles for a Kurdish self and its identity.

Conclusion

Focusing on what voices *do* (affordances) rather than on what they *are* (essence), this chapter has continued to question the seemingly natural link between voice and the interiority of the self, so central to modern ideologies of voice. In a context where subjects lend their voices to express the pain of others and where disembodied voices have the capacity to touch their listeners, the voice functions less as a necessary or natural conveyor of personal feeling. Rather, voices emerge as mobile implements capable of distributing affect, in this way drawing subjects into their fold, establishing relations of pleasurable exchange, and engaging experiences of dispersal and loss. As I have argued, for those Kurdish women who know how to wield it, the voice in this way offers itself as a powerful technology, one they are able to employ strategically in order to call forth embodied and affective responses among listeners. Because the voice constitutes here an affectively powerful force that is, nevertheless, not in any inherent way attached to the self and interiority of its bearers, it is able to function akin to a service, provided by those with the necessary vocal skills for those needing to come to terms with pain, loss, and bereavement.

In addition, I have suggested that where voices are understood as affectively potent, mobile instruments rather than as personalized expressions of the self, there does not exist a necessary, qualitative leap between the "natural" voices animating face-to-face communication and those mediated by modern sound technologies. Here, no authenticity is lost, no potencies spoiled when voices become imprinted on magnetic tape or resound from metallic loudspeakers. Quite to the contrary, as this chapter has demonstrated, the seemingly uprooted, disembodied voices brought into circulation by modern sound technologies do not lose their social potency, instead presenting themselves as crucial resources for addressing the harms done by gendered kinship arrangements, colonial dispossession and dispersal, and histories of flight and migration.

While mediation as such might not diminish vocal force and potency, its specifics nonetheless matter for the kind of effects voices are able to have. As we have seen, the ways in which modern sound technologies are able to make voices seem near when their bearers are far, immediate when they are in fact highly mediated, were crucial for the kinds of social labor Kurdish voices were able to carry out. It was thus thanks to the specific acoustic qualities produced by tape-recording technology that Fadime's cassettes were able to create a sense of intimate proximity with her misery and hardship among those who listened to them, with lasting effects on social relations in her village. Similarly, when Radio Yerevan's producers mobilized recording technology to project an "authentic" sound of Kurdishness, they contributed to making an overarching Kurdish culture and identity imaginable. The facts of technological mediation may thus not have diminished vocal potency, but they have enabled voices to do novel kinds of social labor. Where tapes are able to sustain a fantasy of access to another's suffering via the recorded voice, this voice becomes easily understood as less a mobile affective vector than the intimate expression of the speaker from whom it originates. And where voices broadcast over the ether begin to point to a shared cultural heritage, they readily come to figure as an index of that culture's collective bearer, the Kurdish people, and its identity. Representational logics, in other words, have provided convenient anchors for voices that modern sound technologies have separated from their bearers on unprecedented scales. In this way they have prominently shaped the kind of social labor Kurdish voices are able to carry out today—labor that the remaining chapters of this book will explore in more detail.

FIGURE 3 **Pain**. Gazîn and Eyşe Şan. (Photo by author)

Voice, Self, and Pain

Ey felekê, çima çima te li min reş kir roj û şevan	Hey destiny, why have you darkened my days and nights
Ey felekê, çima çima te li min reş kir hemî zeman	Hey destiny, why have you darkened all my times
Ey felekê, ey felekê, çima wiha kir ey felekê	Hey destiny, hey destiny, why have you done this, hey destiny
Ey felekê, ey felekê, çima wiha kir ey felekê	Hey destiny, hey destiny, why have you done this, hey destiny

It was a cold winter night in a small mountain village only several kilometers away from the Iranian border when Gazîn's voice brought forth these words clad in grief and sadness, wavering between a sense of resignation and a spirit of angry accusation. Her strong voice readily took possession of the village house's large living room, extending its dense presence even into the farthest corner, laying claim to those who had assembled here late that cold winter night. Seated on cushions arranged along the walls of the spacious room were the female members, neighbors, and friends of one of the village's affluent families. The male family members, including our host, sat around the coal stove in the little anteroom, out of sight yet well within the ambit of Gazîn's pervasive voice, which—apart from the occasional clinking of tea glasses and the sobbing of a child—reigned over the house.

Uxur berxê min şehît xistin	They have made Uxur, my lamb, a martyr
Destê xwe bi xwîna wî şuştin	They have washed their hands in his blood
Mervan berxê min şehît xistin	They have made Mervan, my lamb, a martyr
Destê xwe bi xwîna wî şuştin	They have washed their hands in his blood
Wan dijminê hov û xwînxwar	Those savage, bloodthirsty enemies

Ez nizanim li ku hiştin	I don't know where they left him
Wan dijminê hov û xwînxwar	Those savage, bloodthirsty enemies
Ez nizanim li ku hiştin	I don't know where they left him

Some of the women's eyes started to fill with tears as Gazîn lamented the violent death of Uxur, her brother-in-law who lost his life only a year after having joined the Kurdish guerrilla forces in the early 1990s. Gazîn's voice went on to relentlessly transform into sound and language the fate of this young man and the pain that it caused her, repeatedly returning to the chorus: "Hey destiny, hey destiny, why have you done this, hey destiny." Gazîn's pain was exacerbated by the fact that there was no grave at which to mourn for Uxur as his body had never been returned to the family. Her voice seemed heavy under the burden of making this death, which had left no material trace, tangible.

Goristana wî nabînim	I cannot find his grave
Li ser bigirîm bilorînim	Where I could cry and lament
Goristana wî nabînim	I cannot find his grave
Li ser bigirîm bilorînim	Where I could cry and lament
Dil û hinav tijî xwîn e	My heart, my insides are full of blood
Rondikê çavê min dibarînim	I let my tears flow
Dil û hinav tijî xwîn e	My heart, my insides are full of blood
Rondikê çavê min dibarînim	I let my tears flow

By now, several of the women listening were silently weeping and Gazîn's eyes, too, had filled with tears. As her voice finally petered out on the last drawn-out notes, one last time calling destiny to account for its merciless course of action, it left in its place a thick, heavy silence. Tea glasses continued to jingle, the child to sob. Then an elderly woman broke the spell, remarking with reference to the daughter of the host, a young woman in her early twenties who was still busy drying her tears, that this young woman's brother, too, had fallen in the mountains. Gazîn nodded affirmatively and declared: "My heart is injured just like hers."

In the previous chapters we saw how voices in northern Kurdistan often defy expectations that they should represent those who pronounce them. Rather than represent personal interiority or will, I suggested, voices often circulate at a remove from their bearers. Recognized as powerful affective forces thanks to their vocal form, voices are traded as a service or commissioned as a means to impact social relations, their acoustic elaboration and narrative conventions detaching them from the idiosyncrasies of individual personality. When Gazîn pronounced "Ey Felekê" that night in the village, her voice was similarly no straightforward index of her interior self. Its capacity to make eyes shed tears and speak to injured hearts derived not only from how it expressed Gazîn's personal suffering but also—and perhaps even more so—from the ways in which its acoustic and poetic form situated it within an established tradition of tragic oral expression that allowed her listeners to tune into and, in a sense, appropriate the kilam for themselves.

As the previous chapter made clear, however, ideas and imaginations of voice in Turkey's Kurdish regions have been changing, not least under the impact of media and technology, as well as the force of the nation-state and its modes of governance. In this context, representational logics have provided powerful new frameworks for making sense of disembodied voices circulating on unprecedented scales, mapping them with increasing ease onto individual selves and collective identities. Yet, as I have maintained, the kilam constitutes a genre that dovetails with such representational logics only with difficulty. Its narrative, poetic, and acoustic qualities frustrate attempts to neatly map the sorrowful sentiments that kilams so routinely express and elicit onto the personal self of those who pronounce them. How, this prompts me to ask, might new ideas about the representational capacity of voices impact the vocal form of kilams like "Ey Felekê"? How, in other words, would a kilam's sonic articulation and textual qualities need to change in order to represent the self and identity of the Kurdish women uttering it—and with what consequences? If voices do not in and of themselves represent anyone or anything, this chapter sets out to track what it takes for voices to begin to reliably stand in for the self.

As should be clear by now, the kilam is a (if not the) key genre available to Kurdish women and men through which to express and elicit sentiments of loss, grief, and tragedy. This means that the kilam has provided an important cultural resource through which Kurdish populations have engaged the harms wrought by colonial violence, expropriation, and flight and through which Kurdish women, in particular, have addressed the injuries inflicted by patriarchal morality and control. Reading through a lens of representational vocality, one might understand the voicing of pain and suffering that the kilam facilitates as an important avenue toward individual and collective healing, allowing the self to speak out about what burdens it. Alternatively, such a lens might cast the voicing of suffering as a key political act that allows people to assert their grievances and resist against the powerful orders of patriarchy and the nation-state. From such a vantage point, Gazîn singing about the fate of her brother-in-law might appear either as a form of therapeutic engagement with terrible loss or as an act of voicing historical injustices that national politics ought to rectify.

Such a reading, however, relies on a very specific (and arguably "modern") understanding of the relationship between voice, self, and pain—one that comprehends the self as endowed with a rich, conflictual interiority for which the voice serves as the prime vehicle of expression, and which it thus comes to

represent. Following Michel Foucault (1998), we may trace this understanding
to the Christian practice of confession with its simultaneous emphasis on in-
trospection and vocal expressivity and the ways in which this legacy has been
taken up, secularized, and institutionalized by the psychological disciplines
throughout the nineteenth and twentieth centuries. While emotional experience has as a result become increasingly privatized within the bounds of the
self-contained individual, these same individuals also constitutively rely on
the public expression of their interior selves for recognition and respite (Asad
2000; Berlant 2008). Not only has this left us with a burgeoning therapeutic
culture that heralds the empowering capacities of speaking out and being
vocal (Schlichter 2014), but it has also inserted a distinct "will to witness and
document suffering" (Chakrabarty 2000, 117) into the emotional scaffolding
of modern subjectivity. As we have come to accept voices as representative of
the will and interiority of their bearers, acts of assuming voice have been imbued with powerful promises as avenues toward political participation, social
inclusion, and personal and collective healing. Our political systems are in
many ways built around these promises, as they rely on people voicing their
grievances, wishes, and ideas as a central impetus for democratic deliberation
through representational organs like councils, parliaments, and truth commissions (Posel 2008; Slotta 2015).

Pointing to the limits that speech runs up against when trying to give
expression to experiences of pain and loss, scholars studying the aftermath of
mass violence and atrocity have offered important critiques of liberal logics
that would cast the voice as an unambiguous route to healing, inclusion, and
recognition (Das et al. 2000; Das et al. 2001; Kleinman, Das, and Lock 1997).
The literature on trauma has thus highlighted how extreme experiences of
violence, whose quality surpasses our frames of intelligibility, have the force
to shatter speech, calling into question not only the coherence of language
but also that of the subject (Caruth 1996; Felman and Laub 1992). Others have
found speech that resists signification to constitute a powerful challenge to
existing power structures. In this vein, Umut Yıldırım (2021) interprets the
refusal of bereaved Kurdish mothers to voice their suffering vis-à-vis mental health practitioners within the Turkish medical system as an assertion of
political critique and a form of decolonial practice (also compare Üstündağ
2019a, b). In her work with Indian women displaced during the 1947 Partition,
on the other hand, Veena Das (2007) has drawn attention to how, when language fails the subject, legacies of violence and loss often become negotiated
in the intimate spaces of everyday life rather than in moments of speaking out
or up. Others have drawn attention to how political grammars of suffering,
such as discourses on heroism and martyrdom, routinely fail to provide an
avenue for expressing forms of loss that are not easily assimilated into het-

eronormative categories of national sacrifice (Buch Segal 2016). Legal mechanisms encouraging the voicing of suffering, such as truth and reconciliation commissions, too, have been critiqued for reinforcing hegemonic frames of the patriarchal nation (Ross 2003), while medicalized discourses concerned with mental health and trauma tend to individualize and pathologize pain and suffering at the same time as they encourage its voicing (Argenti-Pillen 2003; Fassin and Rechtman 2009).

The attention to language and its limits fostered by this literature has been a productive site to question commonplace assumptions about the therapeutic value of "raising one's voice." It has laid bare how the promise offered by the liberal polity to recognize and remedy suffering once it is voiced operates within very tight discursive frames that frequently cast as unintelligible painful experiences that defy the gendered norms of the national order and, in this way, deny them recognition (Butler 1997). The voice, however, has largely been taken for granted in this literature as that which by default represents the (political) will of individuals or collectives, even if it might occasionally fail the subject or be refused public acknowledgment. Yet accepting the link between voice and self as self-evident means that we can gauge what happens when painful experience gets translated into voice only in relation to whether or not pain and the subject associated with it are successfully granted recognition. Doing so elides not only how voiced pain has effects thanks to its acoustic qualities and aesthetic style, but also prevents us from interrogating how voices come to stand for specific subjects and their pain in the first place—and what effects such representational logics may have.

In this chapter, I do not limit my analysis to an exploration of the politically and socially sanctioned grammars that are available to express pain in northern Kurdistan and how these might enable or foreclose recognition. Rather than taking the voice for granted as representative of the self and its will or interiority, I ask what shape voices need to adopt before they can carry out any representational labor at all, and what consequences their doing so entails. I proceed by first detailing how voices were for many of my interlocutors less tame objects capable of faithfully representing their inner selves than powerful forces called forth by experiences of pain and suffering that often transcended the boundaries of singular subjects. I further trace how long-standing repertoires of Kurdish oral tradition reflect this fragmented relation between voice, self, and pain, but also show how this vocal aesthetics has been changing such that voices increasingly feature as expressive vehicles for singular individuals and their (painful) interiority. In the last part of the chapter, I turn to the lives and work of two Kurdish women singers to delineate the stakes that are involved when the voice comes to represent the private self. This leads me to suggest that voicing personal suffering is not simply liberating (or healing), but that it inscribes women in novel arrangements of vulnerability and exposure.

Of *Deng* and *Derd*, Voice and Sorrow

Recall Asya, whom we encountered as the singer of the lament for Hozan Feraşîn in chapter 1. She would often tell me that she considered herself not actually a dengbêj, but rather a derdbêj. This was a play of words, where Asya drew on the phonetic similarity between *deng*, the Kurdish word for "voice" as well as "news, word, repute," and *derd*, meaning "sorrow." By substituting *derd* for *deng*, Asya implied that she was first and foremost a teller (-*bêj*) of sorrows rather than someone recounting history or relaying information. In this way, she articulated the widespread idea that dengbêjs' oral repertoires have their origin in the narration of pain and suffering. For her, as for many of the women I spoke to, this also meant that this oral tradition was fundamentally gendered because, as she put it, "all pain falls upon women." Women, she said, are the ones who are routinely married against their will, and once married they are expected to adapt to their husband's wishes, have low status in family hierarchies, work hard, and might experience violence in their in-laws' household. According to Asya, this intimate familiarity with pain and suffering makes women and not men the real masters of the kilam, even if it is men who are mostly celebrated as famous dengbêjs, while women's voices are often described as immodest or shameful when they resound in public. This was a common sentiment. Gulbahar, a female singer associated with the Dengbêj House in Diyarbekir, a municipality-funded institution seeking to support and showcase Kurdish oral culture, similarly explained that "dengbêjî is the work of women" because "women have expressed the sorrows, the moaning and grieving (*kalîn û nalîn*) of their hearts through dengbêjî." Like Asya, she identified patriarchal kin relations as one major source of women's suffering but also highlighted the fact that state violence routinely takes away Kurdish women's husbands, brothers, and children, further increasing their pain and hence their propensity to pronounce sorrowful kilams. At the same time, both women were certain that things were changing for the better. Asya thus told me that harmful "customs and traditions" (*orf û adet*), including those that decried women raising their voices in public, were thankfully on the wane, while Gulbahar asserted that "the old times have gone, and compared with thirty years ago women are slowly progressing."

Gulbahar's and Asya's accounts of how Kurdish women's singing has its origin in unwanted marriages, harsh household hierarchies, and the tolls taken by state violence may easily be taken to suggest that women raise their voices out of a therapeutic impetus, seeking to overcome the traumas inflicted by patriarchal communities and authoritarian states. Their accounts also carried echoes of women's rights discourses that equate women's coming to voice with resistance against "backward" cultural traditions and social progress. Construing the act of voicing in this way as either a form of therapeutic overcoming or an act of gendered resistance, however, relies on understanding the voice as a vehicle that is at the ready disposal of sovereign subjects seeking to express their will and opinions, their inner thoughts and worries. This is an understanding of voice as a transparent channel of communication, one whose form matters little for the content it is going to transmit. It is also an understanding in which voice and self neatly map onto each other, the former giving ready expression to, indeed standing in for and representing, the latter. Kurdish oral repertoires, however, are rooted in quite different understandings of both the subject and its voice. Raising one's voice and pronouncing sorrowful kilams was for my interlocutors, particularly for those of older generations, often less a willful choice than the result of pain quite literally usurping their voices. It was also an act that testified to selves that were less bounded and self-contained than distributed and relational, suggesting constellations of voice, pain, and self where these elements do not overlap nearly as tidily as we may expect.

Fadime, for instance, responded to my question about what would make a skilled dengbêj by explaining that one could only become a dengbêj if one had experienced hardship, which could stem either from love (*aşk*) or from despair (*keder*). Everyone has the potential to become a dengbêj, she said, the only condition being that you must have experienced profound sorrow. "If I told you to sing right now, would you be able to? No. But if you had sorrows, then you would sing." Most of the women I encountered had indeed been catapulted into singing kilams by extremely painful experiences. Asya only began to sing after her husband passed away and her ailing elderly mother was imprisoned on political grounds. Fadime took up singing, as we saw in chapter 2, after having been married as a second wife to a much older man. The mother of a friend only began to pronounce kilams after her son left for "the mountains" to join the Kurdish guerrilla forces.

Pain appears as a profoundly transformative force in these life stories: a force that draws out the voice, almost independently of personal intent or will, only to render it capable of touching others. As if pain first had to sediment into the body, burning, as local idioms put it, the heart and other internal organs, in order for the voice to rise up. Those who raised their voices without having passed this minimum threshold of painful experience were in the eyes of my older interlocutors mere performers, employing a term in Kurdish, *hunermend*, that was commonly used to refer to professional musicians who are hired for events like weddings or circumcision celebrations.[1] These musicians typically work in groups of two or three and perform mainly

danceable strans to the accompaniment of an electronic org and other instruments like the tembûr. Such performers, Asya explained, just "sing and sing."
Unlike dengbêjs, they sing "from their mouth," while the latter sing with the
force of their minds (_beyin_) and hearts (_dil_). Fadime similarly reproached
such *hunermend* performers for merely learning kilams by heart—if they
sang them at all—stringing one stanza to the next without understanding
much of a kilam's content and meaning. Implicit in her comment was the
idea that one might very well master the technicalities of singing kilams, but
unless one had experienced the drama and tragedy of misfortune one would
not be able to reach out to and touch others with one's voice, no matter how
well trained.

That the women I encountered sometimes talked about the way in which
kilams "came" to them, rather than being purposely composed, is another
expression of the way in which pain appeared as a catalyzer of voice in these
contexts. During a visit to Gazîn's native village, for example, one evening
we were sitting in the large living room of one of the village's new, two-story
concrete houses, surrounded by a group of women and girls keen to hear
Gazîn sing. At some point during her impromptu performance Gazîn was
asked how many kilams she had composed (literally "brought out," *derxistin*)
throughout her life. Gazîn replied that assembling new kilams—rather than
interpreting long-transmitted repertoires—was difficult. Even though she
was a seasoned dengbêj, the kilams she had composed did not even amount
to a dozen. One, she explained, "came to her heart" (*hat dilê min*) when
she witnessed the brutal evacuation and subsequent burning of Çorsin, the
neighboring village of her in-laws, by the Turkish army in 1992:[2]

> When the villages were burnt, our people were killed by the state in those vil-
> lages. They had set fire to all the villages, and we went there to rescue them,
> we went there to help. My sister was there. The village was so empty; [you
> could hear] the cries and wails of children and people. And there, suddenly
> something came to my heart. [. . .] I sat down right there and a kilam arrived
> (*hat*). I sang about the village. They fled, scattered everywhere. They left their
> houses and became migrants. This is one time when [a kilam] arrived (*hat*).
> Another time I went somewhere and two people, in front of my eyes were . . .
> two people were martyred. In front of my eyes. I held on (*girt*) to one there.
> This was another time when I could make (*çêkirin*) a kilam. Only when your
> heart has burnt a lot you can [make a kilam]. If that's not the case, then you
> can't.

The "arrival" of kilams during these scenes of brutal violence was not a matter of Gazîn making a conscious choice to recount what she was witness-

ing. Instead, the events imposed themselves on her as testimony to be voiced. Rather than Gazîn actively stepping forth to bear testimony, here it was the testimony that made itself be borne witness to.[3] The horror of burning villages, fleeing relatives, and maimed bodies demanded a response, eliciting Gazîn's skilled voice to find expression in a genre predisposed to give sonic shape to sensations of loss, grief, and painful anger. Loss and the pain it implied in this way translated into vocal intensity, becoming a driving force for political testimony as well as poetic expression.

These observations qualify how the vocal potency I outlined in the previous two chapters has to be understood. There, I argued that voices become socially efficacious through the way in which genre affectively charges aesthetic form. Here, however, we see that for a voice to have the capacity to act upon others—for it to successfully transmit pain and suffering—technical training in the modulation of pitch, tone, and rhythm, exhausting knowledge of lyrics and matching *maqam*s, or extensive habituation through listening was not enough. In addition to a trained voice and an accustomed ear, pain would need to accumulate in one's body so as to provoke vocal expression. The self that emerges from this constellation is one constantly remade by the forces of pain and suffering such that its propensity for voice stands in direct correlation with such misery. Less a stable entity who employs her voice to express the ups and downs of her inner life, this is a subject remade in its vocal capacities at each instance of violation.

We are thus confronted with a vocal aesthetics where neither voices nor the selves they ostensibly represent are stable, making it difficult to read women's voicing of pain in any straightforward way as forms of therapeutic "speaking up" or as self-assertive expressions of personal will or grievance. What is more, many of my interlocutors made clear that their own experiences of pain and suffering were constitutively tied to the fate of those they loved and cared for. Consider, for example, how the mother of a friend once told me that she thought I was lucky to not have children, since "every person that enters your life becomes a burden for you. Their sickness, their sorrows, they will all become your own sorrows." Herself a mother of four children, this woman implied that children function as extensions of the female self, such that whatever loss and injury befalls them will directly fall back onto the mother. As James M. Wilce has noted for Bangladesh, the experience of loss is in that sense "an index of connectedness" (1998, 43) or, as Nadia Seremetakis finds in her work on rural Greece, a force that "opens one to the outside" (1991, 116).

Another way of putting this is that women's selves become extended as a result of their reproductive labor and the intimate relations of love and care it entails, a process that Suad Joseph (1993, 2005) has described as an expression of "patriarchal connectivity."[4] Drawing on her research in a working-class neighborhood in Beirut, Joseph argues that women's selves become entangled with those of loved and significant others in ways that reflect patriarchal hierarchies prioritizing male gender and seniority. This means that women learn how to see their own wishes and pleasures reflected in those of others, whose desires they routinely adapt and cater to, in the process often giving precedence to male and older relatives. What this extension of the female self though sustained investment in care work also means is that women become particularly predisposed to pain and suffering, given that the relationships in which they are entangled are at constant risk of loss and rupture. This was certainly the case in the context at hand, where the risk of losing loved ones was all too real. While daughters part from their parents' household upon marriage or are recruited by state institutions keen to assimilate them into proper Turkish femininity (Turkyilmaz 2016), sons are likely to be conscripted into the army, or to migrate to make a living elsewhere. Children may join the Kurdish guerrilla forces, become the victims of political violence, or be hit hard by the economic deprivation rampant across Kurdish geographies.

If experiences of pain and suffering were understood to be the result of how female selves become entangled with the fate of loved ones whom they nourished and cared for, these experiences were also considered key for drawing out women's voices and making them pronounce sorrowful kilams. Inversely, this meant that younger, unmarried, and childless women who might have mastered the technicalities of singing kilams but had not yet become enmeshed in these expansive and potentially injurious relations of care were not considered true dengbêjs. As Asya might have put it, their voices had not yet transformed from *deng* into *derd*. Rojîn, a twenty-seven-year-old singer from Qers (Tk. Kars), clearly knew of the objections that might therefore be raised against her aspirations to train herself in dengbêj repertoires. "Just because I am young there's no rule saying that I cannot sing *uzun hava*," she noted during our interview, referring to the Turkish folk genre that bears strong resemblance to the Kurdish kilam and is often used as a proxy for the Kurdish genre when speaking in Turkish. I picked up the thread to ask whether she had ever been confronted with objections regarding her young age and the fact that she had not yet seen enough sorrow. She laughed knowingly. "Yes, yes, they say that you have to mature (*pişmen lazım*), that your voice needs to settle (*oturması lazım*), that you still need to suffer (*çekmen lazım*)." She thought this view was thoroughly misguided, however, since "as they say, whatever you are at age seven, you remain at age seventy." While for my older interlocutors the self and its vocal propensities underwent crucial changes over the course of a lifetime in response to being exposed to pain and suffering, Rojîn rather saw the self as a stable entity that all it took to express was a skilled voice. Even though she acknowledged that suffering was necessary for becoming a good dengbêj, for her this was a question of endowing vocal expression with sincerity. She thus told me that her skill in singing kilams was related to the fact that she had lost her father as a child and that her singing therefore came "from the heart" (*yürekten*). Unlike older women, however, Rojîn did not see the pain of her father's death as compelling her to raise her voice. For her, performing mournful kilams rather remained a choice that she had taken up to flesh out her profile as an aspiring Kurdish singer.

For my older interlocutors, by contrast, raising one's voice and intonating a kilam was often more akin to a bodily need rather than a joyful or liberating moment of self-expression. This was brought home to me one morning when witnessing an exchange between Gazîn and her daughter. While the rest of the family had long finished breakfast, Gazîn lingered at the table, humming and singing to herself. Not much time passed before she was reproached by her daughter, who had already started doing the morning's dishes, for not helping her with the household chores. "So here you are, sitting there enjoying yourself (*keyif yapıyorsun*)," the daughter remarked ironically. Gazîn responded: "My inside is burning, my dear, I am not enjoying myself. I am telling my sorrows." For Gazîn, raising her voice to pronounce kilams was not a matter of *keyif* or carefree enjoyment, but rather an urge strong enough to temporarily displace household commitments. Her sorrows demanded expression, it seemed, seizing her vocal abilities and making her body their instrument of articulation. And yet at stake was less the spontaneous expression of an inner, "true" self than the employment of an aesthetically highly elaborated, conventional genre—the kilam—to give voice to sentiments firmly embedded in a cultural aesthetic of gendered hardship.

Not all kinds of pain, however, equally possessed the force to find their way into voice and language. I also encountered women who refused to bear witness to their pain, women who seemed to dwell in "those hazardous regions where representation encounters its limit in human language" (Nichanian 2003, 111). There was the woman in Arçak (Tk. Erçek), for example, known as a formidable dengbêj in her youth, who had stopped singing ever since her son had committed suicide eight years ago. Or the woman in Kop (Tk. Bulanık), who had ceased singing after both her brother and his son died in a traffic accident and who intonated a kilam for the first time in twenty-seven years upon my asking. For these women voicing pain seemed to have become impossible, constituting an experience of such an order, perhaps, "that beyond it there remains only a speech in pieces, splinters and fragments" (Nichanian 2003, 112). Or, to the contrary, perhaps these women's pain had receded and no longer possessed the force that would make its way into voice.

On the other hand, there were also forms of pain and suffering that were not easily translated into vocal form because there existed no cultural or political

grammar to accommodate them. Such was the case for forms of sexual violence occurring in the context of marriages, extended kin relations, police inter-
rogations, and military campaigns, which women recounted—if at all—only
in hushed tones, with muffled voices, or during cathartic confessional outbreaks
among intimates. While I witnessed how knowledge of sexual violation could
covertly circulate among close circles of female friends and relatives, recounted
only to those privy to the secret depths of a personal life story, I did not hear of
such experiences translated into the form of a kilam. This "poisonous knowledge" (Das 2000) with its risk of upsetting the patriarchal logics of both family and nation was too dangerous to be turned into lasting sound objects with
the capacity to circulate.

The kilam, this goes to show, provides women with an aesthetic frame
and cultural idiom through which to express socially sanctioned experiences
of pain and suffering, including some of the injuries that patriarchal kinship
arrangements entail as well as the colonial violence that has so insistently
wreaked havoc in Kurdish lifeworlds. Yet the genre is rooted in a world where
voices are not tame objects at the disposal of sovereign subjects. Here, rather,
vocality is something that forces itself upon a subject from the outside; it is less
a choice than an obligation enacted by the forces of pain and violation. This is
also a world where female selves are constitutively tied to their kin and kith, to
close and loved ones, blurring the boundaries between one's own pain and that
of another. It thus complicates any inclination we may have to read voices as
speaking for clearly defined, self-contained individuals or collectives.

Relational Selves

When considering long-standing, "classical" repertoires of kilams, we find
ample evidence for the relational enmeshment of women's selves with significant others—often male—which Joseph's patriarchal connectivity fosters. Such
repertoires allow tracing how the female voice becomes a vehicle to express
both the pain of others and that of the self and are thus helpful for mapping out
shifting constellations of voice, pain, and self in Kurdish contexts. In many of
the much-loved and well-known kilams recounting historical tribal disputes,
military campaigns, or tragic love stories, female voices make a routine ap-
pearance, even when those kilams are pronounced by male performers. They
do so primarily by way of the reported voices that permeate the narrative of
many pieces. In many long-standing kilams, women can thus be heard lamenting the tragic fate that has befallen a loved one, such as a son, husband,
or lover who will often also feature as the protagonist of the narrative in question. These types of kilams exemplify how female agony is caused by the loss
of a significant other—typically male—whose hardship (if not death) becomes

the source for women's own pain, testifying to the relations of love, care, and kinship that so constitutively make up female selves in this context.

Consider, for instance, the following extract from a long-established kilam about the betrayal of Evdilê Birahîm by his half-brother, Emînê Ehmed, during the early years of the Turkish republic. Background to the betrayal is the two brothers' competition for leadership of the Reman tribe. While Emîn is known for a history of collaboration with Ottoman and later Turkish authorities—a history that includes assistance in the 1915 genocidal violence against non-Muslim communities and in the suppression of the 1925 Sheikh Said uprising—his brother Evdil enjoys fame for his fierce opposition toward state authorities. The dengbêjs of the region celebrate him in their popular epics for having assassinated a particularly cruel commander of the Turkish army. Following the assassination, Emîn reports his half-brother to the authorities and watches him being arrested and beheaded alongside eleven other men in the village of Barislê, in the province of Êlih. The story has been transmitted through a well-known kilam that sees the two brothers' mother, Perîxan, lament the betrayal that pits one of her sons against the other and leads to the brutal desecration of Evdil's dead body.[5]

Belê wey li minê, wey li minê, wey li minê, wey axa ey	Oh woe is me, woe is me, woe is me, oh lord
De rabe kuştiyo bê heyf maye	Rise up you murdered but unavenged one
Kula li ser kula lawo, derdê ser derdayê	Grief upon grief, pain upon pain, oh
Kula Emînê Ehmed roja bênderê Barislê, birayê xayîn dil de maye wey ax-ey, wey	The grief caused by that treacherous brother Emînê Ehmed on the threshing day in Barislê remains in the heart
Perîxanê dibê Hesîne lawo, esker rabû ji xopana Girîdaxê lawo, lê serejêr e	**Perîxan says**, Hesîn my son,[6] the soldiers set out from that doomed Girîdax, coming downwards
Mi dî Emînê Ehmed derketî ji qereqola Êlihayê bi sê tîpa lawo, lê esker pê re ye	I saw how Emînê Ehmed left the military post of Êlih with three squads of soldiers
Heyfa min li kuştina Evdilê Birahîm bavê Ehmed nayê	My heart does not burn for the killing of Evdilê Birahîm, father of Ehmed
Heyfa min tê li vê heyfê, min dî bi qeflê xulaman girtin, laşê vî xweşmêrî kişandin lo bi erdê	But my heart does burn for this: I saw how a group of servants dragged the body of this man of courage on the ground
Welê ji devê Evdilê Birahîm bavê Ehmed derxistin lawo cotek lo diranê zêr e	They pulled out a pair of golden teeth from the mouth of Evdilê Birahîm, father of Ehmed

Serê Evdilê Birahîm, bavê Ehmed jê kirin, birine şarê Diyarbekir bi xwe re, lawo birine bajêr e	They cut off the head of Evdilê Birahîm and took it with them to the city of Diyarbekir, they took it to the city
Belê wey li minê, wey li minê, wey li minê, wey li minê, wey li minê, lo wey axa ey	Oh woe is me, woe is me, woe is me, oh lord
Lê kuştiyo lo bê heyf maye	You murdered but unavenged one
Kula li ser kula, lawo derdê li ser derdayê	Grief upon grief, pain upon pain, oh
Kula Emînê Ehmed roja bênderê Barislê birayê xayîn di dil de maye wey ax-ey	The grief caused by that treacherous brother Emînê Ehmed on the threshing day in Barislê remains in the heart

Even though kilams like these are often intonated by male dengbêjs, thanks to the way in which they cite the speech of their female protagonists, women's experiences and observations are in many cases central to the narrative. In this case, we thus see how the voice of Perîxan, the grieving mother, becomes the driving force of the kilam. It is through her painful recollections (introduced by "Perîxan says . . .") that we hear the story of the fateful betrayal. Perîxan's pain, however, is crucially bound up with the fate of her son, whose brutal killing takes center stage in the kilam's narrative. What we see here is what Iris Jean-Klein (2000, 101–102) might refer to as a "cross-subjective" exercise of pain between mother and son, where it is the mother who mediates, interprets, and articulates her son's suffering. Like the Palestinian mothers who Jean-Klein argues play a crucial role in turning their sons into admired resistance fighters by narrating their courageous deeds, so does Perîxan contribute to the making of Evdil into a celebrated hero through her account. As such, Perîxan's voice holds what Jean-Klein calls "subject-constitutive authority" (108): it is her narration that endows her son with the moral status of a courageous fighter. In the process, she constructs herself as fundamentally entwined with the fate of her son, projecting what Marilyn Booth (2013, 56), in her study of Egyptian women's turn-of-the-century autobiographical writings, has described as a "semi-decentered self."

Importantly, while Evdil's fate is transmitted primarily through the kilam's lyrics, Perîxan's own suffering rather finds a home in the piece's sonic elaboration. In the text, it appears explicitly in just a few formulaic expressions, including "grief upon grief, pain upon pain" or "woe is me." More than such wording, though, it is the acoustics of the kilam that embody Perîxan's grief. Melismatically elongated lines ending in plaintive "ey"s pervade the entire piece, intensifying in those recurring lines where grief is explicitly named as befalling the female self ("woe is me"). For Kurdish listeners, these acoustics

are easily associated with the sounds of wailing and lamenting, characteriz-
ing the kilam as an expression of female suffering in the face of overwhelming
tragedy. While its narrative content testifies to male bravery and defeat, then, it
is the kilam's vocal elaboration that gives acoustic substance to Perîxan's pain.

Yet it is not only in the long-transmitted, epic repertoires often performed
publicly by male dengbêjs that women's pain appears as rerouted through the
tragic misfortune of male relatives. When women raise their voices in private
to pronounce their own, personal kilams, they, too, routinely do so in ways
that constitutively tie their pain to that of significant others. The elderly Yezidi women in Armenia, for instance, whom Amy de la Bretèque (2013) worked
with, locate the reasons for their burning hearts in the deprivations experienced
by their sons and husbands engaged in hard manual labor in Russia, in the hardship of relatives doing their military service, or in the misfortune of loved ones
struck by illness or death. My interlocutors in Wan, too, would often attribute
the pain that burnt their insides to the fate of family members forced to migrate,
of imprisoned sons and daughters, or of loved ones who lost their lives in the
decades-long war. The elderly mother of a friend, for example, once performed
the following piece for me when I visited the family's spacious home on the out-
skirts of the city, surrounded by small fields and gardens. In this very intimate,
personal kilam she reflects on a visit to her daughter, incarcerated in one of
Istanbul's high-security prisons for her activities with the Kurdish movement.

Lawiko dîno [. . .] **dibêm** ez ê Wanê ketim, ax ez ê Wanê ketim heya Stembola şewitî berejêr e	You foolish boy [. . .], **I say**, I left Wan, oh I left Wan for the damned Istanbul
Ax **min go** bejna qîza min evdala Xwedê zirav e mîna spîndara nav bajêr e	Oh **I said**, by God, my daughter's figure is slim like a poplar tree in the city
Ax zirav e mîna spîndara nav bajêr e	Oh she is slim like a poplar tree in the city
Wez ê dibêm payîz e, were li kêleka min rûne, qasekê kul û derdê qîza min ê ji min re bêje, dilê min hayê	**I say**, it is autumn, come and sit next to me, tell me of the pain and sorrow of my daughter
Ax dilê min hayê, ax lo dilê'm hayê	Oh my heart, oh my heart, oh my heart
Bêje ez ê Wanê ketim heya Stembola şewitî şev e, şev lerizî	**Say**, I left Wan for the damned Istanbul, it is a shivering night
Ax **min go** şev e, lo şev lerizî	Oh **I said** it is a shivering night
Ax **min go** dizê Tirka li qîza min qelizî	Oh **I said** the Turkish thieves have ambushed my daughter
Ay stêrka sibê li min derizî	Oh the morning star cracks
Ez ê heta pê zivirîm [. . .] bi Xwedê dê heps û zindana da birizî	Until I return to her [. . .], oh God, she will perish in prison

Dilê min hayê, ax lo dilê'm hayê	Oh my heart, oh my heart
Dibê ez ê Wanê ketim heya Stembola şewitî dar û mêş e	**(S)he says**, I left Wan toward the damned Istanbul with its trees and woods
Ax la dar û mêş e	Oh the trees and woods
Dibê jê difûrin kul û êş e	**(S)he says**, I am filled with pain and grief
Dil û cîgera min evdala Xwedê ji ber diêşe	Oh God my heart and insides feel pain
Dilê'm hay, dilê'm hay, o ey, o ey, o ey, o ax lo dilê'm hayê	My heart, my heart, oh my heart, oh my heart
Ez ê Wane ketim heya Stembola şewitî dar û sincî	I left Wan for the burnt Istanbul with its trees and sesame
Qîz û xortê me evdala Xwedê sor narincî	Our daughters and sons, by God, red like a sour orange
Dibê Xwedê li dizê Tirka tu sal û zemanan nehêle ji xwe re Tirkiyê da bizewicî	**(S)he says**, may God never let the Turkish thieves marry in Turkey
Ax dilê'm hayê, o ax lo dilê'm hayê	Oh my heart, oh my heart, wey

This elderly woman occasionally sang this and similar pieces to herself while doing chores in and around her house as a means, she explained to me, of alleviating her sorrows. Here, she narrates her travels to Istanbul, where she visited her daughter Ceyhan in prison and which she describes, using familiar lyrical imagery, as damned (şewitî, lit. "burnt"), with cold nights that make you shiver. Like the female figures in countless other kilams, Ceyhan is "slim like a poplar tree," underlining the injustice of her condemnation to a cruel prison regime that, the mother fears, will make her daughter perish before she can return one more time. She is left yearning for her beloved Ceyhan, her heart and liver aching. All that is left to her is to wish destruction upon those who have taken Ceyhan away from her, denying them reproductive capacities and the stability of married intimacy ("may God never let the Turkish thieves marry").

And yet, as much as this kilam tells of a specific event—the Istanbul prison visit—this is no straightforward narrative. The kilam resembles a succession of impressions loosely strung together around the force of painful sensations, rather than a chronologically or thematically ordered story line. This is in large part the result of how the singer employs what seems like a fragmented pattern of reported speech (highlighted in bold above), where she shifts from reporting what is presumably her own voice ("I say," "I said") to reporting her own actions through the voice of another ("he/she says") to employing an imperative ("speak"). Similar to the Yoruba praise poetry analyzed by Karin Barber, the kilam in this way comes to slide around a number of shifting personal pronouns with the effect that "no voice can be identified as a stable centre" (2007, 131). Rather than a coherent story told by a self-contained subject, we are thus confronted with a series of fragments depicting what might more aptly be described with Walter Benjamin as "memory as it flashes up at a moment of danger" (2007b, 255).

As in the kilam about Evdil, here, too, we see a mother's suffering arise as the effect of what has befallen her beloved child, even if that child is now a daughter rather than a son. Compared to the classic epic, though, in this kilam the mother's experience is more explicitly portrayed. Ceyhan's mother appears not merely as an outside observer of the story, as Perîxan did, but we get a sense of her embodied experience, her feelings and sensations arising from the prison visit. More so than the lyrics, however, it is the kilam's sonic elaboration that conveys to listeners something of the intense suffering that my friend's mother experienced. When performing the kilam for me, her high-pitched, soft voice was trembling, testifying to the effort it required to translate her pain into acoustic form. Several times throughout the piece her voice began to trail off, as if she were about to break into crying. Plaintive "ax"s recurred in nearly every line, reinforced by expressions like "ey" and "hayê" that powerfully indicate suffering and grief to Kurdish listeners. Once again, then, it was the sonic form of the voice—the kilam's plaintive notes and lamenting tones, the trembling melismas, onomatopoetic expressions, and icons of crying—that carried the burden of expressing the suffering female self, while narrative content rerouted that suffering through the hardship befalling a significant other.

With these observations in mind, let us now return to "Ey Felekê," Gazîn's kilam about her brother-in-law with which I opened the chapter. On the one hand, the way in which the kilam ties voice to pain through poetic imagery and narrative themes resonates with what I have described so far. Here again, a woman's pain is entangled with that of a male relative, and the female voice gives expression to the relational experience of suffering this entails. Familiar poetic imagery helps Gazîn evoke the tragedy of violent death and sudden loss: fate (*felek*) is invoked as the harbinger of unjust misfortune, while the enemies impart death out of their "savage and bloodthirsty" character, leading to eyes shedding tears and hearts filled with blood. Similar to Perîxan, moreover, Gazîn's pain stemmed not only from Uxur's death but also from the mistreatment of his body. With the body withheld from the family any structured form of mourning, let alone closure to his death, had become impossible, adding a sense of despair to the piece.[7]

And yet "Ey Felekê" also marks a radical departure from the vocal aesthetics of long-standing kilams. The latter, we saw, rely on the evocative power of vocal sound to transmit affective intensity, specifically where women's emotions are at stake. But in "Ey Felekê" the affective weight shifts from vocal sound to the semantics of narrative content and poetic imagery. The irregular meter and rhyme of the classical kilams give way to short verses with regular rhyme and rhythm, emphasizing narrative coherence instead of fragmented story lines. Gone are the melismatic elongations and onomatopoetic expressions, instead giving way to a somber simplicity that focuses listeners' attention on the semantic content of the words in their rhythmic succession. Gone, too, is the repeated change of narrative perspective effected through reported speech that we saw appear in many of the classical kilams. Instead, a singular "I" and its feelings stand at the center of the narrative. The returning chorus introduced by the main theme, "Ey Felekê," underlines this centrality of the subject, creating regular recursivity instead of the narrative fragmentation that often marks more conventional kilams. Even though the female subject-in-pain thus remains tied to the tragic fate of another, subjective feeling and semantic content come to the fore while the voice as a sound object in its own right recedes.

What we see here, I suggest, are changes in vocal sound and aesthetic with potentially far-reaching implications. As Khaled Furani (2012) has argued, the acoustics of speech and poetry are inseparable from the making of subjectivity. As he shows in his work, while Arabic poetry used to be bound to strict rules of rhyme, meter, and rhythm—all means to measure poetic sound—in the twentieth century Palestinian and other Arab poets instead opted to set their work in prose. The resulting retreat of metered sound in favor of visual metaphors, Furani maintains, goes hand-in-hand with the imagination of the poet as a sovereign subject, uncontrolled by the limitations of formal poetic convention. In similar ways, I propose that the retreat of acoustic elaboration in a kilam like "Ey Felekê" allows for the emergence of a self that, although still impacted by the fate of kin and loved ones, newly stands at the heart of vocal expression, its emotional interiority now the main focus of the narrative. Where the voice used to function as an instrument of affective excitation thanks to its acoustic embellishment, here we see it morph into a much tamer object whose chief function becomes the expression of the subject's inner self.

When Voice, Self, and Pain Converge

"Ey Felekê," then, suggests the emergence of new constellations of voice, self, and pain—constellations in which these three elements begin to overlap, with the voice turning into a privileged means to express an increasingly bounded and self-contained individual self and its suffering. Erik Mueggler (2014) has observed a similar shift, comparing funerary lamentations of China's Yi people from the 1990s with those performed two decades later. While earlier laments were highly formalized and—similar to kilams—incorporated multiple voices in their narrative to lay out intricate sets of kinship relations centered on the deceased, laments from the 2010s came to focus on the lamenter's personal experiences of sorrow and hardship. One might read such a shift as a form of liberation, as both Yi and Kurdish women being finally able to use their voices to express and make heard their own troubles and pains, rather than having to attend to the desires and wishes, the pain and suffering, of others. But once voices begin to unequivocally stand in for the self, this also entails new expectations, demands, and, not least, vulnerabilities. Especially in contexts where the public presence of female voices retains patriarchal discomfort, vocal expression that can be read as faithfully representing women's innermost selves requires new means of "balancing competing ethics of self-expression and self-restraint," as Zuzanna Olszewska (2015, 7) writes in her ethnography of contemporary Afghan poets.

In what follows, I flesh out this observation by turning to the life and work of Eyşe Şan (1938–1996), a twentieth-century Kurdish singer whose vocal performances brought her immense fame while also exposing her to situations of acute vulnerability.[8] Eyşe Şan was extraordinarily popular among the women singers I knew. This popularity, I suggest, is related to the novel ways in which Eyşe Şan employed her voice in order to express personal pain. Her figure therefore provides a fruitful point of departure for exploring the hopes and aspirations, but also the frustrations and contradictions that emerging arrangements of voice, self, and pain entail. Today Eyşe Şan's life story is often read as that of a woman who defied political repression, thanks to singing in Kurdish at a time when this was met with sanction and censorship in Turkey, and who courageously stood up to the restrictive norms of patriarchal custom that denounce women singing in public as immodest or shameful ('eyb, şerm). Tapping into this narrative, the 2010s saw Kurdish-led municipalities and cultural organizations in Turkey greatly invest in promoting her heritage, organizing festivals in her name, dedicating parks to her memory, and naming women's centers after her.[9] Implicit in this celebration of Eyşe Şan as a figure of political and feminist resistance lies an understanding of voice as the direct and immediate expression of personal identity, agency, and will. But as I have outlined, classical Kurdish repertoires project a very different alignment between voice and self, one where both voices and subjects are fragmented in such a way that they frustrate any attempts at neatly mapping one onto the other. Rather than taking the convergence of voice and self for granted, therefore, here I approach the life and work of Eyşe Şan as testifying to the complex process through which voice, pain, and self have begun to overlap in northern Kurdistan, and explore some of the consequences this has entailed.

Pain was a theme that marked Eyşe Şan's life, forming a continuous subcurrent to a career that took many turns. Eyşe Şan's autobiography, penned in 1984, thus begins with the note that the purpose of her writing was to document "my life of pain and sorrow" (Oremar 2012, 25). Misfortune, she asserts, marked her life from the very beginning, being born in the same year (1938) in which Mustafa Kemal Atatürk passed away. Atatürk, whom Eyşe Şan calls a "great man" and whom she greatly admired, was the founder of modern Turkey, who laid the groundwork for the country's assimilationist policies toward its Kurdish populations and under whose rule any vestiges of Kurdish autonomy were brutally crushed. Eyşe Şan's sympathies for the Kurdish political struggle notwithstanding, professions of political loyalty to the Kemalist regime that Atatürk founded recur throughout the text of her autobiography, upsetting contemporary tendencies to see her as an unambiguous icon of Kurdish ethnonational resistance and hinting instead at the complex and at times contradictory affective attachments that mark Kurdish subjectivity in modern Turkey.

While Eyşe Şan's self-understanding as a woman deeply marked by pain and suffering rehearses well-established cultural tropes, the very fact that she chose to document her misfortunes via the genre of autobiography testifies to the ways in which novel imaginations of subjectivity thrive on and productively reshape existing cultural forms and genres (Barber 2007). Here, the "existential continuum" (Seremetakis 1991, 115) of female pain turns into personal experience worthy of lasting documentation through a genre that paradigmatically puts the individual self at the center of reflection. As such, the autobiography simultaneously mimics, foreshadows, and rehearses the ways in which Eyşe Şan would employ her voice throughout her life, adapting existing genres and formats to create new forms of vocal self-expression.

Born in 1938 into a large and well-known Kurdish family in Diyarbekir, Eyşe Şan acquired familiarity with the narrative patterns, acoustic conventions, and poetic figures of Kurdish oral tradition through her father, an acclaimed dengbêj. At the same time, she also immersed herself in the tunes of Turkish folk songs as these were popularized over the airwaves of the young republic. When Eyşe Şan's father passed away when she was only nine, the family was plunged into hardship. Eyşe Şan was subsequently married, at the age of fifteen, to an older man as second wife. It is this experience that she retrospectively identified as what propelled her to raise her voice to pronounce "songs of pain and sorrow" (Oremar 2012, 41), rehearsing a trope we have seen is widespread among Kurdish women of her generation.

Yet Eyşe Şan refused to settle into a life of pain and hardship. Attracted by the promises of republican modernity that began to unfold in Diyarbekir at the time, she left her husband and began to work as an office clerk first with Turkish Airlines and then with an American petrol firm. Feeling that these positions exposed her to too much male attention as a young, single woman, however, she eventually opted to work as a seamstress and left Diyarbekir for Antep, the center of Turkey's textile industry. It was in Antep, at a distance from tight networks of kin and community, that Eyşe Şan began to engage with the professional music industry. Her first contacts were with Radio Antep, where she recorded repertoires of Turkish folk songs before moving on to Istanbul to record several vinyl records with Kurdish and Turkish repertoires later in the 1960s (Reigle 2013).

The 1971 military coup, however, put an end to the short-lived period in which Kurdish voices circulated with relative freedom in Turkey. The tightening political climate, being taken advantage of by profit-driven music producers, and dreams of prosperity and fame kept Eyşe Şan on the move. In 1972 she migrated to Germany, where she stayed for three years, earning a living through manual labor while performing in Turkish clubs at night, as well as once with the BBC. At the same time, her voice began to gather fame among Kurdish audiences in Turkey and Iraq, eventually leading to an invitation from Radio Baghdad's Kurdish section, which Eyşe Şan took up in 1978. There she collaborated with some of the most well-known Kurdish singers and musicians at the time, realizing a number of recordings that were to significantly shape Kurdish public culture, and remain popular to this day.

But the public exposure of her voice also rendered Eyşe Şan highly vulnerable. It led to trouble with her employers at a post office in İzmir, the Turkish metropole on the Aegean coast, where she settled after her return from Germany. In the eyes of her employers, Eyşe Şan's public singing at nightclubs and on the radio had called into question her moral respectability. This led to her employers moving her to a post several hundred kilometers inland in the provincial town of Kütahya, forcing her to leave her two adolescent children in İzmir. Her career as a singer also led to the rupture of relations with her family in Diyarbekir, chiefly her brother, who perceived her as having tainted the family's image through her singing. The rift was so deep that Eyşe Şan's brother did not allow her to come visit their mother on her deathbed. When Eyşe Şan herself died of cancer in 1996, her body was interred in İzmir, with only a handful of people attending the funeral. In her will Eyşe Şan had stated that she wanted to be buried in her beloved Diyarbekir, but her family refused to grant her this last wish, because in their eyes she had diverged too far from the norms of respectable femininity during her life.

Today Eyşe Şan is widely celebrated as one of the iconic voices of traditional Kurdish music. Yet if we look closely at Eyşe Şan's repertoire, what we see is less an unambiguous expression of "traditional" vocality than experimentation with novel vocal forms. Here, established narrative and poetic conventions are creatively adapted to give expression to constellations of voice, self, and pain that significantly differ from those I have explored above. Looking at the pieces that Eyşe Şan composed herself, we see that most of these songs constitute responses to and reflections on personal experiences of misery and sorrow. Eyşe Şan wrote songs that reflect on the hardship she suffered as a second wife, the pain she experienced when her family prevented her from visiting her dying mother, and the longing she felt throughout her life for her hometown of Diyarbekir. Pain and suffering, this makes clear, remain at the heart of female vocal expression, very much in line with the vocal aesthetics I have outlined so far. As we have seen, in classical oral repertoires, women's pain would typically be rerouted through the fate of another, leading to "cross-subjective" acts of voicing. In Eyşe Şan's repertoire, by contrast, we see how the voice tends to become a more immediate means of expression for the personal pain of the female self. This is the case, for instance, in the piece "Qedera Min Ev E" (This Is My Fate), which Eyşe Şan reportedly composed in response to a falling-out with her daughter and in which she bemoans the misery that she claims has marked her life (Oremar 2012, 109).

Qedera min ev e, carek çênabî	This is my destiny, nothing ever works out
Min ji kê re çi kir, ew kir xirabî	No matter what favors I did for others, they returned harm
Emrêm hat û borî, bi vî ezabî	My life has passed with this torment
Betilîm hevalno, betilîm êdî	I am tired, my friends, I am just tired
Emrêm hat û borî, rojek xweş min nedî	My life has passed and I have not seen a single nice day
Min rojek xweş nedî, tim ewr û tarî	I have not seen a single nice day, always clouds and darkness
Li min ne havîn hat û ne buharî	Neither summer nor spring ever arrived for me
Qeder li min bûye ew gurê harî	Destiny has been a rabid wolf to me
Betilîm hevalno, betilîm êdî	I am tired, my friends, I am just tired
Emrêm hat û borî, rojek xweş min nedî	My life has passed and I have not seen a single nice day
[. . .]	[. . .]
Eyşe Şan im ev e her dem halê min	I am Eyşe Şan, this has always been my plight
Xwedî kir mezin kir, bûn dijminê min	I brought [them] up, but they became my foes
Heval çi dipirsî, kûr e derdê min	What are you asking, friend, deep are my sorrows
Betilîm hevalno, betilîm êdî	I am tired, my friends, I am just tired
Emrêm hat û borî, rojek xweş min nedî	My life has passed and I have not seen a single nice day

What the song shares with long-established oral repertoires is how the actions of others, particularly children, become the source of the female self's pain and suffering. But very different from those repertoires, it is the female self and her emotionality that stand at the center of attention here, embodied in the figure of the mother who finds herself depleted by her children. Remarkably, moreover, female emotionality is no longer just confined to the acoustic elaboration of a song, as I have argued happens in the longer-standing repertoires. Here, the suffering female subject is directly articulated in the lyrics, through expressions like "I am tired" or "I have not seen a single nice day." Note, moreover, how these expressions are not relayed in the form of reported speech, as is the case in some of the other kilams we have seen, where the reporting of different characters' voices worked to detach the utterance from the singer and prevented a singular subject position from emerging. Here, by contrast, we have a clear-cut subject around which the song is structured and to which the singer's voice gives direct expression. The acoustics of this piece, too, are very different from the classical repertoires with their trembling and lamenting voices. In "Qedera Min Ev E" the voice is acoustically much less elaborated. Regular rhyme and meter as well as structural simplicity have the effect of putting the enunciating subject and the sentiments she pronounces at center stage. The voice is here less a sound object in its own right than a relatively neutral channel for expressing narrative content, precisely that content where we now find the emotionality of the subject expressed.

What is also notable in this song is that in the last verse Eyşe Şan mentions her own name, in this way directly claiming the song and the emotions it expresses as her own. This is quite a radical departure from those repertoires in which the conventionality of poetic expression and melodic structure works to detach voice from self, as we saw in previous chapters. Here, the insertion of the singer's personal name has the opposite effect and further tightens the link between voice and self.

It is important to note that "Qedera Min Ev E" is not in any way representative of all of Eyşe Şan's repertoire, which is extraordinarily varied and versatile. Her own compositions include kilams that do follow long-established forms and conventions, featuring elements of reported speech, dialoguing voices, strong melismatic embellishment, and traditional narrative patterns that highlight relational forms of subjectivity where the voice does not directly map onto the enunciating self. Other songs refer to current affairs and political issues, lamenting historical injustice and celebrating Kurdish resistance. In Eyşe Şan's repertoire, vocal embellishment intersects with acoustic plainness, lyrical elaboration with poetic simplicity, testifying to the complex imbrication of different imaginations of voiced pain and suffering selves. There is no clear linear path here that would lead from vocal elaboration to simplicity, from relational to bounded selves, from tradition to modernity. Rather, we are confronted with a multiplication of ways in which voice, self, and pain may articulate, leading to creative experimentation and hybrid forms that are hard to contain within neat

classificatory schemes. What is more, Eyşe Şan gave expression to her sentiments in both Kurdish and Turkish. In fact, some of her most personal songs
are written in Turkish, as is her autobiography. While this certainly attests to the
efficacy of Turkish state policies aimed at linguistically assimilating its Kurdish
populations, it also highlights the complexity of Kurdish subjectivity in Turkey
today, which defies simplistic models of ethno-linguistic identification.

For many of the women I encountered in and around Wan in the mid-
2000s, Eyşe Şan was a personality that resonated. The hardships and sorrows
her voice transmitted struck a familiar chord with many, particularly those
who had similarly experienced fallings-out with family over their singing,
and others who could empathize with her difficulties as second wife and
single mother. Eyşe Şan's dedication to pursue her interest in singing, and
her refusal to bow to social norms and family pressures, made her a much-
admired figure among my interlocutors. What is more, the novel articulations
between voice, pain, and self that become apparent in Eyşe Şan's work also reverberated in my interlocutors' voices and found an echo in their repertoires.
Consider, for instance, the following piece by Gazîn, who often compared her
own life as a singer with that of Eyşe Şan, given that she, too, had at one point
been rejected by family members, taken advantage of by profit-seeking music
producers, and felt a general lack of social recognition. In this simple yet intimate song, Gazîn gives expression to some of these sentiments.

Ez Gazîn im, ez dengbêj im	I am Gazîn, I am a dengbêj
Ez ne ker im, ez ne gêj im	I am neither deaf, nor am I mad
Derdê dilê xwe dibêjim	I tell the sorrows of my heart
Kesekî dengê min nabihîze	Nobody hears my voice
Derdê dilê xwe dibêjim	I tell the sorrows of my heart
Kesekî dengê min nabihîze	Nobody hears my voice
Ez Gazîna dilbirîn im	I am the heartbroken Gazîn
Dil û hinav tijî xwîn in	My insides are full of blood
Weke Xecê, weke Zîn im	I am like Xecê, like Zîn
Li ber zulma van dijmina	In the face of the enemies' cruelty
Erdek nemaye ez biçim	There remains no place for me to go
Li ber zulma van dijmina	In the face of the enemies' cruelty
Erdek nemaye ez biçim	There remains no place for me to go
Ez Gazîna nav gundiya	I am Gazîn amidst the villagers
Ez bêrîvan nav bêriya	I am a milkmaid on the pastures
Wekî quling diqeriyam	I cry out like a crane
Li ber zulma van dijmina	In the face of the enemies' cruelty
Bûm hêsirê, serê çiya	I have become a captive in the mountains
Li ber zulma van dijmina	In the face of the enemies' cruelty
Bûm hêsirê, serê çiya	I have become a captive in the mountains

The song very movingly focuses on the loneliness of the singer, who recounts how she is telling her sorrows, crying out like a crane among villagers to achieve recognition for her pain, but nobody hears her voice. In her disappointment she ends up turning to the mountains, the paradigmatic site of freedom from social convention in the Kurdish popular imagination and site of the Kurdish armed struggle. Gazîn further likens herself to Xecê and Zîn, two heroines of early modern Kurdish literature who engaged in tragic struggle and ultimately death rather than accepting the compromises demanded from them by society. In the tale of star-crossed lovers Mem and Zîn, it is tribal politics that prevents the two lovers from uniting. An evil conspiracy first leads to Mem's death, with Zîn dying soon after while mourning Mem at his grave. Xecê, on the other hand, defies her family in her love for courageous but poverty-stricken Siyabend. The pair eventually elopes, but when he dies falling off a cliff while hunting, she chooses to follow her lover into death. While Gazîn saw in Xecê and Zîn like-minded spirits for how they struggled against the conventions imposed by their families and communities, the sense of self she articulated in her song was in many ways quite different from that projected in the classic epics. As Lila Abu-Lughod (2000) has argued, such epics situate their protagonists within a force field of larger fateful powers, focusing on the tragedy that ensues when individuals rise up against these powers, rather than on the development of the characters' inner life. While emotionality is not absent from such narratives, it manifests externally in the ample description of tears, bodily reactions, or natural occurrences like thunderstorms. Modern cultural genres like the novel or television drama, by contrast, focus on depicting the inner being that is the subject of tragic emotions—a concern that is clearly central also to Gazîn's song.

The vocal aesthetics able to accommodate this concern turns out to be very similar to how Eyşe Şan employed her voice in "Qedera Min Ev E." As in the latter piece, so in Gazîn's song, too, we no longer find elements of reported speech that would detach voice from self, but instead encounter a subject who uses her voice to directly express her personal frustrations. This overlap between voice and self is further highlighted through Gazîn putting herself center stage in the song. Not only does she name herself in the first line as the song's enunciator and protagonist ("I am Gazîn"), but that very name enacts the convergence it announces: Gazîn being a self-chosen stage name derived from the Kurdish words for shout or call (*gazî*) and reproach (*gazin*), it performed the very identification between self and voice that the song's force relies on. And yet the actual acoustics of this voice that both named and defined the enunciating self were rather plain and subdued. Similar to what we observed in both "Ey Felekê" and Eyşe Şan's song, here the voice no longer constituted a performative instrument in its own right. Regularity in rhythm and meter, a uniform verse structure, and consistent rhyme instead combined with clear articulation and slow tempo to allow the lyrics and the account they gave of a plagued inner self to come to the fore.

But what the song also makes clear is that this equation between voice and self, where one literally comes to define the other, leaves the subject acutely vulnerable. Judith Butler (1997) has argued that the viability of the subject is directly tied to the recognition of one's voice as falling within the boundaries of what is considered legitimate, intelligible speech. If somebody's speech is not recognized as such—for instance, if speech gets labeled as asocial or psychotic rambling—then the person's very status as a subject is thrown into doubt. As Butler writes, "the consequences of such an irruption of the unspeakable may range from a sense that one is 'falling apart' to the intervention of the state to secure criminal or psychiatric incarceration" (136).

What this chapter's discussion makes clear, however, is that it is only once the voice has been rendered coterminous with and representative of the subject that the voice's social recognition can become as central to the subject's survival in the way Butler describes it. When Gazîn highlights how she is heartbroken because "nobody hears my voice," and how she ends up captive in the mountains because she does not receive a response to her crying out, she poignantly expresses the anxieties and vulnerabilities that arise from a constellation where the subject increasingly relies on the public acknowledgment of her voice and what it pronounces in order to maintain integrity and well-being. Similarly to how the genre of the novel signals a new imagination of the private self at the very moment that it offers that privacy up for public consumption (Bakhtin 1981b), Gazîn's piece points us to the complex entanglement of the intimate self with a public from which it stands apart and on which it depends for recognition. It also indicates that, in a cultural context where the public audibility of women's voices has often been regarded as a potential violation of patriarchal norms of female modesty, the stakes of this entanglement are particularly high for women. Once voices are less mobile vehicles of affective excitation than sound objects that directly stand for the enunciating self and her private interiority, raising one's voice in public conjures new risks and vulnerabilities, but also promises new forms of recognition and reward.

Conclusion

This chapter has explored how articulations of voice, pain, and self have been transforming in Kurdish contexts, and how such change is related to the emergence of novel understandings of subjectivity. In many classical kilams,

the voice testifies to the embeddedness of the female subject in expansive relations of nurture and care, which render women particularly predisposed to
the infliction of loss and tie their pain to the (mis)fortune of others. In these
repertoires, the voice functions as a vector of women's relational experience
of pain not so much because of what it narrates as because of how it sounds:
voices transmit female pain as they tremble and quiver, lament and wail. But
I have also traced the emergence of a very different kind of vocal aesthetics in
which the voice as sound object recedes into the background. Instead of moving listeners through its sonic features, here the voice features primarily as a
channel for the transmission of semantic content, which in this way comes
to bear the weight of emotional expression. While the voice used to testify to
pain that transcended the boundaries of individual interiority, in these more
recent repertoires we are confronted with a more bounded subject-in-pain
for whom the voice represents first and foremost a means of self-expression.
Voice, self, and pain thus come to converge—and voices begin to represent.

Let me be clear that in outlining these different articulations of voice, self,
and pain I do not mean to suggest a model of linear succession. "Traditional"
repertoires in which cross-subjectively experienced pain constitutes relational
selves remained both readily available and were highly valued by many of my
interlocutors. Novel articulations of voiced pain draw from and build upon such
older modes, reshaping and resignifying them in complex ways rather than simply replacing them. What is more, neither Gazîn nor Eyşe Şan is necessarily
representative of Kurdish women and their desires and aspirations in general.
They may, in fact, be considered rather exceptional for how they have employed
their voices in ways that have not only opened up new imaginations of self and
other but also entailed significant risks of censure, violence, and misrecognition.
And yet, even if these two women do not embody a broader norm, their lives
and work have allowed hearing and pronouncing voices in novel ways.

Understanding the voice as a primary vehicle for the expression of individual interiority not only opens up new ways of imagining and inhabiting
the self; it also endows the voice with new forms of value and significance,
turning it into a key benchmark for political agency, identity, and resistance.
Once promises of social recognition and political participation are tied to
"having a voice," voices easily become overdetermined sites of conflict and
debate. But how can voices be made to belong to those pronouncing them?
And how have Kurdish women sought to leverage the value that comes with
having a voice? It is to these questions that I turn in the next chapter.

FIGURE 4 **Inscription**. Voices captured on cassette tape. (Photo by author)

4

Claiming Voice

In April 2012, on one of the first warm spring days of the year, I visited Fadime in her new home in a large state-run container camp, to which she had been relocated several weeks earlier. The two heavy earthquakes that hit Wan in October and November 2011 had severely damaged Fadime's simple mud-brick house, which was located in one of the poorer neighborhoods of the city. Like most of us who stayed in Wan over the winter, Fadime had passed more than three bitter cold months living in a tent pitched in the front garden of her house together with her adult son, fearing that the continuously shaking ground might cause the structure with its numerous cracks, some as wide as a hand's palm, to collapse entirely. During this time, Fadime left most of her sparse belongings inside the damaged house. A carpet, bedding, and several cushions, a small electric heater and a portable burner, tea, a teapot, and sugar, were all that accompanied her into her temporary shelter—as did her tape recorder and a selection of her most cherished tapes, assembled inside a shoebox.

This assemblage of life-sustaining and assuaging objects had also made its journey to the brand-new container to which Fadime proudly welcomed me on this spring day. Her new abode of twenty-one square meters was one of thousands, lined up in seemingly endless rows on a vast empty plot of land along Wan's main arterial thoroughfare toward the airport. Lined with gravel, the straight pathways between the containers teemed with life on the day that I visited. Children had made the expansive space around their new homes their playground, and several women were busy hanging up laundry to dry outside. Some families were still moving in, while those who had already arrived observed the busy comings and goings, taking in the first warm sunrays of the year.

When I arrived at Fadime's container, I found her listening to a cassette tape together with an acquaintance from her old neighborhood who had been relocated to the same camp. As the two women explained to me, the male voice that I heard emanating from Fadime's cassette recorder was recounting the famous Kurdish epic Mem û Zîn. Without waiting for the end of the epic, the neighbor soon left us, and I spent the afternoon with Fadime in her sparsely furnished container, listening to cassette tapes, and discussing the intricacies of Kurdish oral traditions. Sitting on the carpet-covered ground, equipped with plenty of tea and the tape recorder, Fadime played for me the voices that had marked her life, voices that had provided her with solace and comfort at some moments, with courage and pleasure at others.

But Fadime was also keen that I record her own voice using my digital voice recorder. In particular, she wanted to sing for me compositions that she said "belonged to her" (-ên min in). These included a dizzying array of pieces ranging from short praise poems for Kurdish politicians like Wan's well-known Remzi Kartal, to songs celebrating International Women's Day or Newroz, to mournful kilams about the recent earthquake, a neighbor's failed romantic love, and Fadime's own hardships throughout her marriage, as well as, finally, several lamentations for relatives who had passed away. Fadime had recorded herself singing these pieces in the past, and now the old tapes turned out to be useful reminders. Some pieces, she said, she had not intonated for a long time, so the recordings allowed her to recall a particular kilam's first notes, the details of a maqam, or a specific rhyming pattern. The sonic snippets spurred her memory, allowing her to reperform her own compositions for the sake of my recording device.

Once we had finished our mini recording session, Fadime broached a topic that was clearly dear to her heart. She explained to me that kilams and other songs said to be anonymous—which includes many if not most Kurdish oral repertoires—did not in fact lack authors. They were only considered anonymous because the author's name had not been recorded, and as a result had been forgotten. As she put it,

These are not anonymous pieces (parça). If the name of the owner had been written down, these wouldn't be anonymous. [...] There are thousands of pieces of which nobody knows who they belong to. There is Payzanok, Herekol, Wê Here. What else? Xalê Qazî . . . I have sung these pieces, but I don't know the owner of a single one of them, nobody knows them. Whoever I ask, and I have asked a lot, nobody knows. If it had been possible, if they had mentioned the name or surname of that person with only a single word within the piece, they wouldn't have been lost. That's how it should be, but these beautiful voices, beautiful words are now lost (kayıp). [...] If my name is written down, nobody can take away my right. If my name is there, even if you put it on the internet, nobody can play it without me, without my permission. Once my name is there, they can't do anything. Then it's mine.

What Fadime was suggesting here is that all songs—or what she simply called here "pieces" (_parça_)—have an owner. To her, songs are created by identifiable individuals, and these individuals deserve to be recognized as the owners of their vocal compositions. Voices, however, are extraordinarily mobile objects. Once pronounced, they are able to circulate in ways that potentially distribute them far from their origins, particularly when mediated by modern sound technologies like cassette tapes, CDs, or that vast and intangible space of the internet. For Fadime, this capacity of voices to circulate entailed menacing prospects of lost ownership, unbridled anonymity, and infringed rights. At the same time, she was very clear about what it would take to counter these risks: mentioning names. Attaching a name to a voice, Fadime maintained, would allow tying that voice to its rightful point of origin. Inserting a name into a song, recording it, or writing it down would establish ownership; it would protect rights and bestow recognition. Inscription, in other words, would make a voice belong.

Unfortunately, however, Fadime lacked the necessary skills in alphabetic literacy that would have allowed her to write down names. Having grown up in a remote mountain village, she had never been to school and was forced to marry an older man at the age of twelve as his second wife. So she asked me to make sure that her voice would not succumb to the same fate as that of so many other Kurdish voices that were deemed anonymous even though they did, in fact, have an owner.

> Whatever you are going to write about me, write my name underneath. Write my name. Dengbêj Fadime. Whenever. Wherever. Because the day will come and we will disappear. You know how many people have disappeared. These people, these songs, so many owners are lost (_kayıp_). And not within a long span of time. Normally there should be their name, only the name, it's not a lot. But it hasn't been given any value, our people are indifferent (_duyarsız_). Especially when it comes to the family, and to us Kurds . . . They oppose it, they don't let us [sing]. So many historical people, writings, pieces, things have been lost. And whatever is left, [other] people have appropriated for themselves.

The fear of loss and disappearance that Fadime expressed here clearly reflected the history of systematic subdual and erasure that Kurdish language, culture, and identity have been subject to in Turkey throughout the twentieth century. In speaking of the _kayıp_, of those who are lost, Fadime equally evoked the specters of the thousands of Kurdish oppositional politicians, journalists, and activists who were forcefully disappeared, with many extra-judicially killed by state security services in a systematic policy that peaked during the 1990s (Göral, Işık, and Kaya 2013). But beyond state and political violence, Fadime also hinted at other sources and actors of disappearance: attitudes of disregard within Kurdish communities, for example, that had left oral traditions unguarded against what she regarded as misappropriation and theft, as well as patriarchal kinship ideologies that prevented Kurdish women from raising their voices.

What strikes me above all about Fadime's statements is an enormous anxiety about the potentialities of disappearance, loss, and demise in relation to the voice as a mobile sound object that easily circulates independently of its origin and is therefore perennially unstable as a trace—always ready to betray, as it were, its point of origin. In the previous chapter I argued that voice and self converge in contemporary Kurdistan ever more frequently, meaning that vocal objects like kilams are with increasing ease understood as expressions of the subject's self and interiority. An equation of voice with self is also foundational for representational politics, which valorize voices as indices of both individual and collective identity, will, and presence, intimately tying political agency and social status to the idea of "having a voice." These new forms of valorizing the voice, I suggest, have increased scrutiny of the ways in which voices may be linked to those who pronounce them, and heightened anxieties of the kind expressed by Fadime, about how that link may be stabilized. At a moment when Kurdish voices—and those of dengbêjs in particular—have acquired unprecedented political, social, and even financial value, how can they be reliably tied to their bearers? What modalities exist for directing and distributing the value that has come to inhere in Kurdish voices? And how can one lastingly lay claim to voices that have not only gained in value but also travel increasingly far distances thanks to modern sound technologies?

One powerful trope through which voices may be tied to selves is the notion of authorship. Ideas about authorship determine how we think about, attribute, and trace processes of cultural production and where we locate the agency that goes into the making of knowledge and artifacts. They influence who we consider eligible to claim status as authors and what we regard as claimable in this way (Biagioli and Galison 2003b; Foucault 1977; Kittler 1985). Understandings of authorship in this way create, as Mario Biagioli and Peter Galison (2003a, 4) write, "economies of credit" or, as scholar of intellectual property regimes Rosemary Coombe puts it, "cartographies for cultural agency" (1998, 6). From the perspective of a politics of voice, I propose that we may usefully approach authorship as a historically and culturally variable notion that constitutes subjects in relation to how they claim and bear a voice.

Modern politics of representation are predicated upon subjects, both individual and collective, having a voice. This means that they simultaneously demand and foster forms of authorship that conceive of voices as objects one can "have"—even own—and that match voices to single, identifiable subjects that these voices thus come to represent. It is only once voices are claimed in this way that they may begin to deliver on the promises that representational politics attach to them.

But being able to claim a voice as one's own is no mean feat, as Fadime's worries indicate. In this chapter, I therefore take a closer look at what happens when voices become objects that need to be claimed as ownable property in order to access their value. I ask how women like Fadime navigated these novel terrains of vocal value and how they went about positioning themselves as the legitimate author-owners of their voices. Doing so, my aim is not only to highlight the conflicts and contestations that arise when "having a voice" becomes a key site for the making of political subjectivity, but also to shed light on the dilemmas and vulnerabilities that these subject positions entail. To make my argument, I will first outline how a politics of pluralist elicitation has invested Kurdish voices in Turkey with novel representational value and in this way rendered questions of authorship an increasingly contested field. The next section will show how resulting ideas about voices as objects that may be owned are rapidly reconfiguring existing logics of reckoning authorship in Kurdish contexts and prompting new strategies for laying claim to voices and their value. As we shall see in the final part, while new ideas about authorship have allowed women to challenge how patrilineal logics grant and accord voice, such ideas have also induced new risks that come with the pressure to become identifiable as the author and owner of one's voice.

Valorizing the Kurdish Voice

After decades of censorship and silencing, Kurdish oral repertoires have over recent years become new sites of value, fueling conflicts over who may lay claim to them and how. This new valorization follows a long history during which Kurdish voices were denied, assimilated, and violently silenced in Turkey, as sketched out in the introduction. As much as the newfound appreciation of dengbêjs and their repertoires has to be understood within the context of Turkey's short-lived pluralist turn of the 2000s and 2010s and the way in which it allowed for hitherto silenced voices to become publicly audible, it is also rooted in longer-standing historical legacies that are intimately tied to early Kurdish nation-building efforts.

Already in the first half of the twentieth century, Kurdish intellectuals had turned to dengbêjs and their repertoires as a source of cultural and linguistic richness that would befit the nation they hoped to forge.[1] While intellectuals initially chose to focus their attention on the "high culture" of written Kurdish literature, including classical poetry, especially in the period following World War I attention shifted toward oral and popular culture as an important source for the documentation of Kurdish cultural heritage (Strohmeier 2003, 151–154). Among the most important efforts in this field were those undertaken by Celadet and Kamuran Bedirkhan, members of the prestigious Bedirkhan family of Kurdish notables, who published a number of influential Kurdish journals from their base in the French Levant in the 1920s and 1930s. Convinced of the need to "showcase the richness and historical depth of Kurdish traditions and cultural heritage" (Henning 2018, 575), the brothers attributed great significance to Kurdish oral repertoires and became invested in the transcription of dengbêjs' sung narratives (Fuccaro 2003, 206–209; Tejel Gorgas 2007, 275).[2] This early emphasis on the significance of oral genres secured dengbêjs and their repertoires an important place within an evolving understanding of a collective Kurdish culture, even though the cultural politics forged by the Bedirkhanis valued such genres mainly for the insights these provided into the Kurdish language, whose documentation and standardization they deemed instrumental for the forging of Kurdish national unity (Yüksel 2011, 65; Klein 2000, 16–17).

The Kurdish political movement that emerged in Turkey from the hotbed of left-wing student politics at the country's major universities over the course of the 1970s, by contrast, was much less enthralled with respected singer-poets than were early nationalist elites. As committed socialists, many members of the movement regarded dengbêjs as symbols of the old feudal and tribal order that the Kurdish people needed to overcome in the name of both social and political revolution (Çakır 2011; Çakır 2019; Scalbert-Yücel 2009). The movement's cultural politics encouraged protest music combining elements of Western rock music, socialist marches, and Anatolian folk music, rather than elderly men and women chanting (hi)stories of tribal warfare, blood feuds, and elopements (Aksoy 2006; Blum and Hassanpour 1996). At stake was the creation of a new art and culture that was to be at once national, democratic, and socialist in both form and content (Scalbert-Yücel 2009). Gazîn remembered this period as the time when there was no more interest "in the old songs." During the 1990s, she recalled, singers and musicians began to make primarily political songs about the ongoing war and its victims, condemning village evictions and the massive migration these caused, and celebrating the PKK's martyrs for their sacrifice to the Kurdish nation. "Their pain went in that direction," Gazîn explained, identifying the suffering caused by political violence and state terror as the force that made emerge a

Kurdish voice steeped in the politics of the present and reverberating with the sounds of armed resistance. Turkish authorities worked rigorously to silence this voice, which consequently circulated in Kurdish lifeworlds mostly in clandestine form, through bootlegged and smuggled cassette tapes, secretly intercepted radio waves, and carefully calibrated satellite dishes receiving television broadcasts from abroad.

Beginning in the late 1990s and early 2000s, however, with the global rise of identity and multicultural politics following the end of the Cold War, things started to change. For one, when Turkey's Justice and Development Party (Adalet ve Kalkınma Partisi, AKP) came to power in 2002 it inaugurated an ambivalent politics of pluralism, which granted greater cultural rights to ethnic and religious groups that had been sidelined by dominant Turkish nationalism throughout much of the twentieth century (Kadioglu 2007; Tambar 2014). These initiatives were partly fueled by Turkey's wish at the time to join the EU and the need to fulfill the legal requirements regarding political and minority rights that were part of the accession procedure. But the initiatives were equally part of the AKP's project to dismantle the institutional hegemony of Turkey's secular Kemalist elites and accord Sunni Islam—alongside neoliberal market policies—a more central place in the nation's public and political life (Savcı 2021). As part of its pledge to strengthen civil liberties and democracy, the government promised that it would finally "solve" Turkey's Kurdish issue and inaugurated a peace process that saw state authorities negotiate with the PKK leadership.[3] In the period that followed, Turkey enjoyed a substantial relaxation of restrictions on civil liberties, which led to a flourishing of cultural production and political activism on the part of a wide range of previously marginalized social actors, including Kurds, Armenians, Alevis, and LGBTQI groups.

While this new regime of multicultural pluralism allowed for and even incited the display of cultural difference in the name of minoritarian representation, it also encouraged a conceptual separation of culture from politics and fostered the commodification of difference (Schäfers 2015; Tambar 2010; Walton 2013). Minoritarian subjects were thus able to raise their voices only under the condition that they would not venture into the realm of "politics." Concretely, this meant that when cultural production could in any way be construed as a threat to Turkey's territorial integrity, the limits of state tolerance would quickly be reached (Karaca 2011, 178). Given that most Kurdish cultural and artistic expression can be construed in this way, Kurdish cultural producers are prosecuted on a routine basis in Turkey, typically under the charge of spreading "separatist propaganda" or under terrorism charges.[4] Since the collapse of the peace process in July 2015, which spelled in many ways the end of Turkey's short-lived pluralist experiment, this has only gotten worse as massive repression has been meted out against the Kurdish opposition in the country.

My interlocutors were keenly aware of the conditionality this imposed on their voices. Asya, for instance, responded when I asked her whether she also sang "political" (*siyasî*) songs that she only did so in front of the appropriate audiences. "Everything knows its place," she added, indicating how Turkey's multicultural regime required of those it supposedly empowered to carefully calibrate their voices and develop a fine-grained knowledge of contexts in order to stay within the bounds of officially sanctioned speakability. And even with such knowledge, raising one's voice remained a risky endeavor. At the time of my fieldwork, for instance, Gazîn had two trials pending against her in which she was prosecuted on charges of terrorist propaganda and incitement to separatism, carrying potential sentences of up to five years' imprisonment, for performing at events organized by the Kurdish movement.[5]

At the same time as Turkey's government embarked on its new regime of managing difference roughly two decades ago, the Kurdish political movement also underwent important changes. Following the arrest of PKK leader Abdullah Öcalan in 1999, the movement increasingly concentrated on attaining political and cultural rights for Kurds in Turkey through a politics of representation within the domain of democratic political institutions and civil society (Akkaya and Jongerden 2012). Successes in municipal elections throughout the 2000s and 2010s gave the movement crucial access to public finances, which became an important source of funding for a wide variety of cultural initiatives (Watts 2010). Dengbêjs featured with increasing prominence in such projects, now with the understanding that the repertoires of these elderly singers harbored the essence of Kurdish cultural heritage and therefore needed to be institutionally supported and safeguarded. This framing of dengbêjs and other elements of rural Kurdish culture had been pioneered starting in the mid-1980s by a number of Kurdish writers and intellectuals—many of them living abroad—who were concerned about linguistic and cultural changes occurring as a result of massive rural-urban migration by Kurdish populations and ongoing assimilation efforts by the state.[6] It was subsequently adopted by the Kurdish political movement, which played a key role in propagating this new view of Kurdish folk culture through its own institutions, publications, and television channels from the late 1990s onward (Çakır 2019, 60–61). The intersection of this "cultural turn" within the Kurdish movement with the Turkish state's newfound pluralist (yet highly paternalistic) tolerance of the early 2000s proved to be fertile ground for a renewed valorization of Kurdish oral repertoires. These repertoires were increasingly promoted as instances of Kurdish (oral) literature and history and thus as key elements of a Kurdish cultural heritage that assimilation policies and large-scale social change had seemingly brought to the brink of vanishing. Within this framework, dengbêjs, in particular, have come to be widely celebrated as among the most authentic embodiments of Kurdish identity and as key "labourers of Kurdish culture" (Çakır 2019, 184).

One of the most prominent outcomes of this development was the opening of a so-called Dengbêj House (Mala Dengbêjan) in Diyarbekir in 2007, run by the local Kurdish municipality and financed with the help of both EU and Turkish state funds. Furnished with a modest monthly stipend, selected dengbêjs were expected to show regular presence at the House, participate in research projects focusing on Kurdish oral traditions, and showcase these traditions to both foreign and local audiences (Scalbert-Yücel 2009). Similar establishments soon followed in other Kurdish towns and cities. Cherished as icons of Kurdish tradition and heritage, dengbêjs have found themselves not only on municipal payrolls, but they are also regularly invited to concerts and festivals, appear on a variety of television channels, have recorded popular albums, and attracted a flurry of research and publications. Arguably, one result of the way in which dengbêjs have essentially been cast as embodiments of a Kurdish past is that they have been able to feature across long-standing political divides. Safely removed from contemporary politics in the eyes of the state and unsullied by the forces of Turkish modernity in the eyes of Kurdish activists, they thus appear with equal frequency in the studios of Turkish state broadcasters and on highly politicized Kurdish TV channels, on festival stages set up by Kurdish cultural activists and on those sponsored by the ruling AKP.[7]

If dengbêjs have thus, in a certain sense, become the collective voice of the Kurdish people, this was also a voice that many felt was at acute risk of disappearance. Dengbêjs appeared like the vestiges of an old order who carried, as I was often told, extraordinarily rich "treasures" (*hazine*) in the form of oral repertoires that had almost miraculously survived the onslaught of the Turkish state's systematic attempts at silencing, denying, and assimilating Kurdish voices over the last century. Because these treasures were confined to the perishable bodies of mostly elderly men and women, everyone seemed to agree that measures of salvation and rescue were urgently needed. As a consequence, the last two decades have seen the emergence of a vast array of documentary and transcription projects aimed at wresting oral repertoires from the bodies containing them. A veritable "archive fever" (Derrida 1998a) has been running rampant as a variety of different actors have come to be engaged in documenting Kurdish oral traditions, ranging from the private endeavors of passionate folklore collectors, armed with not much more than tape recorder, pen, and paper, to professional undertakings on the part of research units, municipalities, and NGOs, often funded by Western donors.[8] These efforts are carried out with a considerable sense of both gravity and urgency. The leaders of an American-funded transcription project focusing on oral repertoires from the Çewlîg (Tk. Bingöl) region, for example, describe their project as "a moral and conscientious obligation, a social and historical responsibility." Given that Kurdish oral culture "has seen neither the opportunity nor the blessing of becoming permanent," they consider its life to be at risk and deem documentary efforts a form of "emergency intervention" (_acil müdahale_) that allows "admitting dengbêj culture into an oxygen tent" (Karasu et al. 2007, 8–9).

My interlocutors at the Women Dengbêjs Association in Wan were similarly invested in the powers of documentation. Worried that their repertoires were doomed to disappearance unless written down, yet lacking in alphabetic literacy themselves, they were keen to solicit my skills in this field in order to lastingly document the many kilams and strans they knew. And so we embarked upon a transcription project that saw me put nearly thirty of the women's songs into writing, eventually producing a modest folder with neat printouts assembled in transparent document pockets that would come to occupy pride of place at the association. Several years later, Gazîn found assistance in a young Kurdish teacher who transcribed by hand over 200 of the songs she knew during painstaking transcription sessions that lasted weeks. Beyond writing in a narrow sense, the women active at the association were also keen to have their voices inscribed through audiovisual technologies. All made regular use of the recording function of tape recorders and cell phones to capture their own or each other's voices, but they also delighted in the prospect of figures like journalists or television crews producing permanent records of their vocal skills and repertoires. Some years before I first met her, Gazîn had even ventured into producing a series of video recordings that were modeled after evening shows on television, where she acted as a host who interviewed a different guest singer in each episode (Schäfers 2019).

What this "archive fever" points to, I believe, is that rendering the voice permanent through forms of inscription holds powerful promises when minoritarian voices are to matter within a context of pluralist representation. Inscriptive technologies allow externalizing embodied repertoires and provide tangible proof of cultural forms. They have the potential to salvage genres that chains of oral transmission from one performer to the next may no longer sustain. And they bestow upon long-denied voices an aura of officiality and authority (Jamison 2016). Yet inscription, at the very moment that it fixes oral texts, also potentially unmoors them from their points of origin. Jacques Derrida calls writing an "iterative structure," one that is able to function independently of the presence of its author, like "a kind of machine" (1977, 8).

Despite its air of permanence, writing may spur the circulation of texts, fixing discourse only in order to detach it from its author, offering it up for distribution, interpretation, and appropriation.

In a context of pluralist politics where voices ought to reliably represent their carriers if they are to deliver on the promises of agency and empowerment tied to them, this is a prospect that requires careful management. As Rosalind Morris's (2000) work shows, modern representational economies are continuously haunted by the possibility that writing may turn from a medium of representation into one of self-referential performativity. In the hands of the Thai spirit mediums Morris frequented, writing easily turned from an abstract means of transmitting semantic content into a form of magic that would draw its power from its own materiality. Ensuring that inscriptive technologies represent, in other words, requires continuous efforts: writing needs to be tamed in order to make its promises deliver. For my interlocutors, writing therefore not only held great hopes, but also prompted new anxieties. It required new competencies that would allow translating voices into inscribed matter. It made owner and authorship dependent on new actors, who wielded specific technologies and know-how, including avid transcribers like myself, but also music producers, camera(wo)men, and project managers. And, perhaps most importantly, it called for new means and instruments that would bind widely circulating and increasingly valuable voices to their points of origin. Assertions of authorship, I suggest, have emerged as central mechanisms to do precisely this: to negotiate how inscribed and recorded voices relate to the subjects who utter them and whom they may thus be taken to represent.

What Makes an Author?

We tend to think of authorship as a relatively straightforward category that matches authors, as the originators of texts, songs, and art pieces, to their works. On closer inspection, however, it becomes clear that neither the category of the author nor that of the work are as stable and straightforward as they may appear. For one, as anthropologist Alfred Gell (1998) makes clear, the agency that goes into the making of a cultural artifact tends to be distributed across a range of human and nonhuman actors, including commissioning patrons and executing craftsmen, but also various ideas and materials. In such a context, how can one delimit who (or what) counts as the author of a work? Recall how kilams, as I outlined in chapters 1 and 2, draw a good part of their affective impact from the way in which they reiterate poetic and musical elements that can be found across countless other pieces. Kilams, I also showed, often incorporate a multiplicity of voices into their narrative, which

allows listeners to tune into the narrative while detaching it from its performer. Attributing such a polyphonic, multitextual artifact to a single author
is no straightforward task. It requires that accumulative and collaborative
relations of cultural production are made to fit into the relatively confined
categories of "author" and "work." Marilyn Strathern's notion (1996) of "cutting the network" might prove useful for thinking through what is at stake
here. If cultural artifacts are the products of a proliferating network woven
by a variety of actors, materials, and ideas, establishing authorship becomes
a question of strategically "cutting" that network. While certain relations of
creativity are acknowledged, others need to be rejected in order to contain
creativity in certain bodies and objects that can then count as, respectively,
authors and their works (Strathern 1999, 2005).

Modern notions of authorship typically posit the individual subject and
their creativity as the single point of origin of a work, thereby radically nar-
rowing down the dispersed network of relations and agencies that sustains
the making of any cultural artifact. As Coombe writes, the modern author is
one "who speaks with a single voice and possesses a singular self embodied
in unique textual expressions deemed to be his 'works'" (1998, 252). When
representational politics require that subjects "have a voice" as a condition
of their political agency, they implicitly rely on such an understanding of authorship and the kind of relation it presumes between voices and those who
pronounce them. Having a voice that will count as politically consequential,
in other words, requires that subjects express themselves through voices that
are able to unambiguously represent singular and bounded selves. Only once
voices become representational in this way can those pronouncing them feature as their identifiable authors and owners, granting them access to the political capital tied to "having a voice."

But at the same time as modern authorship vests creativity in single, identifiable individuals, it also brings into being a realm of cultural production
driven by collective yet anonymous creativity. This bifurcation is perhaps
most clearly institutionalized in modern copyright legislation. Under such
legislation, to qualify as a work of authorship, "a text must have been created
by an identifiable individual or individuals . . . and must exhibit 'originality'"
(Jaszi and Woodmansee 2003, 198). If an individual can legitimately claim to
be the originator of a work, they qualify simultaneously as authors and owners of that work, which in this way becomes a form of property. But where
no individual author comes forward to claim a work it falls into the public
domain, meaning it will be considered as belonging to an imaginary collective such as "the people" or "the nation" (Goodman 2002, 89–91). Copyright
law in this way enacts a conceptual divide between, on the one hand, the cel-

ebrated authorship of the creative individual—which we typically recognize as art—and, on the other hand, an anonymous creativity brought forth by an abstract public, relegated to the realm of culture or heritage.

If my interlocutors were going to "have a voice," then, they would need to claim authorship over their voices on the grounds of either the individual or the collective terms offered by modern understandings of intellectual property. Their voices, however, were actually steeped in logics that reckon creativity very differently from those underwriting contemporary notions of authorship. As scholarship of music and oral repertoires across a variety of Middle Eastern contexts makes clear, in such contexts works tend to be valued less for their originality than for how they creatively interpret existing patterns and fit within long-standing performance traditions. Authorship—and the authority associated with it—derives here from the continuity of transmission and the traceability of descent, a wide-ranging principle that Andrew Shryock (1997) has conceptualized as the "genealogical imagination." Not only has this idiom shaped how cultural production is understood and practiced in many contexts across the Middle East, but it functions as a powerful trope of (patriarchal) authority more broadly. From tribal affiliation to national belonging to the transmission of Islamic knowledge, principles of genealogical descent—mostly traced through the male line—anchor and legitimize a vast range of social facts.[9] In the realm of oral and musical performance, genealogical principles inform the prevalence of long-standing master-disciple relationships—as is the case, for instance, among performers of classical Turkish music (Gill-Gürtan 2011)—and they vest authority in repertoires that are traceable through chains of transmission, like the North African repertoires of Andalusi music, whose origins practitioners trace all the way back to the Muslim presence in Spain (Glasser 2016). But such principles may also help to anchor musical knowledge in specific localities and the communities inhabiting them, as is the case at Turkey's Black Sea coast (Elias 2016).

Similar principles can also be seen at play in Kurdish contexts. Certain kilams, for instance, are associated with the names of authoritative dengbêjs who are imagined as key nodes in the transmission of oral repertoires to subsequent generations. Other pieces are understood as belonging to particular regions or localities based on their specific intonation, accent, melodic elaboration, or instrumentalization. These genealogical idioms of reckoning authorship attribute creativity to a point of origin—be it a person, locality, or community—but, differently from modern understandings of authorship as property, they do not restrict the communal use, interpretation, and adaptation of cultural forms. Rather than celebrating such forms as fixed expressions ("works") of a single author's creative inspiration ("their voice"), genealogical models encourage continued interpretation by performers while rewarding fidelity to transmitted traditions (Bryant 2005; Gill 2017).

But the genealogical anchoring of oral repertoires in certain places or persons is undergoing important changes, changes that speak of the appeal that the property logics associated with modern authorship hold in contexts where voices promise access to new forms of value and authority. At Turkey's Black Sea coast, for instance, songs and dances used to be closely associated with specific valleys thanks to subtle variations in lyrics, performance style, and instrumentalization. As anthropologist Nicolas Elias (2016) has noted, these genealogically traced variations are rapidly falling victim to a culture industry that is intent on marketing a single, uniform Black Sea culture to audiences across the nation. At the same time as local repertoires have acquired new value as expressions of the nation's (or region's) cultural heritage, they have, as a result, become increasingly standardized (see also Öztürkmen 1998).

In a similar way, dengbêjs' repertoires, too, are more and more perceived as representing an overarching, homogeneous Kurdish culture rather than as locally rooted and genealogically traced corpora of oral genres. Take, for instance, the way in which the term *dengbêj*, which used to be specific to the northern Kurdish region of Serhed, has come to function as an umbrella term replacing local performer designations elsewhere. In the past, performers of Kurdish sung prose or poetry outside the Serhed region would locally be known by different designations, including *stranbêj*, *şaîr*, and *mitirb*. While these terms used to indicate specific, locally rooted performance traditions, as Argun Çakır (2011, 50–53) has noted, in recent decades more and more of these performers have decided to call themselves dengbêjs. Given that the figure of the Serhedî dengbêj has become emblematic for how Kurdish culture and tradition as a whole are imagined in Turkey today (Çakır 2011, 2020), even performers of repertoires that significantly differ from the performance traditions prevalent in Serhed stand to benefit from referring to themselves in this way. After all, the term *dengbêj* is widely recognized among audiences across Turkey and readily indexes cultural authenticity, itself a prime value and marketable commodity.

Less and less understood in terms of local or regional forms of belonging and descent, the voices of Kurdish singer-poets have thus come to embody what is today easily imagined as a single, collectively held cultural heritage. This development, I suggest, is the result of how representational politics encourage thinking of voices from within a logics of property, such that voices become things that one can "have" or, indeed, own. These logics attribute voice either to individuals—single author-owners of texts, songs, artworks—or to an anonymous collective, that ominous "public domain" imagined by intellectual property legislation. While the modern, individual author speaks with a single voice to express their singular self, dengbêjs represent the collective counterpart to this figure, their voices now indexing an overarching Kurdish culture, history, identity.

Claiming Ownership and Countering Theft

Once voices can be owned, however, they may also be stolen. And, indeed, fear of theft and misappropriation shadowed my interlocutors' engagements with oral genres, precipitating a range of responses with a view to asserting and defending what they saw as their rightful ownership. Such fears not only reflect how voices are increasingly viewed as property in Kurdish contexts—as things one can have or own, either as an individual or collectively—but also speak of the conflicts and contestations provoked by the valorization of voices as representational vehicles that promise social status, political authority, and increasingly also financial profit. If access to these promises required claiming voices as property, this meant that my interlocutors were faced with the challenging task of fitting voices steeped in a genealogical ethos into the very different logics of intellectual property. Navigating this terrain required that my interlocutors would find novel ways of "cutting" the manifold relations of influence and borrowing that marked their repertoires, making sure that their voices would reliably point back to themselves as their identifiable author-owners.

A first set of anxieties concerned forms of collective theft. Throughout my fieldwork, women of all ages and backgrounds, singers or not, repeatedly told me about how men had stolen the art of dengbêjî from them virtually wholesale. Women, this widespread narrative held, were the real originators of the kilams that dengbêjs sing, even though they were today hardly recognized for this. Because women are particularly predisposed to experiencing profound pain and suffering, it was they, I was told, who had sung the first sorrowful kilams in a faraway past. Over the course of history, however, men appropriated the practice from them, claimed it as their own, and prohibited women from singing under the pretext of concerns about female modesty and familial honor. Through this misappropriation, men were now able to gather fame and profits that should in fact belong to women. Asya recounted this story of theft in the following way, locating the origins of dengbêjs' repertoires in the systematic denial of women's wishes and desires by patriarchal marriage practices and the suffering this causes: "Dengbêjî comes from women, but men have appropriated women's heritage (*mîrat*). [. . .] Women used to be exchanged in marriage (*berdêl*), they would be given to old men. When men killed each other, they would give women as compensation (*jin pêş xwînê ve didan*). So what would a woman do then? She would sit down and with her thoughts and feelings she would sing dengbêjî. But now men have appropriated our legacy. They are the artists, the dengbêjs, they sing at concerts, and they even receive money for it." Gulbahar, the female singer associated with Diyarbekir's Dengbêj House whom we met in the previous chapter, was similarly convinced that, as she asserted, "dengbêjî was invented by women." She imagined the process of men seizing women's repertoires in the following way: "One [man] would say to the other, at so-and-so's funeral, this-and-that woman sang in such a way that she melted people's hearts. And from there they [men] seized it and took possession of it. They added a few things and made it into dengbêjî. It's the work and labor of women, but men took it away. For women it became prohibited, while for men it has been free."

Such claims about women being the actual originators (and therefore rightful owners) of dengbêjs' oral traditions were typically made with regard to repertoires that my interlocutors would describe as anonymous or *gelerî* in Kurdish, meaning literally "of the people." These were the kinds of folk repertoires not attributable to an individual author, which modern property logics therefore ascribe to the public domain as a seemingly uniform, collective property holder. Women's claims to ownership over these anonymous repertoires, then, can be thought of as gendered acts of "cutting the network" of that ostensibly general, homogeneous public imagined by intellectual property legislation. By underlining the work, labor, and suffering that women had invested in shaping oral performance traditions, both Asya and Gulbahar highlighted the injustice of men now solely profiting from these traditions' recent valorization under the banner of cultural heritage. They highlighted that the seeming anonymity of a collective creative actor like "the people" in fact obscured differentiated spheres of cultural creativity. As such, their allegations made a crucial intervention in a politics of representation that readily colludes with patrilineally defined notions of community in order to accord voice. In a context where the seemingly anonymous repertoires of dengbêjs have become increasingly valuable as indices of cultural authenticity and tradition, women's stories of wholesale theft laid bare the patriarchal privileges that structure what modern property logics construe as the undifferentiated creative force of a collective like "the people" (compare Goodman 2002).

In addition to claiming voice as collective author-owners, women also advanced claims to voice through that other route offered by modern property logics, that of individual authorship. It was in that sphere, too, that fears of theft were ripe, often concerning kilams that a particular singer had crafted herself, for instance, in response to a specific event or to reflect on personal experience. Such suspicion of theft arose, for example, when in the fall of

2012, together with Gazîn, I visited Sînem, a female dengbêj based in Erdîş
(Tk. Erciş), a small town on the other side of Lake Wan. Erdîş was close to
the epicenter of the 2011 earthquakes that devastated the region, and the town
had been hit hard by the disaster. Like many other dengbêjs, Sînem had made
her own kilam about the event. When she sang it to us during our visit, Gazîn
cried out that Sînem's kilam was exactly like one she had heard only recently
being performed by a male dengbêj in Wan. Adil, Gazîn was sure, must have
gotten the piece from Sînem. "And when I asked him," Gazîn recalled, "he
even claimed it was his own!" She was appalled at what she felt was yet another time a male dengbêj tried to accrue fame for himself on the back of a
woman's accomplishments. Sînem acknowledged Adil might have gotten the
piece from her; after all they were distant relatives and he might have overheard her singing it somewhere. Still, Gazîn insisted, that did not give him the
right to pretend this piece was his own: "He could simply have said, I learnt
this from my friend Sînem."

During our afternoon recording and chatting in Fadime's temporary container home, when Fadime had urged me to write down her name whenever
and wherever, she had advanced similar suspicions of theft. Just recently, she
told me, her daughter's sister-in-law attended a wedding where a male singer
performed a kilam that Fadime said was in fact hers. She was certain that the
wedding musician must have overheard her performing the song elsewhere,
then learned it himself—perhaps he had even secretly recorded her singing—
and was now performing the song as if it were his own. What outraged Fadime most was that he had done so without asking her permission (*izinsiz*),
meaning he was gathering fame and popularity by passing off someone else's
labor as his own.

Given the way in which kilams routinely borrow from, refer to, and cite
other pieces, however, accusing someone else of theft and claiming a kilam as
one's own was a less straightforward task than it might seem at first sight. As
much as Sînem's and Fadime's kilams might have been original with regard to
what they recounted—in Sînem's case the 2011 earthquakes and how Sînem
experienced them—the form they took would invariably draw upon a pool
of poetic expressions and melodic elements widely shared across kilams and
other oral genres, such as laments, epics, and lullabies. While genealogical idioms would appreciate such borrowings as fidelity to an established tradition,
property logics can only ever perceive them as instances of unlawful copying
or plagiarism that throw into doubt the originality of the author. Claiming
ownership over the "tissue of quotations" (Barthes 1977, 146) constituted by
a kilam, therefore, would require radically cutting the network woven by the
genre's various cross-references, borrowings, and citations.

In order to get a better sense of the challenges that kilams posed for advancing ownership claims, below I reproduce one stanza of Gazîn's own kilam about the 2011 earthquakes. It illustrates the extent to which even kilams that relate a unique event or experience draw upon established textual themes, which I have visualized here by marking in bold elements that can frequently be found in other kilams and oral genres.

Wî de min got dewran e, dewran e, dewran e, dewran e, dewran e, dayê li min bûye fermanê	**Oh I said these are bad times, bad times, bad times, bad times, bad times, mother a verdict was cast upon me**
Wî de [. . .] du he[zar] yanzdanê bîst û sisiyê Eylolê	On [. . .] twenty-third September two thousand eleven
Wî de berê vî payîzê min ê dema bala xwe lê didaye, wele min ê kirîbû kar û barê zivistanê	Before this autumn I had turned to and occupied myself with the pre-parations for winter
Li ser serê me digeriya **ewrekî reş û tarî**, ewrê erdhejiyan e, **dayê dewran e**	**A dark black cloud** hovered above us, the cloud of earthquakes, **oh mother these are bad times**
Wî de **dema min ê berê xwe nê dida** li erdê Erdîşê Wanê temame bi gundanê	**When I turned toward** Erdîş and Wan and all the villages
Wele çawa xirab biye li van bînan û xanîyan û malanê	Oh how all these buildings, houses, and homes have been destroyed
Wele zarê tête zarokanê, qeyrê diçe dayik û babanê, hewar diçe ma-mostanê, **dayê li me bûye fermanê**	Oh children are wailing, the cries reach mothers and fathers, the calls for help reach the teachers, **mother this is a verdict**
Wî de **dema min ê berê xwe nê dida** li erdê Erdîşê Wanê temame bi gundanê	**When I turned toward** Erdîş and Wan and all the villages
Wele tête dengê axîn û nalînê zarokanê binê van axanê, **dayê dewran e**	The crying and wailing of children emerges from below the ground, **mother these are bad times**
Wî de şûna axînê nalînê wanê torba tijî kevir kirine, gotine 'Eva heqê wan Kurdan e'	Instead of crying and wailing they filled up bags with stones and said 'This is what those Kurds deserve'[10]
Ax dewran e, dewran e, dewran e, dewran e, dayê ferman e, ferman e, ferman e	**Oh mother these are bad times, bad times, bad times, mother it's a verdict, a verdict, a verdict**

As the above illustrates, nearly half of the stanza's lyrics is composed of textual elements that one can find across a wide variety of oral traditions. Note that these are mainly the poetic motifs that lend the account its affective impact and in a sense frame those sections that recount the event of the earthquake in more factual terms. Beyond this more general resemblance to other oral traditions that draw on the same pool of poetic motifs, one can also identify more direct forms of resemblance with specific other kilams. For example, Gazîn's kilam shares its key motif and leading line "Dayê dewran e" (Mother these are bad times) with a well-known kilam also called "Dewrane" that is widely attributed to Şakiro (1936–1996), one of the most important male dengbêjs of his generation. Even closer associations can be made with Kurdish iconic singer Şivan Perwer's song "Helebçe," a lament for the victims of the 1988 Helebçe (Ar. Halabja) massacre, Saddam Hussein's gift gas attack in northern Iraq that cost the lives of several thousand Kurdish civilians. In his piece, Perwer describes the attack as a verdict (ferman), which features in the song's plaintive refrain in ways that closely resemble Gazîn's piece above (li me ferman e, "a verdict is upon us"). The way in which he evokes the crying and wailing of children and their parents that emerges from the town (li jêr tê qîreqîra zaroka, hawara dayik û bavanê) is similar to the expressions employed by Gazîn (zarê tête zarokanê, qeyrê diçe dayik û babanê, hewar diçe mamostanê), as is the melodic delivery of the piece. Finally, Perwer's song carries a parallel political charge, accusatory of anti-Kurdish state violence and mournful for its victims.

A genealogical ethos would likely value the parallels between Gazîn's, Perwer's and Şakiro's pieces as evidence for a continuing tradition of oral performance that gains its strength from how different pieces reference each other. From the perspective of modern understandings of intellectual property, however, those very same parallels are easily construed as instances of plagiarism, just as the similarity between Sînem's and Adil's, or between Fadime's and the wedding singer's, kilams could suggest instances of theft. For Gazîn, Sînem, and Fadime to be recognized as the rightful authors (and owners) of their kilams, therefore, instances of resemblance and borrowing between kilams would need to be downplayed or disavowed. Only by "cutting" proliferating relations of influence and continuity would these women be able to claim a status as the single originators of their work. The accusations of theft advanced by Gazîn and Fadime against, respectively, Adil and the wedding musician can be understood as precisely such gestures of cutting, which prioritized the women singers' labor in assembling their kilams over genealogical lines of borrowing and transmission. In this way, the accusations turned what genealogical logics might have valued as instances of creative borrowing within an existing tradition into acts of unrightful misappropriation.

As far as her own repertoires were concerned, Gazîn took even more radical steps of cutting genealogically traced lines of borrowing and exchange. In 2012, she decided to register a legal claim to copyright over more than thirty pieces she considered her own through the Professional Union of Owners of Musical Works (Musiki Eseri Sahipleri Grubu Meslek Birliği, MSG), one of Turkey's two principal institutions managing musicians' copyright claims. Gazîn had long felt that others were profiting off her voice, but had only recently learned about copyright legislation as a potential way of protecting herself. She was one of the few female dengbêjs of her generation who had successfully entered the music industry and could proudly count over a dozen albums as her own. Most of these albums had been produced by the same company, one of the first Kurdish music production firms that entered the market after the lifting of the language ban in the 1990s. When Gazîn came to Istanbul to record her first albums in the early 2000s, she was unfamiliar with the workings of this industry and had no idea of her rights and entitlements as a singer. During that first trip to the studios, she was made to sign papers she did not understand and could not even read, and then encouraged to sing numerous songs that the company later released staggered on several albums without her knowledge. Even though some of these albums became bestsellers, Gazîn was never paid any royalties, something she found out she was entitled to only much later.

As Amir Hassanpour (2020b) has argued, the widespread exploitation of Kurdish musicians by music companies and producers of the kind Gazîn experienced is directly linked to the separation of voice from body that modern sound technologies enable. Where in the past oral and musical performances were bound to the physical presence of the artist, "singers and performers were owners of their labor power" (Hassanpour 2020b, 31). But once the sound of voices and instruments was able to circulate independently of their performers thanks to vinyl records, radio waves, and audiotapes, music could be turned into a commodity sold in a market, raising new questions about the ownership of these circulating voices and fostering contestations over the distribution of their value. Copyright legislation, of course, arose precisely when similar questions began to be asked with regard to writing after the printing press allowed for the unprecedented circulation—and commodification—of books in early modern Europe (Chartier 2003; Rose 1993). At a moment when inscriptive technologies spurred the circulation of texts, copyright legislation provided a means of binding these texts back to their points of origin, positioning the author (rather than, say, the owners of printing presses) as the central beneficiary of the value accruing from their works.

When Gazîn found her own voice transformed into a marketable commodity in the early twenty-first century, copyright legislation once again promised to secure the tie between voice and self. By the time I met Gazîn over a decade after her first contact with the music industry, she was well aware that she had been ruthlessly exploited while others had made a handsome profit selling her voice. Asserting copyright presented itself as a way of redressing this injustice: by producing a legal tie between herself and her voice—a tie that voice recording technologies had loosened—it would direct the surplus that her voice produced back to herself, allowing her to take possession of monetary profits and social recognition that had been unjustly withheld from her.

Among the songs that Gazîn registered with the MSG, the majority were widely circulating and well-known "anonymous" pieces—both kilams and strans—that were steeped in precisely the networks of genealogical transmission that claims to ownership would likely cut or, at the very least, redirect. Only two of the kilams that Gazîn registered were her personal "compositions" in a narrower sense—one of them being "Dewrane," the song about the earthquake—but as we have seen even such compositions brimmed with the traces of adjacent works. These were repertoires, in other words, that did not lend themselves easily to making any clear pronouncements about original authors or unambiguous owners. Being able to claim originality, however, was not necessarily what was at stake in Gazîn's claim of ownership. In registering herself as the legal author (and thus owner) of these pieces, Gazîn did not claim to have single-handedly composed all these songs from scratch. She readily acknowledged that she was not the original creator of these repertoires, which she knew were widely circulating and which she had herself picked up from other singers. What her claim did set out to achieve was rather to channel any returns that the circulation of her voice might accrue when interpreting these repertoires—be they in the form of status, fame, or financial profit—back toward herself, thereby preventing other actors from accessing the value attached to her voice. While Gazîn chiefly had greedy music producers in mind whom she sought to cut out of the networks of value accumulation linked to her voice, her act had potentially farther-reaching consequences as it cut through the accumulative and collaborative patterns of cultural production that have historically sustained Kurdish oral repertoires.

Even though Gazîn was the only woman I knew who went this far in defending her voice as her own, the concerns driving her were by no means unique. Fear of misappropriation and theft was widespread among my interlocutors, who felt they were at acute risk of missing out on the value that their voices had come to possess. If they were going to have a voice, it became increasingly clear, they would have to invest in laying lasting claim to it, ensuring that their voices, when circulating, would reliably point back to themselves as their point of origin, so as to duly carry out their representational labor. Making a voice one's own, however, required new forms of reckoning relationships of cultural and knowledge production, cutting out actors and relations from networks of oral transmission that a genealogical ethos would have valued as points of reference and authority. Representational politics, with their requirement that minoritarian subjects ought to "have a voice," in this way encouraged the carving up of previously communally owned and utilized repertoires into passionately defended domains of both individual and collective ownership.

The Promises and Perils of Unveiling

If politics of representation rely on subjects having a voice, for those voices to do the crucial work of representing those to whom they ostensibly belong, ownership needs to be unambiguous and identifiable. In a cultural context where the public exposure of women's voices was easily considered immodest or shameful, however, this representational imperative presented a delicate issue. Preventing voices from unambiguously pointing to those enunciating them has historically constituted an important mechanism enabling women to raise their voices without drawing accusations of impropriety across a variety of patriarchal contexts. Among the Awlad 'Ali tribe in Egypt, for instance, the formulaic nature of poetry allows women to express intimate sentiments without becoming identifiable as their bearer (Abu-Lughod 1986). In Yemen, female poets make use of the separation between voice and body offered by sound technologies like the radio or audiocassettes to achieve public audibility without exposing their identity, or they use pseudonyms to destabilize the link between themselves and their voices (Miller 2002). Among female Afghani poets, pen names similarly represent a long-standing technique that functions "as a symbolic veil, allowing their words to circulate while preserving their privacy" (Olszewska 2019, 178).

Kurdish oral genres, too, provide ample opportunity to veil the identity of an enunciating subject. Features including stock poetic formulas, reported speech, and fluctuating personal pronouns constitute a rich cultural repertoire for distancing an intimate utterance from the individuality of its speaker. Likewise, sound technologies that allow for the circulation of disembodied voices, as well as pseudonyms, were available to and used by Kurdish women as a means to raise their voices while hiding their personal identity. In a context where voices not tied to identifiable subjects are hard to conceive as forms of political agency and representation, however, such forms of vocal veiling represented an increasing liability. As Amanda Weidman (2021, 6) has noted, "the combination of a single individual's body, voice, name, and authorial will or intention can create a potent sense of presence" that has enormous benefits in contemporary cultural industries, translating among others into recognition, fame, or profit. Concomitantly, with the kilam having gained considerable value in today's Turkey within the salvage politics of tradition, becoming identifiable as the author-owners of these oral repertoires represented an important opportunity for Kurdish women to tap into circuits of political and social authority and stake a claim to profits many felt were bypassing them. In this context, disentangling body, voice, name, and authorial will in order to achieve anonymity had become a double-edged sword for female singers. While it allowed navigating a complicated and shifting terrain where expectations of gendered modesty and desires for audibility intersected, it carried the risk of preventing women from gaining social recognition for voices endowed with growing significance.

At the Women Dengbêjs Association in Wan, at least two women had released music recordings under a stage name in order to prevent their voices from being identified with them personally. These included Gazîn and Zehra, a younger singer of pop genres whom we briefly met in the introduction. Both had taken on stage names when they began to record their first albums in the early 2000s with the aim of shielding themselves from their families' disapproval by hiding their real identities. By attaching a different name to the women's voices, these pseudonyms stabilized the separation between voice and emitting body that modern recording technologies enable. In a sense, they worked to reroute Gazîn's and Zehra's voices via a false track that pointed not to themselves as the voices' point of origin but to a fictional persona. But when Gazîn's tapes eventually became widely popular, this rerouting meant that she was unable to lay claim to her fame, even though she would regularly hear her own voice wafting through the open windows of the neighbors whenever they played her cassette. Recalling this period of secrecy years later, it became clear that Gazîn was deeply hurt by having to pretend that this popular voice did not belong to her. She would have liked to take pride in it and garner the praise and recognition that her vocal skills promised to accrue for her. By the time I met Gazîn, she was a widely recognized singer and no longer kept her various musical engagements secret from her family. Everyone knew of her public appearances, and some in the family even took pride in her accomplishments. Getting to this point of acceptance, however, had taken many years of strife and struggle that had stretched family relations almost to the point of breaking.

By attaching an alias to her disembodied voice, Gazîn had been able to make forays into the music industry that may otherwise not have been possible, earning her voice widespread exposure among Kurdish audiences in Turkey. And yet, she regarded the need for women to hide their identities in the first place to be an injustice, unbefitting of the times we were living in. Like Fadime, whom we encountered at the beginning of this chapter, she was convinced that women ought to take possession of their voices and unveil their names and identities. In fact, Gazîn was certain that much had already improved and that it was only a matter of time before Kurdish women would (and could) lay unequivocal claim to their voices. As she had asserted the very first time I met her, "now it is not like it used to be in the past. We can say 'this is me, this is us.' Today we can show our existence. Women's voices can no longer be hidden."

   Esen, a young English teacher from the provincial town of Mûş with whom I had a long conversation about this matter, shared the view that hiding Kurdish women's identities through means like stage names prevented them from laying claim to what rightfully belonged to them. Like so many others, Esen, too, was convinced that dengbêjs' oral repertoires had in fact originated with Kurdish women but had over the course of history become unrightfully appropriated by men. In Kurdistan, she explained, because male dengbêjs had appropriated female repertoires, women's works were effectively being ventriloquized by men's voices. This, she asserted, resembled the way in which the works of female authors in Europe used to circulate under male pen names in the past. Kurdish oral repertoires were, from this perspective, like artworks with wrongly attributed provenance, waiting for their relationships of creation to be redrawn so that Kurdish women could emerge from their hidden authorship—just like their European counterparts had a century ago, setting society upon a path to advancement and progress.

   In both Gazîn's and Esen's accounts women becoming the identifiable authors and owners of their voices featured as a crucial step toward achieving female emancipation and leaving behind restrictive traditions that seemed inappropriate to the current times. As such, their accounts carried the echoes of those narratives of modernity that so insistently tie social progress to the unveiling and exposure of women's bodies and identities, particularly where Muslim women in or of the Middle East are concerned. Not all women I encountered, however, shared this faith in the promises of unveiling. In particular, women embedded in social networks less connected to the Kurdish political movement encountered my research with suspicion, worried that their practice of singing kilams might be exposed, leading to potentially dreadful consequences including family fallings-out, social condemnation, or violent disciplining. It took my repeated assurances that I would guard their anonymity by using pseudonyms throughout my work, that I would record but their voice, not their image, and that I would not share those recordings with any third parties to convince some of these women to let me make an audio recording of their voices. To them, the ability of pseudonyms and sound technology to obfuscate the link between their voices and personal identities represented less a "backward" obstacle to a modernist ideal of unveiling than a reassuring commitment on my part. While women like Gazîn, Fadime, and Esen championed women publicly claiming ownership of their voices, for others the risks that doing so entailed appeared all too concrete. Gaining voice, this goes to show, was an undertaking that did not simply produce empowerment and emancipation, but came with its own perils and risks attached.

Conclusion

What does it mean to "have" a voice? Many of my interlocutors were intensely worried about their voices disappearing, getting lost, or being misappropriated. Having a voice appeared in this context as a laborious and contested achievement rather than as self-evidently given. This chapter has explored the efforts that some Kurdish women invest in laying claim to voices as their own. The desire to do so, I have argued, is animated by the rise of a pluralist politics of representation in Turkey. Such politics intimately tie political subjectivity to having a voice and rely on voices unambiguously representing those who utter them. Voices feature here as the personal property of their bearers, whether individual or collective, belonging to those who raise them and founding their agency.

If representational politics are embedded in a specific ideology of voice, this chapter has explored how such politics have reconfigured the ways in which people relate to their voices in Kurdish contexts. With the Kurdish voice having acquired prime representational value as an index of minoritarian culture and identity, questions of who can legitimately lay claim to this valuable token have gained in social and political significance. While contemporary politics of representation require that voices unambiguously belong, dengbêjs' repertoires are historically embedded in a genealogical ethos that traces authorship along lines of transmission that meander, branch out, and diverge. Yet these logics, I have argued, are being reconfigured. As more and more value is vested in being able to claim exclusive ownership over a voice, vocal objects are being wrenched from their genealogical entanglements so that they can be matched to an identifiable owner.

In the struggles that ensued, gender represented a key fault line, as women were keen to claim their share in the value Kurdish oral traditions have accumulated. Doing so meant challenging patrilineal logics that have historically determined how voice, and the authority attached to it, are accorded. At the same time, however, laying claim to a voice came with high stakes. In a context where the public exposure of women's voices retains patriarchal discomfort, the imperative that voices ought to reliably represent those who enunciate them posed specific gendered risks. While becoming identifiable through one's voice could open a path to social recognition, even fame, and financial profits, it also risked exposure to moral censorship. For women, gaining voice thus represented a double-edged sword, simultaneously promising access to circuits of value and authority and generating new forms of vulnerability. The final chapter will further investigate how such vulnerabilities take shape when Kurdish women take up voice in public.

FIGURE 5 **Public Voice**. Performing on November 25 in Wan. (Photo by author)

5

Making Voices Matter

In March 2012, Gazîn, Fadime, Seda, and Minever, all active members of Wan's Women Dengbêjs Association, set out on a trip to Istanbul, more than a thousand kilometers to the west. They had been invited by the rector of one of Istanbul's fine arts schools to perform as the main act at the university's annual celebration of International Women's Day taking place on March 8. The invitation occurred in the context of a wave of solidarity with Wan's residents on the part of civil society organizations across Turkey following the two heavy earthquakes that had hit the town in the fall of 2011. It was also a distinctly feminist gesture by the university's female rector, who sought to give a platform to a group of women whose struggle for voice resonated with her own ideals and that of Istanbul's women's rights activists more broadly. I had been involved in establishing the relevant contacts that eventually led to the invitation, and it was through further contacts in Istanbul's artistic and activist circles that we were able to expand the trip into a one-week schedule packed with events: in addition to the concert on the university campus, the women had been invited to participate in a seminar at Istanbul's conservatory, perform at a major Kurdish cultural center, and appear at several smaller music venues.

As it turned out, the presence of the Kurdish women singers garnered an extraordinary amount of attention. Not only were the concerts they played during that week all sold out, but journalists of different liberal and left-wing media outlets vied with each other for interview opportunities, while Kurdish television channels were keen to document as much as possible of the women's stay in the city. Arguably, a good part of the appeal stemmed from how both the women themselves and the media portrayed the trip as a long overdue act of coming to voice on the part of women whose voices had been silenced for far too long. Here was a group of mostly elderly women, with their white, see-through headscarves and colorful dresses that so readily indicate Kurdishness in Turkey, who spoke of how they had wrestled with and eventually broken what they described as "the chains" imposed on them by a traditional society. In one interview with the press, for instance, Fadime put it this way: "In the past, it was forbidden for our women to sing songs. But we have broken the proscription. I have struggled for music all by myself" (Tahaoğlu 2012). To another journalist, she said: "Even if not as much as in the past, women's singing as dengbêjs is still regarded as immodest (*ayıp*). They think they are protecting us this way, but what they are doing is damaging our freedom. We have broken the chains to come here" (Karakaş 2012).

Hailing from a geography that Istanbul's liberal middle classes readily associate with patriarchal communities and conservative traditions, in their outspokenness the women contradicted widespread preconceptions about silenced and oppressed Kurdish women, perennial victims of their own tribal communities. As Ayşe Öncü (2011) writes, the Kurdish "east" constitutes a "semi-real, semi-imaginary geography" (49) in the Turkish public imaginary, which is "inscribed in dualistic opposition to the dominant order at multiple layers—geographically remote, backward, unchanging, pre-capitalist, tribal, simultaneously untamed and rebellious" (52). Kurdish women appear in this imaginary either as powerful yet cruel matriarchs or as victims of the harsh codes of tribalism they desperately try to escape. What arguably brought the group of women singers from Wan such admiration and applause in Istanbul, then, was how their stubborn insistence on raising their voices indicated their courageous resistance against the restrictive conventions of their own culture. Here, the voice and its public audibility effortlessly symbolized women's emancipation from the weight of patriarchal custom and tradition. Having a voice, speaking up, and acquiring public presence were perceived as powerful indicators of agency and empowerment, pregnant with associations of women struggling for self-determination and emancipation in the face of retrogressive norms holding them back. This narrative about the emancipatory powers of speaking up and the importance of gaining voice is, of course, in many ways a familiar one. Not unique to Istanbul or Turkey, it is a compelling motive that links voice to identity, emancipation, and resistance. Promising agency and empowerment to those who raise their voices, it informs political discourse, policy making, and civil society engagement. And it powerfully animates the dreams, aspirations, and desires of minoritarian subjects in many parts of the world.

Yet as I set out to show, raising one's voice in public is not as unequivocally empowering as it may appear. Once voices become publicly audible, they have to reckon with the exigencies of hegemonic frames and expectations that structure public spaces, and that may mishear, misrecognize, or otherwise curtail those voices. Such frames determine limits of speakability at the level of semantic content, regulating what can and cannot be said in both overt and covert ways. But they also determine what kind of a thing we take the voice to be and how we understand its efficacy as a social and sonic force. "Ideologies of voice" (Weidman 2006, 2014a) regulate what ontological status and consequently what kind of potency we ascribe to voices; they stake out the parameters within which voices operate. How we frame and understand, indeed how we "hear," voices renders us attuned to certain vocal qualities rather than others. It encourages the cultivation of particular dispositions of hearing and sensing voice and suggests what aspects of voice should garner attention. Ideologies of voice participate, in that sense, in the formation of what Jacques Rancière (2010) might call a particular "distribution of the sensible," influencing how voices are able to shape subjects and how they may forge social relations.

As previous chapters have made clear, the repertoires that Gazîn, Fadime, Seda, and Minever had come to perform in Istanbul draw a large part of their social appeal among Kurdish audiences from the affects that they are able to solicit, particularly where middle-aged and elderly listeners are concerned. The kilam, we saw, constitutes a form of melodized speech that is associated with the tragic and lamentable and that women use to recount personal experience and other nonfictional accounts. This is a genre that possesses extraordinary social potency: kilams are able to make listeners shed tears, they induce sensations of touch and burning, and generate flows of pain and sorrow between relational selves. These effects, I argued, are intimately tied to the genre's specific sonic and aesthetic qualities—what I also called *voice as form*—including the vibrating melismas that voices perform when they descend at the end of lines, the densely poetic accounts they weave, and the melodic patterns they follow.

But if reigning ideologies of voice do not account for such qualities and potencies, this has consequences for the kind of social labor voices are able to carry out. In this chapter, my aim is to ethnographically trace what happens when voices whose social potency depends on the modulation and stylization of vocal form come to resound in contexts that can only ever hear them as metaphors for female empowerment and cultural resistance. What happens when the focus of attention shifts from the voice as an efficacious force in its own right to the voice as a symbolic token standing for agency and empowerment? How does this shift influence how voices gain force and carry out social labor, what kinds of subjects they are able to shape, and how they draw communities together? By attending to two concrete occasions when the voices of Kurdish women became publicly audible, I hope to move beyond a dichotomy of voice versus silence, where voice all too readily translates into agency, and silence into suppression. Gaining (public) voice, I argue, is not inherently or inevitably liberating, but defines and delineates voices' reach and efficacy in specific ways.

As I set out to critically scrutinize the ways in which voices become delimited and even curtailed in spaces that tend to perceive them primarily as metaphors for agency, empowerment, or resistance, my aim is emphatically not to tell a history of decline. Casting the metaphorical framing that contemporary ideologies of voice encourage as a form of impoverishment that would deprive formerly powerful voices of their sonic and affective force might be an easy task. But we need to recognize that even if voices are "heard" first and foremost as metaphors, they still constitute sonic, material forces. This means, first of all, that they may have unforeseen effects. Vocal sound always has the potential to be sensed and interpreted in ways that defy the ideological frameworks in which voices are placed, exceeding or subverting the hegemonic significations ascribed to them. Second and perhaps more importantly, if voices always retain a sonic and material presence, the question becomes how certain sonic characteristics lend themselves to certain forms of ideological signification more than others. As Sarah Bakker Kellogg underlines in her ethnography of liturgical singing in the Dutch Syriac diaspora, "at issue is not whether material voices have agency, but how a voice can have different kinds of agency in relation to shifting historical conditions" (2015, 433). Put differently, even if voices are cast primarily as metaphors, within this ideological framing voices still have particular effects (or "agency") thanks to the way in which they do (or do not) sound. Scholarship on the sensory cultures of secularism has amply highlighted this point, showing that secular regimes do not simply deaden the senses, but fashion sensory cultures that favor certain forms of sound, sight, touch, and smell over others.[1] Here, I follow the lead of such scholarship to ask how contemporary politics encourage a certain vocal aesthetics that is particularly amenable to the representational demands that such politics put forward. How, in other words, does a voice have to sound to successfully function as an index of its bearer's self, agency, and empowerment?

To make my argument, I first consider in some more detail the concert on International Women's Day in Istanbul, before then turning to a second performance by the same group of women, this time in Wan. Even though both events traded in discourses of women's rights and empowerment, they represented very different strands of women's activism and were animated by ideologically diverging political agendas. While these two events thus represented different regimes of speakability, I suggest that they shared an appreciation of voices as metaphorical figures and as a result ended up conditioning and delimiting the women singers' voices in similar ways. Making voices audible, this leads me to suggest, is not simply a technical question of amplifying vocal sound, but a process of making that sound intelligible, ascribing it meaning, and shaping the contours of its social potency.

Calibrating the Kurdish Woman's Voice

Let me begin by returning to March 8, 2012, when the women from Wan were scheduled to perform at one of Istanbul's public universities to mark International Women's Day. The concert was part of a busy three-day schedule of events at the university that included a variety of seminars and panel discussions on topics ranging from women's right to the city to gender equality at contemporary Turkish universities. A day before the concert, the event series had been launched with the opening of a photo exhibition entitled "The Wan Earthquake and Women" (Van Depremi ve Kadın) in the university's lobby. Photographs of Wan's ruined cityscape, portraits of women against the backdrop of cracked house facades, and snapshots of life inside tents, containers, and other emergency shelters brought a world that seemed very far away into the halls of this buzzing academic institution. The images had been taken by a team of women photographers from the university's own photography department whom the administration had sent to Wan several weeks earlier to document the impact of the earthquake on the lives of women and, at the same time, to photograph the four invited women singers in their home environments. Their large portraits now occupied part of the wall space in the lobby, alongside written panels informing viewers about the history and practice of Kurdish oral traditions (part of which I had been asked to prepare), as well as short life stories of each woman, culled by the organizers from interviews I had conducted in Wan ahead of the concert.

In those interviews, all four women had emphasized their upbringing in rural settings as crucial for nurturing their passion for the sung words of kilams and strans. Seemingly untouched by popular culture and state policies, the village emerged from their narratives as the paradigmatic location of Kurdish oral culture—as the natural milieu, as it were, of the authentic Kurdish voice. And yet the village also appeared as a space saturated with patriarchal custom intent on stifling precisely that voice. The life stories exhibited in the university hall hinted at family disputes, rejection, and domestic abuse that had shadowed the women's lives in their rural homes because of their obstinate insistence on raising their voices. At the same time, however, the panels also suggested a cautious sense of progress, indicating that the stories' protagonists had been able to resist the oppressive weight of tradition (firmly associated with rural contexts) and were now inhabiting a present marked by greater freedom and self-determination (squarely situated in the city). Fadime's life-story panel, for instance, related that moving from her village to the town of Wan had "reduced her family's control a little," such that now, following her husband's death, Fadime "can finally live her dengbêjî more freely. Now she no longer has to sing secretly in barns and stables." Gazîn's life story, on the other hand, underlined the importance of personal struggle in the achievement of social progress, relating how she had to travel to Istanbul in secret in order to record her first cassette tapes but had eventually "made the men of her family accept her passion for dengbêjî and did not give up, despite all obstacles."

A desire to publicly raise one's voice in order to express one's inner self emerged from the exhibition's panels as natural and intuitive, rendering the struggle against social forces that would seek to curb this desire equally natural, if not inevitable. This powerful and in many ways familiar narrative directly linked the audibility of women's voices to the retreat of patriarchal norms and structures, validating liberal values of self-assertion, choice, and agency (Mahmood 2001). It not only structured the exhibition in the university lobby, but also marked the subsequent concert and in fact framed the women's entire stay in Istanbul. Its key themes were reiterated in the interviews the women gave to the press, in the op-eds that were written about their appearances, in the way in which organizers introduced them on stage. As such, it decisively shaped how the voices of the women singers from Wan would become intelligible during that week in Istanbul and how listeners would consequently engage with them.

And yet, even if the women themselves readily underlined how they had broken "the chains" imposed on them in order to raise their voices and resisted the "customs" and "tradition" that had stifled their lives, often in the same breath the women also attested to rather different trajectories of vocal expression. For example, during several interviews both Gazîn and Fadime traced their urge to raise their voices back to how they had suffered as young brides in their in-laws' households or to the grief they had experienced when losing a loved one. We can sense here the reverberations of a configuration of voiced pain I discussed in detail in chapter 3: a configuration where experiences of pain and misery are able to call forth women's voices, sometimes almost against their will, rather than voices featuring as tame instruments at the disposal of self-possessed subjects.

What I want to draw attention to is the ease with which liberal understandings of voice are able to make intelligible to themselves and feed off understandings of voiced pain that speak of these different genealogies. The centrality of female pain in long-established Kurdish approaches to the voice becomes easily resignified within what Lila Abu-Lughod (2013) has described as "the new common sense" that women's rights represent today and the massive expansion of policies, budgets, state institutions, and civil society organizations that this has fueled, including in Turkey. While female voices would typically have emerged from a profound intimacy with pain and suffering, uttered in the context of

Istanbul's liberal public they have become intelligible as a means of resisting backward social constraints and as proof of Kurdish women's desire for freedom and emancipation. Long-standing themes of pain and suffering have in this way come to take on new meanings and shape new sensibilities, channeling voices to do novel kinds of social labor—labor that relies more on voices' capacity to represent abstract concepts like emancipation and liberation than on their capacity to move listeners to tears or burn their hearts.

In contrast to the photography exhibition, whose opening had attracted only moderate attention, the concert on March 8 drew a large audience. By four o'clock, the university's lobby was packed with an astoundingly diverse crowd for a university event. Apart from students, I spotted university staff ranging from the vice-rector and professors to administrative and service staff. Many students had brought their families, including mothers and fathers, younger siblings, nieces, and nephews. Children ran back and forth in front of the stage, while attendees who did not find a place in the main space of the lobby itself had moved up onto the surrounding mezzanine gallery. I made out familiar faces I knew from several women's organizations active in Istanbul, as well as journalists from a variety of media outlets, including several camera teams from different Kurdish television stations who were eventually asked to leave, since the university administration deemed their presence politically too sensitive.

When the event finally started, the excitement in the hall was palpable. Gazîn and Seda moderated the show, with Seda, being the youngest in the group and thus most fluent in Turkish, doing most of the talking. She began by expressing the group's gratitude for the invitation and stressed how honored they were to have the opportunity to present their culture in Istanbul. Seda in this way voiced what all those present instinctively knew, namely, that the Kurdishness that the women represented through their language and attire was structurally other to this space of bourgeois education in the heart of Istanbul. The platform that the women had been given was clearly for performing minoritarian difference, and the women were well aware of this and of the political sensitivities it entailed.

Both Seda and Gazîn further congratulated all present for International Women's Day and underlined their commitment to the promotion of women's rights. Fadime then began to intonate the first piece, a sorrowful kilam about a woman's unhappy marriage. The strong guttural tones and drawn-out melismas embellishing the end of each line generated a heavy atmosphere. This was underscored by the instrumental accompaniment, here chiefly the wailing of the duduk, a type of oboe, and the subdued sounds of the stringed tembûr, provided by three male musicians whom we had recruited in response to the women's fears that their singing alone might bore or strain the audience. For now, these fears seemed unfounded, as the audience was listening attentively. The women took turns with the microphone, alternating between "heavier," only minimally accompanied kilams they sang solo and fast-paced, danceable strans sung in chorus that were carried forward by the upbeat rhythm of the percussion and the melodic lead of the tembûr. It did not take long for the audience to tune into those joyous beats, enthusiastically clapping and many also singing along, suggesting that a considerable number of the university's Kurdish students had shown up for the performance. By the end of the concert the hall was a teeming dance floor with large rounds of line dances that picked up the rhythm of the upbeat strans, privileging embodied knowledge of rhythm and tempo over linguistic familiarity.

While the occasional glitch—a microphone mishandled, a chorus slightly out of tune, an entry missed—spoke of the women's distance from the professional music industry (only underlining, perhaps, what many perceived as attributes of authenticity), this does not mean that the performance was not thoroughly planned. The Kurdish woman's voice was carefully staged and calibrated, making sure it would not violate the limits of speakability that at once framed and lent legitimacy to the event. Being personally involved in the concert's organization, I witnessed firsthand the effort spent on making sure the women's voices would not overstep any significant boundaries. According to the university's rector, this was the first time a Kurdish music concert took place as an official event at a Turkish state university. The concert was, in other words, a "sensitive" occasion, and the university administration was cautious, wanting to prevent political controversy.

Several times in the weeks before the concert, organizers had urged me: "Please, make sure they won't sing anything political!" I spent those weeks in Wan working with the women on their repertoires and searching for songs that would fit the occasion of International Women's Day as conceived by the university administration. These were songs, we all understood, that were to feature "women's" and not "political" issues, the latter referring to the Kurdish struggle for political rights and the decade-old war that has been waged with more or less intensity in the Kurdish regions over the last four decades. The organizers further insisted that the precise number and succession of songs that were going to be performed would be fixed in advance and that no improvisation should take place. In addition, they asked me to transcribe all selected songs and provide Turkish translations, which were printed in a booklet that was distributed during the concert free of charge. As much as the intent may have been to enable Turkish audience members to understand the Kurdish lyrics of the performed songs, this was certainly also a means for the university to ensure that the women did not venture into the contentious realm of the political.

That a Kurdish music concert could take place at a Turkish state university at all owes much to the ways in which Turkey's pluralist turn of the 2000s and 2010s opened up novel space for the display of minoritarian difference. The anxiety that arose about taking up that space, however, also speaks of its ambiguous limits. As I outlined in the previous chapter, the elicitation of Kurdish and other, hitherto marginalized voices was tied to the implicit condition that they would not challenge dominant narratives of national history and belonging (Tambar 2010, 2014). As much as the display of cultural, linguistic, and religious difference was encouraged, that difference was also actively folklorized, producing "a tamed version of diversity, one that is clearly divorced from political claims" (Karaca 2013, 167). Gazîn, Fadime, Seda, and Minever were evidently familiar with how this pluralist regime at once encouraged their coming to voice and delimited their voices' range. Thus, even though all four were closely engaged with the Kurdish movement and well versed in its repertoires of "political" songs, on March 8 they readily provided a spectacle of innocuous cultural heritage paired with politically palatable ideas of women's rights. Even though they were at times uncomfortable with the imperative to depoliticize their performance—experiencing a lingering feeling of betrayal vis-à-vis the Kurdish political movement—they were also excited at the recognition that was offered to them in return. Applauded for their voices and encouraged in their struggle for emancipation, the women suddenly enjoyed a fame they had hardly ever dreamt of. Fadime poignantly summed up the resulting sense of accomplishment when, several days after the concert, we were relaxing at the house of a friend who asked the women from Wan how they had experienced the event. Fadime told Nilüfer about how we had had dinner after the concert at the university restaurant, sitting at long tables decked with white tablecloths, overlooking the Bosphorus with the Asian shore glimmering in the distance, and being served by waiters in black suits. Think about it, Fadime told Nilüfer, men not only served us, but they also laid out the table, and they will even wash the dishes. "It's at that moment that I thought that we have made it. In the past we were not even allowed to eat in front of our fathers-in-law!"

But calibrating the Kurdish woman's voice so that it would fit into the limits of the pluralistic space offered in Istanbul involved not only a delimitation of what that voice was going to say, favoring repertoires with "folkloric" or "women's" content over "political" ones. It also required modulating that voice according to the aesthetic sensibilities of Istanbulite university students, staff, and broader publics. Concretely, this meant creating a sound that would suggest authenticity of expression without overburdening the senses, while at the same time being able to signify the women's emancipatory endeavor. Already in Wan the singers had thus decided that it was going to be important to perform at least as many danceable strans as sorrowful kilams. They feared the ballads might bore the majority Turkish audience, whose members were unlikely to understand the lyrics or appreciate their dense poetic associations. Once displaced from its original context, the genre risked losing much of its affective potential. This potential arose, after all, from the interplay between an affectively attuned and sensorially alert audience, on the one hand, and the genre's sonic characteristics, on the other. Strans, by contrast, with their regular rhyme and rhythm, repetitive lyrics, and upbeat tunes, promised to transcend the linguistic and cultural specificities of performance contexts more easily.

In addition, the women decided to reduce the length of the kilams they were going to perform to a "manageable" three minutes, even if this was going to cut short or render unintelligible their narrative content, and opted to accompany the kilams with musical instruments so as to mitigate the intensity of the a cappella voice, which they worried might strain the ears of Istanbulite listeners. Doing so, they were careful not to have themselves accompanied by the electronic synthesizers and orgs that music producers often choose when marketing dengbêjs' repertoires to Kurdish audiences. Instead, they preferred accompaniment by musicians playing acoustic instruments, including the tembûr and erbane (a large frame drum, also known as def), as well as the wooden bilûr flute and the duduk—all instruments that are readily associated with Kurdish repertoires in Turkey and easily evoke a sense of folk culture and traditionality. The resulting acoustics were coarse and brittle enough to sound authentic yet at the same time palatable to Turkish audiences, who would not necessarily be receptive to the kilam's poetic qualities, narrative details, and affective potency. These acoustics were able to take on the weight of signification, staging at once Kurdish cultural heritage and the coming to voice of ostensibly silenced Kurdish women.

Vocal sound, this goes to show, was not simply eclipsed in a context where voices were valued to such a large extent for their capacity to index female empowerment and resistance. It was, rather, harnessed to turn the voice into a powerful metaphor, contributing to the fashioning of a sensory culture where voices can be appreciated for what they symbolize over and above, say, how they are able to transmit sensations of pain and suffering or even what they communicate.

Unruly Sounds and Marginal Affects

But what goes amiss when the voices of Kurdish women are always already read as a "barometer" (Deeb 2009, S115) of their bearers' societal status? At what expense do we read the voice as a metaphor for female agency and empowerment (or, alternatively, as one for cultural authenticity and tradition)? For one, we have seen how the liberal public in which the women's voices resounded in March 2012 effectively shut out contentious politics, failing to acknowledge the histories of state violence that have shaped Kurdish oral genres and that contribute to proliferating the pain and suffering kilams routinely give expression to. Here we see how the new common sense regarding the primacy of women's rights and well-being all too easily comes at the expense of inquiring into the historical and political trajectories of unjust gender relations, "blaming culture for bad behavior" (Volpp 2000) rather than addressing how colonial histories have shaped gender injustice and fueled gendered forms of violence.

Yet, as we have also seen, the disciplining of the Kurdish woman's voice during that week in Istanbul went beyond delimiting what can be said. At stake, in other words, was not only where the limits of the speakable were going to be drawn, but also how voices were going to sound. Disciplining the voice was in that sense also a question of fashioning a particular acoustics. If voices have "agency" not just because of what they communicate but also because of how they sound, this fashioning of vocal sound needs to be recognized as socially consequential. The women dengbêjs' decision to cut the length of their *kilams*, their choice of instrumentation, and their reluctance to perform pieces with intense vocal elaboration all contributed to creating a certain type of voice, one equipped with certain affordances and not others, with the capacity to affect listeners in certain ways and not others. As I have suggested, this was above all a voice whose sound would be amenable to carrying out representational work, featuring as a sign that could indicate women's agency and empowerment, cultural diversity, Kurdish difference.

The propensity to enlist (if not efface) vocal sound in the service of broader representational enterprises is one we encounter across a wide range of contemporary contexts. Pooja Rangan (2017a, b), for instance, has pointed out how documentary films contain and delimit the voices of those whom they portray—typically disadvantaged or marginalized subjects—by making these voices audible in specific ways. Through features such as dubbing, subtitling, or voice-over, Rangan argues, documentaries foreground voices' referential content at the expense of their actual sounds, "subordinat[ing] sonic disturbance to verbal information" and "limit[ing] the expressive range of vocalization" (2017a, 285). Only once voices are made intelligible in this way as rational expressions of thought and opinion rather than incoherent sound can they feature as evidence for the proper subject status of those who utter them, a move that in turn allows the documentary genre itself to become a means of "giving voice" to the ostensibly voiceless.

As Rangan underlines, one crucial effect of how media frame voices and

make them intelligible is that they fashion specific habits of listening, impact-
ing the way in which audiences engage with voices' sonic materiality and affective potential (see also Hirschkind 2006). In previous chapters I outlined
how in Kurdish contexts, voices are often valued for the affective intensity
that their sonic elaboration is able to evoke among audiences and for the way
in which they are able to draw subjects into a shared field of pain and suffering. But in a context where the voice is "heard" primarily as a metaphor
for gendered or cultural liberation, such engagements with the affective and
acoustic potentialities of the voice are easily limited or sidelined. Where audiences have been trained to interpret voices as metaphors rather than to
be receptive to their specific pitch and modulation, to their reverberations
and melismas, the potential of voices to viscerally impact their listeners risks
being curtailed. Where listeners perceive empowerment and emancipation
rather than the condensed force of a life of pain and suffering, a kilam will
only with difficulty make tears roll down cheeks, or ignite hearts and livers.
Where kilams are signs waiting to be read, their efficacy requires the mediation of printed booklets that explicate semantic meaning, rather than mani-
festing itself in burnt hearts and touched bodies.

Calibrating and disciplining voices, however, can only ever be so successful. Even if they are "heard" primarily as signs and metaphors, voices are always also sonic objects, and sound waves possess the remarkable capacity to
affect bodies and evoke sensibilities (Eidsheim 2015). While the hegemonic
frames in which the women's voices resonated during their trip to Istanbul
may have sidelined these sonic potencies, their voices nevertheless managed
to unfold force fields that bypassed and occasionally even challenged established frames of listening and relating to voices. The very fact that it did not
take long for the audience on March 8 to tune into the upbeat strans that the
women performed by clapping along and forming large rounds of line dances
attests to the power of vibration, rhythm, and pace in fashioning visceral
states that representational frameworks find hard to capture (Henriques 2010).
At the same time, this spontaneous, embodied engagement also speaks of
the shared nature of musical repertoires and sensibilities across Anatolia, the
eastern Mediterranean, and the broader Middle East. Kurdish strans thus
resemble not only Turkish danceable folk songs in their rhythmic structure
and melodic progression, but also Greek and Armenian repertoires (to name
just a few), allowing for forms of spontaneous attunement that defy ethnic or
linguistic divisions.

While repertoires of rhythmic and metered strans might appear more
conducive to such embodied engagement than kilams with their dense semantic content, poetic associations, and free meter, the latter genre, too, was

able to address audiences in Istanbul on an embodied level thanks to shared acoustic habits and sensibilities that span the broader region. Even though they may not have understood the lyrics, several Turkish friends told me, for instance, that the voices of the women singers intonating sorrowful melodies deeply impressed them. They recounted how hearing the women pronounce their kilams touched them, made them shiver, or impacted their insides (_iç_). Given that similar patterns of associating certain musical characteristics with a certain affective range recur in musical repertoires across the wider region, my Turkish friends' seemingly intuitive access to the sentiments transmitted by the Kurdish women's repertoires is not all that surprising. Key characteristics of the kilam, including the free-metered, recitational passages, the descending melodic patterns, and the melismatic embellishment of extended vowels and syllables, can thus also be found in the Turkish genre of _uzun hava_, where they are equally associated with loss, longing, and tragedy. But parallels can also be drawn farther afield, for instance, with Arabic repertoires such as the _mawwal_ (Reynolds 1995) or with repertoires performed by Armenian epic singers (_ashugh_).

But the voices of Wan's women dengbêjs escaped the prevalent tendency to be "read" first and foremost as metaphors not only thanks to their appeal to broader cultural and acoustic sensibilities. In the shadows and at the margins of the dominant frames that orchestrated their presence in Istanbul, the women's voices were also able to address more specific listening habits. There was, for instance, the man from the university's cleaning staff, whom I noticed taking a break in the lobby a day before the concert, attentively watching a documentary that was part of the photography exhibition. The thirty-minute documentary traces the friendship of Gazîn and a young female dengbêj from Gever (Tk. Yüksekova) in Turkey's far southeast.[2] In addition to filmed interviews with both women, it features long stretches of both protagonists intonating a number of plaintive kilams. After some time of silently watching the film, the middle-aged man pulled out his cell phone. I do not know who he called, but I could overhear snippets of Kurdish, spoken excitedly into the cell phone. While I was not able to capture much of the conversation, his subsequent gesture was explicit: he held his cell phone, with whoever was on the receiving end of the line, close to the screen showing the documentary in loop. The aim was, clearly, to catch some of the sound waves—the lamenting tones and sorrowful melodies of the women's kilams—and transmit them to wherever this man's interlocutors were located. Perhaps he wanted to communicate some of his excitement at having encountered familiar sounds and voices in an environment as unlikely as a Turkish state university. Or perhaps he had a mother, aunt, or grandmother who was herself proficient in the art of pronouncing kilams and *stran*s and wanted to acquaint her with the two singers he saw on screen.

This man was not the only one to employ contemporary sound technology to amplify beyond the boundaries of Istanbul the soundscape woven by the women during their trip to the city, drawing on the plaintive tones of their kilams to sustain and nourish intimate relations with close ones. When Gazîn, Fadime, Seda, and Minever gave their first concert in Istanbul, two days before March 8, two young Kurdish women similarly used their cell phones to transmit some of the momentum of hearing familiar Kurdish sounds, voices, and melodies back home to their families. The occasion was a concert I had organized in a small bar run by a friend. Situated in Beyoğlu, the heart of Istanbul's entertainment area, this was a location frequented by secular and left-wing university students and young professionals. The dengbêjs had at first been skeptical about the location. This was a crowd the women were not familiar with, and they did not know how the audience would react to their music and expertise, or whether those in attendance would be receptive to the affects the women's voices were meant to induce.

Contrary to their fears, the women were received with enthusiasm by Istanbul's young cosmopolitan audience. This enthusiasm was in all certainty fueled by what the women from Wan and their voices stood for: the struggles against patriarchal custom they were waging, the "strange land" they had come from. They were fascinating because of the authenticity they communicated, and the pristineness their voices conveyed. By contrast, the two young women who stood at the back of the room that night had a different experience, excitedly speaking in Kurdish on their cell phones, turning their phones toward the loudspeakers and transmitting nearly the entire concert live to whoever was on the other end of the line. When the somber kilams gave way to exuberant strans, they timidly asked whether it would be appropriate to ululate—a vocal gesture that powerfully communicates joyfulness and exuberance across Middle Eastern geographies. Once the girls began to utter their trilling cries, others in the audience quickly fell in, filling the packed space with an effervescent energy that soon translated into clapping and dancing.

For these two young women, we may presume, the voices of Gazîn, Fadime, Seda, and Minever were not so much metaphors for abstract notions like female liberation and cultural authenticity as sounds they were intimately familiar with. These were voices they had perhaps grown up with, voices they knew how to react to in acoustic and embodied registers. Their excitement probably arose not from the pristine authenticity the women conveyed to some in the crowd, but from their experience of encountering the sounds of home and intimacy in a place as unexpected as Istanbul's Beyoğlu neighborhood. And as they pulled out their cell phones, technology once again provided—as it had for the cleaner at the university—a way of making the affective currents and embodied sensations provoked and sustained by those voices travel, nourishing and sustaining relations of kinship and affection in the process.

Voices, these examples show, are difficult to discipline in finite, stable ways. Their sounds and reverberations resist fixation within representational frames. They may at once symbolize abstract concepts or values *and* speak to the senses, signify empowerment and cultural authenticity *and* provoke visceral responses. Nonetheless, the ways in which we frame voices does matter for the social labor voices are able to carry out. While hegemonic frames may not be able to fully contain vocal sound, they significantly shape its uptake, encouraging certain habits of listening and engaging over others. Where voices are primarily understood as metaphors standing for abstract liberal values—signposts to demarcate a desired transition from unfreedom to freedom, from tradition to modernity—they are able to function as affectively efficacious sound objects only at the margins: during the hushed moments of a cleaner taking in the sounds of a documentary, or of two young Kurdish girls timidly taking out their cell phones at a concert.

Radical Politics, Symbolic Voices

One thing that the events of that week in Istanbul make clear, then, is that liberal politics of women's rights and empowerment do not simply "give voice" to previously silenced female subjects. As much as these politics may accord voice, they also shape and condition women's voices, fashioning particular sensory cultures that allow voices to carry out certain kinds of social labor while sidelining or marginalizing others. To further explore how the framing of voices may enable or foreclose certain forms of vocal labor, in this section I turn to a second occasion when the voices of Kurdish women were put on public display in the name of women's rights. This second event will take us from a context of liberal multiculturalism to one of radical Kurdish politics, governed by very different norms of public speech than we encountered during the women's trip to Istanbul. And yet, even if imperatives to depoliticize Kurdish cultural content moved into the background here, women's voices once again became intelligible and gained value primarily through what they were able to symbolize rather than through their acoustic elaboration or affective potentialities. If public audibility is indeed the pinnacle of political agency and empowerment, it functions less as a neutral mechanism, state, or quality that would simply make sound become publicly available to the senses. It emerges, rather, as process that shapes, conditions, and where necessary curtails vocal sound (Rangan 2017a).

Only eight months after their trip to Istanbul, the members of the Women Dengbêjs Association were invited to perform at yet another occasion set within the global women's rights agenda. November 25 is recognized worldwide as the International Day for the Elimination of Violence against Women, and in Turkey, women's organizations throughout the country put on a variety of events, rallies, and performances to protest against high levels of gender-based violence.[3] In Wan as in other Kurdish towns, it was the Kurdish women's movement who would typically organize protest rallies on the occasion of November 25, and that year the local organizers in Wan had decided to invite the women dengbêjs to perform some of their repertoires at the event, which would also feature speeches by Kurdish women's rights activists and politicians.

As protestors filed into the public park where the rally was held, exuberant protest music filled the air. The organizers had set up a large sound system next to a flight of stairs that served as an improvised stage for those who were going to raise their voices on this cold November day. Soon the park was packed with women of all ages, from young children to elderly grandmothers, many of them wearing colorful dresses and sporting shawls and bands in green, red, and yellow, the Kurdish "national" colors. The crowd carried banners and posters with slogans ranging from "Woman, Life, Freedom" and "My body, my decision" to "Stop women's killings, stop solitary confinement"[4] and "Freedom for Öcalan," referring to the head of the PKK and his conditions of imprisonment. Clearly, the limits of speakability were drawn very differently here than they had been during the events in Istanbul only a few months earlier, where "politics" had been rigorously excised from the women's performances. The rally began with a minute of silence in honor of those who had fallen in the PKK's armed struggle, a common practice at pro-Kurdish events that served as a stark contrast to the high-spirited atmosphere created by the vibrant, fast-paced Kurdish protest songs that had dominated the soundscape until this point. Then, several female politicians of the Kurdish Peace and Democracy Party (Barış ve Demokrasi Partisi, BDP)[5] took to the stage. In their speeches, they hailed the strength and courage of Kurdish women in the face of decades of state-sponsored violence, condemned the current government for its conservative policies on questions of gender and sexuality, and did not fail to demand freedom for Öcalan. The rights of Kurdish women, they made clear, could only be achieved in the context of a broader struggle for Kurdish political and cultural rights.

When it was finally the dengbêjs' turn after over an hour of speeches by female politicians and pre-recorded protest music, Gazîn briefly addressed the audience, adding her own condemnation of how women's wishes and desires were routinely sidelined in Kurdish households. "We don't want only women but also men to understand this issue well," she began. "All of this is because of suppression and violence. We always say 'it's the men,' but all this is happening to us because of a lack of education. They marry girls by force. We don't like this. May nobody get married against their will (*bê dilê xwe*) anymore. May our small girls not be married to old men of seventy, eighty years anymore! We will now sing kilams for you that have been sung from the past until today about women, young girls, who are married to men of seventy, eighty years." Gazîn then began to intonate "Xalê Cemîl" (Uncle Cemîl), a well-known kilam in which a young girl called Werdem grieves over having been promised in marriage to a man three times her age. Gazîn had previously released "Xalê Cemîl" on a cassette album, and it was probably the song she was best known for among Kurdish publics in Turkey. Recall how in chapter 2 Adnan's mother recognized her as the singer of that particular kilam and requested an impromptu performance over the phone. As we saw on that occasion, this was a kilam capable of founding social ties between virtual strangers, animating amicable relationships by transmitting a shared world of female suffering in the face of patriarchal kinship arrangements.

Set up as a dialogue between the young bride and her future husband, the kilam gives precedence to the woman's voice as she is lamenting her fate. She bemoans how the desire of this man who could be her father will beset her destiny, making her a "victim of old men" and the topic of villagers' idle talk and rumors.

[Werdem]
Xalê Cemîl, Xalê Cemîl lê wez gune me
Lo lo Xalê Cemîl mi go emrê te nê çûye çil û pênca, ax lo ez çarde me
Lo lo Xalê Cemîl mi go wele ez ê ne layiqê gotin û xaberdana ax la [mirdarê] fenanê te me[6]
Xalê Cemîl, Xalê Cemîl ax wez gune me
Ax emrê te nê çûye çil û pênca, ez çarde me

[Cemîl]
Lê Werdem Xanimê vê sibê li diyarê lê Xerdîlekê
Mi go ez heyrana bejbilindê, lê qam kinikê[7]
Mi go tu nê guhê xwe nede gotin û xeberdana ax la fesadiya xelkê

[Werdem]
Uncle Cemîl, Uncle Cemîl, have mercy with me
Hey Uncle Cemîl, I said, you are forty-five years old, oh I am fourteen
Hey Uncle Cemîl, I said, I don't deserve the talk and insults of a dirty man like you
Uncle Cemîl, Uncle Cemîl, oh have mercy with me
Oh you are forty-five years old, I am fourteen

[Cemîl]
Hey Lady Werdem this morning in the region of Xerdîlek
I said, I adore your tall posture

I said, don't listen to people's idle talk and gossip

Bila Xwedê mirazê min û te bike,   May God fulfil our wish, one night
şeveke payîza tu nê li ser sîngê min   in autumn you will lie on my chest
peya be mîna qasidê lê korfelekê   like the messenger of damned fate[8]
Werê gidî lê, gidî lê, gidî lê, gidî lê, hey   Oh dear, oh dear, oh dear, oh dear, oh
Lê Werdemê hey, de bab gawirê, dê   Hey Werdem, you are the daughter
ecem e   of a Christian father, and an Ajam
                                            mother[9]

[Werdem]   [Werdem]
Xalê Cemîl min go tu mezin î şûna lo   Uncle Cemîl, I said, you are old, you
bavê min î   are like my father
Lo lo Xalê Cemîl mi go tu mezin î   Hey Uncle Cemîl, I said, you are old,
şûna ax lo xalê min î   oh you are like my uncle
Lo lo Xalê Cemîl mi go tu nê nebe   Hey Uncle Cemîl, I said, don't be-
sebebê bayîsê lê qedera min î   come the culprit of my destiny
Werê Xalê Cemîl, Xalê Cemîl, ax ez   Uncle Cemîl, Uncle Cemîl, oh I am
birîndar im, birîndarê kesê kal im   wounded, I am the victim of an
                                            old man

Once the last melismatic elongations of Werdem's sorrowful account had dis-
sipated, Gazîn passed on the microphone to the next singer. One after the other,
the women performed kilams that, like "Xalê Cemîl," offered highly emotional
accounts of women's painful experiences. The kilams focused on the loneliness of newlywed women separated from their natal families after marriage,
conflicts with their husbands and marital kin, or the burdens of domestic work.
Similar to the songs for March 8, this selection was thoroughly premediated,
although the concerns in selecting what to perform were situated somewhat
differently than during the Istanbul concert. Ahead of the Wan rally the women
had reasoned that long-standing kilams about female pain and misery would
raise awareness of Kurdish women's predicaments, making for a fitting program item at an event that was held to protest violence against women. They
had consciously chosen songs that spoke of women's suffering from patriarchal
kinship arrangements, making this suffering palpable through their plaintive
melodies, the strong melismas, the extended "ah"s and "lo"s that permeated the
flow of their narrative. As the women performed these songs on stage, however,
the audience did not indicate being profoundly affected by the plaintive voices
and sorrowful sounds wavering through the park. Here, there were no eyes
shedding tears, no melting hearts and burning livers. Rather, the assembled
crowd whistled and applauded enthusiastically after each song, relaying the
exuberant spirit of triumphant struggle and unbroken resistance that the politicians' speeches and the intermittent protest pop had stoked.
    After the rally, I returned with the singers and a few other friends to the

Women Dengbêjs Association to warm up and discuss the event. A palpable sense of disappointment reigned among the women. They felt they had not been given a prominent enough place during the program, with their performance scheduled at the very end, which meant not only that they had to wait for their turn for what felt like an eternity in the biting cold, but also that there was not enough time left for them to perform the entire program they had prepared. In fact, one woman did not get to sing at all because the organizers decided to cut the singers short, given that the politicians' speeches had run over time. When the women did not immediately comply with the demand to stop singing in the midst of their performance, the organizers simply turned off their microphone just as Gazîn was about to intonate a new song. Instead, they turned on high-volume Kurdish pop music, in this way signaling the end of the rally.

Now, warmed up by tea and biscuits, the women bitterly complained about this gesture, which they perceived as a serious lack of respect. Gazîn vented: "They asked us to participate as singers, but instead of letting us sing they played recorded music all throughout! Why would you do that if you have live music sitting right there?!" Minever, too, was upset with how the organizers had handled the rally: "If this was about violence against women it should not have been a joyful event as if it were Newroz or a wedding. This should have been a time for mournful songs." The other women agreed that the rally had been too celebratory for an occasion as somber as the struggle against high rates of gender-based violence. The high-spirited sounds of Kurdish resistance pop and fiery voices of women politicians had drowned out the sorrowful kilams they had so carefully chosen for the occasion. They were dismayed that the organizers had neither recognized nor acknowledged their efforts and that their voices had, as a result, failed to resonate with the assembled audience. Differently from March 8, this was an audience that should have been receptive to the specific vocal modulations, poetic register, and onomatopoetic expressions that render the kilam such a powerful genre, only augmenting the women's disappointment at having failed to establish a bond of resonance with those present.

Their disappointment was also nourished by a bitter sense of having, somehow, been betrayed. Wasn't it the women's movement's mission to empower women by giving them voice? How come, then, that the organizers felt entitled to literally stifle the voices of those who represented their constituency? In this context, it is important to know that questions of gender equality stand very much at the heart of the Kurdish political struggle in Turkey. Contrary to many other nationalist liberation movements,[10] the Kurdish political movement tightly links women's to social and political emancipation, insisting that a society is only as free as its women are. As a much-referenced quote by the movement's charismatic leader Abdullah Öcalan has it, "the Kurdish woman liberating herself will be Kurdistan liberating itself" (1993). Questions of gender equality and

women's rights are not just subservient or adjacent to the cause of national liberation, but have over the last three decades become increasingly central to the
movement's overall struggle. The movement understands patriarchal structures
of oppression to be directly linked to the forces of both capitalist exploitation
and state violence, requiring a three-pronged struggle against capitalism, state
power, and patriarchy all at once. This understanding of an organic and necessary interlinkage between women's and sociopolitical emancipation ensures
that "women's issues" occupy a central place within Kurdish politics in Turkey.
The movement thus defends key feminist standpoints in political debates, practices a system of male-female co-leadership, and has built up strong, autonomous women's institutions where it has had the opportunity to do so. Active
resistance and struggle are central to its vision of female being and becoming
and cultivated through a wide range of political and educational activities.[11]

The gendered suffering that the women narrated on November 25 through
their kilams, however, does not easily fit into such a framework. The intimacy
with pain and its centrality to female subjectivity that the women's repertoires
spoke of were to a certain extent at odds with the movement's vision of the resisting and resilient Kurdish woman, who struggles against suffering rather than em-
bracing it, and defeats pain rather than rendering it the foundation for social ties
and subjectivity. At the same time, the way in which the women's microphones
were simply cut off in the midst of their performance suggests that the discrep-
ancy here concerned not only narrative content or ideological vision, but also
aesthetic form and sensibility. The instance in fact highlights, I contend, strik-
ingly different approaches to the voice as a form of intervention in public and
political spheres. For the rally's organizers the voices of the women they had
invited to perform that day seemed to function primarily as a metaphor: that elderly women whose voices had been limited to domestic and all-female spaces
in the past were now able to make their voices audible at a public rally signified
the Kurdish movement's success in remaking the gendered fabric of Kurdish
society and working toward women's emancipation. What is more, insofar as
the women's age, attire, and repertoires squarely positioned them as representa-
tives of Kurdish cultural heritage—they were, after all, celebrated as authentic
dengbêjs—their presence on stage also powerfully symbolized that Kurdish traditions were, after all, compatible with women's rights and empowerment.

The women themselves, however, regarded their voices less as metaphors
for abstract ideals than as a means to make a concrete intervention in their
community. Performing the genre of the kilam, they sought to employ the
specific sonic and poetic qualities of their voices and draw on the affective
potencies of the genre in order to render female suffering tangible to those
assembled. They sought to make hearts burn and tears flow as a means of

viscerally transmitting something of the experience of female suffering from patriarchal kinship arrangements and domestic violence. It was through embodied knowledge and emotional impact, in other words, that they hoped to reshape opinions and practices in Kurdish public and private settings.

Organizers and performers thus imagined the voice in divergent ways. Where the voice stood as a metaphor for notions like female emancipation and cultural heritage on the one hand, it was valued for its sonic and sentient capacities on the other. In that sense, the Kurdish organizers of the rally on November 25 in Wan found themselves less diametrically opposed to Istanbul's liberal feminists who had organized the March 8 event than their ideological differences might at first suggest. Both shared an understanding of voice that effortlessly translates public audibility into emancipation, agency, and empowerment. Whether a voice is audible or not—whether it is "on" or "off"— matters more within such a framework than the form that such audibility may take. That the organizers bluntly shut off the women's microphone once they deemed their time to be over poignantly illustrates how, where voices occupy primarily a metaphoric position, the mere fact of momentary audibility becomes sufficient for voices to carry out their ideological work. For the singers, by contrast, precisely the specificities of vocal form—the voice's pitch and tone, volume and modulation, poetic and lyrical elaboration—were crucial for their voices to unfold their affective potential and envelop their listeners in relations saturated with sorrow and suffering.

Kabir Tambar has argued that contemporary forms of pluralism, including in Turkey, manage difference by simultaneously inciting its public display and "disciplin[ing] the boundaries within which [it] is permitted to authenticate itself" (2014, 12). What Tambar further underlines is that the disciplining of difference that is at stake in pluralist contexts concerns not only what can be displayed, but also how such display takes shape. In terms of a politics of voice, this means that the question is not only whether the subaltern *can* speak (Spivak 1988), but also what form the subaltern's voice is able to take on when it does speak, what affective and embodied sensibilities it is able to induce and sustain when it becomes audible, and how it comes to impact its listeners in this way (compare Gal 1989). Both in Istanbul and in Wan, I have demonstrated, when Kurdish women took up voice in public, their voices were made intelligible—and gained value—first and foremost with regard to their capacity to symbolize women's agency and empowerment, or cultural authenticity and tradition. Hegemonic frames of audibility meant that the women's voices were staged and perceived by many as metaphors, a framing that sidelined and marginalized the kind of social effects that these voices may also have had thanks to their acoustic elaboration, lyrical density, or poetic associations. Gaining voice, this makes clear, is an endeavor shadowed with risks: as we saw on both occasions, in Wan and in Istanbul, when minoritarian subjects take up the invitation to raise their voices, they also submit their voices to public scripts that, in rendering them intelligible, at once condition, delimit, and if necessary curtail them.

It is important to underline that in making this argument my aim is not to chart a story of vocal impoverishment. When I argue that contemporary ideologies of voice encourage approaching voices as metaphors for abstract values rather than as aesthetic and affective forces in their own right, my intention is not to provide a nostalgic reading of once powerful voices that modernity has stripped of their potency. Voices, rather, are always already disciplined by ideologies of voice, which govern what we take voices to be, how we understand them to function, and what social labor we consequently allow them to carry out. The fact that a voice may be disciplined does not therefore deprive it of its "agency." Quite to the contrary, it is as a result of how voices are framed that they are able to carry out certain kinds of social labor and not others.

Such a perspective allows us to recognize, on the one hand, that where voices are valued for their acoustic qualities and affective potentiality these voices are not in any way freer or more authentic than where this is not the case. As I outlined in previous chapters, among Kurdish audiences dengbêjs' voices are often cherished for the affects they are able to provoke. In such contexts, too, voices are framed or disciplined in the sense that they become intelligible within culturally and historically shaped frameworks that allow these voices to have specific social effects, such as inducing sensations of pain and suffering, while inhibiting other types of expression, including the voicing of sexual or other forms of violence that easily upset reigning patriarchal ideologies. On the other hand, we also need to acknowledge that the dominant framing of the women's voices as metaphors during the two events in Wan and Istanbul did not just foreclose or shut down vocal agency. Instead, it enabled these voices to take on certain, albeit new or unfamiliar forms of social labor. Calibrated in the ways I have outlined, for instance, on March 8 in Istanbul the voices of Gazîn, Fadime, Seda, and Minever contributed to shaping the acoustic contours of Turkey's ambiguous pluralist experience, determining what Kurdish difference and female empowerment would sound like in twenty-first-century Turkey. In Wan, the women's voices similarly gave sonic shape and substance to Kurdish oppositional politics, acoustically materializing the movement's political stance aimed at putting women's issues front and center within its political undertakings. Yet the affective intensities sustained by the women's voices also questioned a notion of public intervention that primarily relies on the communication of referential content and the mobilization of voices as metaphorical figures rather than as sound objects in their own right. Voices, this suggests, carry out social labor and gain political currency with respect to how they sustain, expand, or challenge particular ways of partitioning the sensible. The question is thus not whether voices do or do not have "agency," but how reigning ideologies of voice delimit the space within which voices can become potent and have social effects.

Conclusion

At first sight, the two events I have investigated in this chapter—on the one hand the performance on International Women's Day in Istanbul, and on the other hand the rally organized by the Kurdish women's movement in Wan— might appear politically and ideologically radically opposed. What I have tried to show, however, are the similarities in how women's voices became staged during those performances, animated in both cases by an understanding of the voice as a powerful index of women's emancipation from restrictive customs and traditions. Rather than accepting at face value narratives that celebrate the coming to voice of subaltern subjects, I have sought to bring into view how acquiring public voice is not simply a neutral, technical procedure of amplification, but an ideological process that frames, conditions, and where necessary disciplines voices. Where contemporary politics of representation "hear" (and celebrate) voices primarily as metaphors for the agency and empowerment of those who utter them, they risk sidelining voices' sonic and affective qualities and thereby curb how voices are able to become socially efficacious. For in the context at hand it was precisely these qualities—the aesthetics of vocal sound and poetic expression—from which much of the social potency of Kurdish women's voices derived, rendering these voices capable of constituting subjects enveloped in expansive networks of pain and suffering, and of drawing together Kurdish communities in the face of violence, dispersal, and loss. Once conceived of primarily as metaphors that are either on or off, either audible or silenced, however, the social labor that voices carry out thanks to their acoustic and aesthetic elaboration risks becoming radically diminished.

Yet no matter how "impoverished" contemporary framings of voice may appear from a sonic and affective perspective, one thing that they undoubtedly achieve is to powerfully imbue the voice with novel forms of value. Once voices symbolize the agency of their bearers, they become a morally dense and politically charged site, warranting bureaucratic management and control while attracting the hopes and ambitions of the marginalized. But precisely insofar as the voice becomes an object of desire and aspiration for the ostensibly silenced, it also risks turning into a site of what Lauren Berlant (2011) might call "cruel attachment." That is to say, the voice and prospects of its audibility animate hopes that keep being disappointed the moment voices are raised. During the performance on November 25, we saw this encapsulated in the moment when the rally's organizers shut off the singers' microphone, thereby dashing the women's hopes that their voices would be able to have a broader impact once publicly audible and amplified. And yet, this did not stop the same group of women from accepting invitations to similar rallies farther down the line, even though comparative scenes kept recurring when their performances were cut short, when precedence was given to other speakers or performers (often male), or when hosts fell dramatically short of expectations regarding hospitality and remuneration. Despite experiencing more than once that being invited on stage was largely a symbolic gesture that more often than not failed to make the women's voices actually matter, they kept—to use Berlant's terms—returning to the scene of hope and desire.

While the trip to Istanbul might have initially appeared more successful than the rally in Wan, given the women's enthusiastic reception by audiences and organizers alike, here too the hopes it had raised quickly vanished. The women had imagined that the trip might be the beginning of further engagements, such as invitations to additional concerts, perhaps even to performances in Europe, or that it might lead to signing a lucrative record contract. None of that materialized, however, and as the women slowly settled back into their lives in Wan, they not only were faced with the everyday challenges produced by chronic economic precarity and political insecurity, but also had to repair family relations that had been upset by their departure for Istanbul, with some of the women's family members convinced that their public appearances had been improper and unbecoming. These setbacks, however, did not stop the women from continuing to dream of how perhaps the next lucky invitation for a concert might finally bring about the fame and recognition they felt they deserved, or hatching plans for how to tap into the seemingly bountiful funding attached to civil society projects of all sorts. Their investment in the promises of the representational economies of multicultural and women's rights schemes did not seem to falter in the face of the routine disappointments they encountered. To paraphrase Berlant, there was an optimism at play here that sustains the fantasy that *this* time we will finally make ourselves heard, *this* time our voices will finally usher us into the recognition so long foreclosed, yet so well deserved. It is an attachment that forces marginalized subjects to return to the scene of desire, to try yet one more time to raise their voices in the optimistic hope of inclusion and acknowledgment. And yet, this attachment becomes cruel when "the object/scene that ignites a sense of possibility actually makes it impossible to attain the expansive transformation for which a person or a people risks striving" (Berlant 2011, 2).

These observations suggest that "gaining voice" is less a straightforward route to empowerment and recognition for marginalized subjects than it might appear at first sight. As this chapter has outlined, new sites and avenues of audibility held out immense promises to those marginalized by the circuits of national politics and patriarchal ideology, propelling Kurdish women from their homes in Turkey's impoverished east to the glimmering shores of the Bosphorus, bestowing them with fame and recognition—at least momentarily. Yet these promises came with conditions attached: acquiring public voice demanded careful consideration of not only what those voices were going to say but also how they were going to sound. It required orchestrating voices so that they would be able to successfully symbolize their bearers' empowerment and agency, in the process potentially sidelining voices' affective force. In a context where women's voices easily triggered patriarchal anxieties about sexual propriety, public audibility also came with specific gendered risks attached, leaving women in the difficult situation of having to negotiate between novel avenues for social status and recognition and the patriarchal backlash this may cause.

Let me be clear that in submitting contemporary politics of representation to critical scrutiny, my aim is not to retract from struggles that seek to open up spaces for those who have been denied the privilege of public audibility. After all, the public remains a space where authority is accorded, value attributed, and opinions articulated in today's world, so gaining public audibility represents a key avenue for those who struggle against injustice, discrimination, and oppression. What I want to draw attention to, however, is that assuming voice and becoming audible is not simply a technical process of volume amplification, but one that ideologically shapes both voices and those enunciating them. As Audra Simpson (2007) has pointed out, where it is impossible for subaltern voices to become audible on their own terms, refusing to expose these voices to the public may be as crucial to the struggles of the marginalized as gaining audibility.

Nonetheless, what I hope this book allows us to grasp is why people like the Kurdish women that populate its pages choose precisely not a path of refusal but remain passionately invested in a struggle to gain voice, even if this struggle keeps running up against disappointment. Recognizing how contemporary politics of representation render the voice a site of cruel attachment for minoritarian subjects highlights the allure that the voice holds in the contemporary world given what it promises to those who bear it. And yet it also underlines the fact that the routine failure of public voice to achieve full recognition or inclusion is not aleatory or coincidental. Rather, this failure is a consequence of how minoritarian voices become structurally vulnerable to empty rituals of public display once they feature primarily as metaphors for agency and empowerment, rather than as sound objects in their own right. Recognizing as much, I hope, may help us explore acoustic arrangements and sensory cultures where desires for voice would take shape as less cruel attachments and where disappointment would be less systematic.

FIGURE 6 **Resonance**. Dengbêj Gazîn and Ashugh Leyli on Akhtamar Island, Lake Wan. (Photo by Serra Akcan)

Resonance and Its Limits

September 2014. Applause erupts inside Istanbul Technical University's large concert hall on the prestigious Maçka Campus, situated at the heart of the Turkish metropolis on the Bosphorus. The several hundred people filling the seats have risen to their feet demanding yet one more song from the Kurdish-Armenian troupe on stage. The group is led by two imposing women, each in the heavy, embroidered costume of her respective Kurdish or Armenian heritage. One is Gazîn, whom we have come to know throughout this book. Here, she shares the stage with Leyli, a well-known Armenian *ashugh*, or singer of epics, now well into her seventies.[1] Both bathe in the applause, bowing over and over again, their faces beaming with joy, pride, and exhaustion. Behind them stand seven younger women in a semicircle, similarly attired in their respective "ethnic" costumes, bearing instruments and holding microphones. The group's rehearsals did not prepare them for these insistent demands by the audience to hear yet another piece, so it takes them a few minutes to coordinate which song to repeat. Then we get to listen one more time to the harmonious interweaving of Kurdish and Armenian tongues, to voices effortlessly complementing each other as they follow the same rhythm, tracing the contours of the same melody.

The concert was the culmination of a project whose planning had occupied nearly two years, and which had taken me along with nearly twenty women—Kurdish, Armenian, Turkish—across landscapes in Kurdistan and Armenia, from Wan to Yerevan and, finally, to Istanbul. Financed by the EU's Support to the Armenia-Turkey Normalisation Process program and carried out by Anadolu Kültür, an Istanbul-based not-for-profit organization that focuses on creating civil dialogue through cultural and artistic activities, the project sought to foster an exchange between Kurdish and Armenian women via the power of their voices. Civil society initiatives focusing on Turkish, Kurdish, and Armenian relations were booming in the 2010s, despite the historically difficult relationship between these communities. Until the 1915 genocide, Kurds and Armenians shared a geography in eastern Anatolia that is today variously identified as eastern Turkey, northern Kurdistan, or western Armenia. Despite a long history of coexistence, some Kurdish tribes became willful collaborators in the genocidal violence unleashed in the early twentieth century by the Young Turk regime against Anatolia's Christian communities, leading to their killing and expulsion from the region.[2] While the Turkish state continues to deny the genocide, Turkey's Kurdish movement has actively sought to mend ties with Armenians in recent years. Kurdish political leaders have apologized for Kurdish participation in the genocide, while Kurdish-led municipalities have become actively involved in safeguarding and restoring Armenian landmarks. Much of this engagement has been fueled by the sentiment, popular among Turkey's Kurds, that both Kurds and Armenians have been victims of the same exclusionary violence perpetrated by Turkish state authorities and thus share a history of suffering.[3]

Building on this sentiment, the 2010s witnessed a plethora of initiatives exploring Kurdish-Armenian histories of coexistence and exchange that were made possible not least thanks to generous European funding. As previous chapters have explored, this was a period when minoritarian and marginalized voices made themselves powerfully heard in Turkish publics, prompted by an unprecedented wave of efforts seeking to engage with the country's multilayered histories of state violence. Anadolu Kültür was a major actor in that field at the time, having developed a particular focus on exploring Turkish, Kurdish, and Armenian relations through cultural and artistic projects. The organization has had to pay dearly for its engagement with issues that remain precariously perched on the margins of Turkish state tolerance: its director, Osman Kavala, was arrested in 2017 and indicted for seeking to overthrow the government during the 2013 Gezi protests, with coup and espionage charges added during the following years. In April 2022, he was sentenced to life in prison without parole.

In promoting an exchange between Armenian and Kurdish female singers, the Female Minstrels project (as it was officially called) sought to harness the power of both gender and the voice in order to address, if not repair, the ruins of Turkey's violent nation-building. It thus tapped into some of the key discourses and assumptions that this book has submitted to critical scrutiny. The project purported to "give voice" to the silenced and marginalized—here Kurds and Armenians—in order to promote their empowerment and ensure their participation in public dialogue. It pinned its hopes on the voice as a means of achieving a more just and inclusive polity. And it focused on the voices of women, in particular, who appeared doubly silenced both by the cultural forces of patriarchy and by the political logics of exclusionary nationalism. Given these ideological moorings, the project provides a useful point of departure for reviewing here some of this book's key arguments. My interest concerns in particular those moments when the project's vision of Kurdish-Armenian vocal harmony ran into obstacles. Those moments of misunderstanding and even failure, I believe, point to the broader dilemmas, ambiguities, and impasses of contemporary mobilizations of voice that *Voices That Matter* has sought to highlight.

Where it had initially been Gazîn's idea to bring together Armenian and Kurdish women singers simply to exchange repertoires and enjoy the sonic echoes of a shared history and cultural sensibility, once taken up by Anadolu Kültür what materialized was a carefully orchestrated "project" in the sense that the civil society sector understands it.[4] This was a project with clearly laid-out goals and objectives, operationalized and budgeted, appealing to international donors and to the liberal values of intercultural dialogue and female empowerment many of them embraced. It had the express aim of exploring the commonalities of Armenian and Kurdish traditions of sung narrative, dubbed "minstrelsy" in the project description, and to emphasize women's central contribution to these traditions. The project envisaged two exchange trips between Armenia and Turkey during which Gazîn and Leyli, each accompanied by a group of younger female singers and musicians, would work on their shared musical repertoires, give a total of three concerts, and record an album. Making the voices of Kurdish and Armenian singers resonate with each other in sonic terms, so went the underlying logic, would ultimately also foster social resonance between the peoples these voices represented. Acoustic harmony was in this way to translate into sociopolitical rapport. The voice featured here as a means to challenge regimes of nationalist history writing and encourage a more genuine, authentic relationship between two peoples that can look back on a long history of cohabitation. As the project application stated, repertoires of dengbêjs and ashughs "display the common past of the [Kurdish and Armenian] peoples," but they "have been neglected and silenced by the official history."[5] Recovering the voices of Kurdish and Armenian women thus became a means to excavate a past of communal coexistence despite the top-down pressures of divisive nationalism.

The project's confidence in the capacity of vocal sound to overcome linguistic, cultural, and historical divides echoes liberal understandings of music as "an acoustical medium that expresses . . . human creativity, intelligence and emotional depth" and entails "positive, blissful transcendence" (Cusick 2008, paragraphs 4–6). It also echoes liberal understandings of voice as a medium that promises hitherto repressed communities and individuals—Kurds, Armenians, women—an escape from stifling regimes of silencing. The project thus drew on and reiterated understandings of voice that this book has set out to critically examine. It promoted the voice as a transparent channel of communication, one that appeared capable of rendering differences commensurable and fostering cross-cultural understanding and exchange. Note how it was less the transmission of meaningful content that rendered voices valuable cultural mediators in this context than their pre-linguistic resonance. It was the simultaneous, harmonious audibility of Kurdish and Armenian voices together that promised to bring about interethnic understanding and dialogue—little import was attached to what those voices would pronounce, or how they would sound. As such, the project is indicative of how classic, liberal understandings of the voice as an index of will, intention, and rational communication have been reformulated under contemporary conditions of neoliberalism, with the voice now increasingly figuring as an index of values that include authenticity, sincerity, and transparency (Kunreuther 2010; Weidman 2014b). Within this context, the singing voice, in particular, is continually naturalized "as a modality that expresses the self in a privileged transparent and direct way" and as a means of accessing sincere emotion and interiority (Weidman 2021, 7).

Much to the delight of the project team, both Gazîn and Leyli repeatedly confirmed ideas about the voice as a transparent and effortless channel of dialogue. Throughout the duration of the project, both singers told us how they enjoyed being able to freely engage in musical exchange and improvisation with a representative of that much-fantasized ethnic "other," with whom, it turned out, they had much in common. They insisted that they instinctively understood each other despite not sharing a language. Both made much of the fact that they conversed as women who had experienced personal hardship and suffering, suggesting they were able to communicate thanks to a shared gendered fate. Gazîn and Leyli also expressed that their understanding stemmed from how the collective pain and suffering of their respective communities—the pain of genocide, persecution, and repression—was ingrained in their voices and provided a shared platform of sensory-emotional resonance. To the project managers, such utterances confirmed a vision of the voice that could sustain interethnic dialogue and ensure the empowerment of minorities and marginalized subjects. Just as the notion of "culture" does in much EU-funded cultural policy, the (singing) voice appeared here as "a source of creativity imbued with moral values that enables peaceful cohabitation" (Karaca 2009, 33).

Given what I have argued throughout this book, however, we may also read Gazîn's and Leyli's proclaimed mutual understanding as reflecting a common appreciation of the female voice as a medium of tragic suffering and pain. As I have shown in chapters 1–3, this is an understanding of voice less as a vehicle of individual self-expression, personal healing, or collective empowerment than as a medium that sets gendered affects related to pain, suffering, and tragedy into motion, touching receptive bodies and enmeshing porous selves. While I have explored the contours of such affective vocal labor primarily with respect to Kurdish contexts, there is much to indicate that it reverberates beyond linguistic and ethnic boundaries and informs a vocal poetics that encompasses, at the very least, eastern Anatolia and the southern Caucasus, if not a much wider expanse of territory across the Middle East. From this perspective, Gazîn and Leyli may well have connected on the basis of a regionally shared sensibility for the vocal elaboration of pain and suffering rather than (or in addition to) an appreciation of the (singing) voice as the expression of personal interiority and emotional sincerity.

Despite Gazîn's and Leyli's professions of mutual understanding and appreciation, however, as the Female Minstrels project materialized in flesh-and-blood encounters it turned out that the much-anticipated encounter between Kurdish and Armenian voices was not as straightforward and harmonious as the lengthy funding applications would have had us believe. As we have seen, the project was based on an idea of seamless commensurability between Kurdish and Armenian voices and the repertoires they pronounce. Three concerts were going to provide proof of this commensurability: the first one in Yerevan, the second one at the annual Armenian church service on Wan's Akhtamar Island, and the final one in Istanbul. During these concerts, the group was to perform a number of songs known to both Armenian and Kurdish audiences—of which there are plenty—with lyrics alternating between the two languages.

But while centuries of Kurdish-Armenian cohabitation have shaped repertoires of vocal expression that closely resemble each other, what the project brought to light were subtle differences in the consolidation of Kurdish and Armenian musical traditions. This quickly became apparent when the group set about rehearsing during the first trip to Yerevan in May 2014. Working with Norar Kartashyan, a professional composer and musician, the group became aware of how seemingly identical pieces were in fact performed slightly differently by Kurds and Armenians. In case of the song "Ninnim" (Arm.)/"Meyrokê" (Kr.), for instance, we discovered that in the Armenian version the voice moves up a quarter tone when intonating the refrain, while in Kurdish the jump is less than a quarter tone. What had seemed like an easy exercise—singing alternately Kurdish and Armenian lyrics to the same melodic base—consequently turned into long and tiring sessions negotiating the subtleties of separately consolidated acoustic traditions.

The Kurdish-Armenian encounter also unsettled other vocal habits. Given the project's aim to highlight the two peoples' shared past, one of the songs the Kurdish side wanted to perform was "Malan Bar Kir" (They Parted and Left), a song that has been read as alluding to the deportations of Armenians that initiated the 1915 genocide. It is a widely known and very popular song among Kurdish audiences. The lyrics speak of neighbors leaving behind empty houses, of separated lovers and aching hearts, of parting caravans and the hardships of migration. Despite the tragic lyrics, the song is often performed as a fast-paced, upbeat stran that has audiences rising to their feet to dance.[6] To the Armenian project participants, the effervescent style in which their Kurdish peers knew the song was unsettling. There seemed to be a grave mismatch between sonic form and semantic content: what to Armenians represented a turning point in their national history, the catastrophe of the genocide, was here transformed into an occasion for joyful exuberance. The young Kurdish women participating in the project, on the other hand, had never even noticed the mismatch. They had not given much thought to what this song might mean, and simply embraced it as a popular dancing song. In the end, the song remained part of the repertoire to be performed at the three concerts, but to give it a heavier, more somber feel Norar insisted on slowing down the tempo and adjusting the timbre of the Kurdish performance.

Voices, these examples make clear, are less transparent media of commensurability than sonic objects that are ingrained in acoustic habits, webs of affect, and social history. As I have argued in this book, genre provides a useful framework for comprehending how voices become inscribed into such pathways. As genre molds vocal sound and textual expression, it inserts voices into genealogies of feeling and relating. Rather than a straitjacket, the conventionality that genre imposes on voices is what endows them with social force. To generic form attach meaning, affect, emotions. The "agency" of voices—their capacity to have social effects—derives from these established pathways of convention. "Malan Bar Kir" could thus elicit sentiments of either exuberance or devastation, depending on how the specificities of its sonic elaboration had become tied to the semantics of historical knowledge in the two different contexts at stake here. And to a skilled listener, subtle but systematic variations in the vocal tonality of a seemingly identical folk song like "Ninnim"/"Meyrokê" could become the signifiers of ethnic difference.

But the notion of effortless vocal commensurability ran up not only against the acoustics of the vocal repertoires at stake, but also against their semantics. The envisioned performance of a number of common songs with the lyrics alternating in Armenian and Kurdish required breaking up the original lyrics in each language. From the project's perspective, this was not much of a problem, since what was important was not what the lyrics recounted but the fact that they were set to the same melodic base in each language and could thus be made to interweave. Gazîn, however, was sincerely distressed seeing how the lyrics of long-standing Kurdish repertoires would be fractured without much attention to their original meaning. "There will be Kurdish audiences watching us and we will embarrass ourselves (_rezil oluruz_)," she protested to the project managers. To no avail: the symbolic value of Kurdish and Armenian voices intermingling prevailed over Gazîn's concern for semantic consistency. We see here what I have argued is characteristic of contemporary regimes of representation, namely, that they incite the voices of marginalized and minoritarian subjects as symbolic tokens for their bearers' presence and agency. As we saw in chapter 5, this means that the mere fact of audibility becomes enough for voices to fulfill their ideological labor. Once their time is deemed over, voices can then simply be shut off or, in this case, their referential content may be truncated, broken up, and rearranged as long as the symbolism of vocal audibility is harnessed.

What the Female Minstrels project thus underlines is that voices do not automatically function as transparent vehicles for understanding and dialogue; they have to be labored on sonically and semantically in order to be construed as such. It is precisely such labor that I have put at the forefront of my investigation in this book. Focusing on what it takes to render voices metaphors for abstract values like agency, understanding, and empowerment, and on the effects that voices have underneath, beyond, and despite such framings, my aim has been to destabilize some of the core assumptions we hold about the voice today. Rather than accepting at face value discourses that celebrate the coming to voice of subaltern subjects, _Voices That Matter_ demonstrates how such discourses operate with a very particular understanding of voice, one that appreciates voices for how they represent the will, interiority, and agency of their bearers, but tends to sideline the sonic and affective quality of voices. Yet it is precisely the elaboration of vocal sound and poetic expression as well as the affects that arise from it that make for much of voices' social effects in the context at hand. As we have seen, the voices of Kurdish women, particularly those of an older generation, gained their social potency once they were stylized according to the genre conventions of the kilam. This particular aesthetic mold imbued voices with the capacity to constitute subjects enveloped in expansive networks of sentiment, and to draw together "communities of loss" (Oushakine 2009) in a context where lasting bonds of cultural and ethnic belonging have been continuously subjected to the forces of violent dispersal and flight. But once voices are conceived of primarily as metaphors indicating the agency and emancipation of those pronouncing them, the specificities of vocal sound and aesthetic elaboration come to matter less than the mere fact of voices being either audible or silent.

Yet the Female Minstrels project underlines not only the limits of contemporary ideologies of voice. It also highlights another central argument of this book, namely, that such ideologies powerfully imbue the voice—particularly the presumably silenced voice—with novel forms of value. Construed as a metaphor for the agency and interiority of those enunciating them, the voice becomes a dazzling object worthy of bureaucratic intervention, governmental management, and well-meaning (if not outright patronizing) elicitation, as much as an object of minoritarian desire, subaltern achievement, and impassioned struggle. In Turkey, it was the political conjuncture of the early twenty-first century that rendered Kurdish, Armenian, and other formerly silenced voices objects of extraordinary value, attended to by a burgeoning civil society sector in the name of empowerment, salvage, and the mending of past injustice. But where voices acquire such value, the question of who is able to claim these voices and the privileges attached to them becomes subject to potentially intense debate. The Female Minstrels project allows us to observe these dynamics up close. For example, as the project took shape I witnessed how Gazîn—having initiated the project—suddenly found herself in a position of considerable authority regarding whom to select as her collaborators. Codirecting the project, she had the power to elevate the voices of others and insert them into prestigious circuits of international funding, civil society, and project management. Such power left grudges, not least among the other women at the Women Dengbêjs Association, who felt they were left out of these new distributive mechanisms of vocal profit.

Paying attention to the novel forms of subjectivity, authority, and social interaction engendered by changing understandings of voice, *Voices That Matter* does not tell a story of impoverishment or decline. When I argue that contemporary ideologies of voice encourage approaching voices as metaphors for abstract values and entities rather than as aesthetic and affective forces in their own right, my intention is not to provide a nostalgic reading of once powerful voices that modernity has stripped of their potency. Rather, this book has demonstrated that voices understood as indices of agency and empowerment come to carry out new forms of social labor, shaping subjects that are increasingly concerned about the recognition of their voices and the selves these stand for, and setting in motion struggles about how to lay claim to voices' novel worth.

Such a perspective sheds new light on contemporary politics of representation and how they engender conflict, anxiety, and disappointment among those they supposedly empower. It allows us to see the limits of a politics that might make voices audible, but routinely fails to address how the prestige and value of those voices is distributed. Taking up voice is not simply a process of representing preexisting subjects and communities. Rather, as this book underlines, assuming voice needs to be recognized as constitutive of the very subjects that voices are subsequently taken to represent. Where voices are increasingly understood as representative of the will, agency, and interiority of their enunciators, subjects come to relate to their voices in new ways. I have traced how Kurdish women have become more preoccupied with voicing their intimate lives, but also more anxious about retaining ownership of their voices as their value increases. Prevailing politics of representation encourage the constitution of subjects that "have a voice," alongside a clearly defined will and interiority that this voice can represent. This may make it difficult to account for forms of subjectivity based on more relational, expansive ties, where voices may not be tied to individual selves but have the capacity to speak for, with, and through others without being anyone's personal property. In this regard, I concur with Amanda Weidman when she writes that escaping the "tyranny of 'identity' and 'expression'" that dominates contemporary politics of voice entails freeing voices "from having to express the truth of the inner self" (2021, 12). As I have underlined, representational imperatives render women vulnerable in novel ways as they become increasingly dependent on having their voices, including the "truths" these express, recognized by an anonymous public while simultaneously having to negotiate patriarchal anxieties concerned with the preservation of female modesty and sexual propriety. As much as "gaining voice" thus opened up novel avenues for social authority and recognition for kurdish women, it also exposed them to new forms of societal scrutiny and patriarchal concern (if not violence).

My critique of the ways in which "voice" is routinely mobilized in contemporary politics of representation is emphatically not meant to downplay the importance of initiatives seeking to amplify and augment voices that were previously suppressed or sidelined. Doing so would be to deny the significance of the voice as a crucial site where political participation and agency are attributed, negotiated, and struggled over in the contemporary world. Voice is centrally entangled with claims for sovereignty and debates over the limits of representation, and as such has a crucial role to play in the struggles of indigenous, dispossessed, and marginalized subjects (Simpson 2007). Yet it is important to remember that gaining voice and becoming audible are not neutral questions of sonic amplification. Taking up voice is a material, social, and ideological process that shapes not only voices but also those enunciating them. It encourages a specific distribution of the sensible, one in which voices can be unambiguously tied to subjects or communities, their sounds always already representative of their bearers' presence and will. But once voices matter not for *how* they sound but for the mere fact *that* they sound, they risk receding into silence the very moment their audibility is celebrated.

Making these arguments, this book holds significance beyond the Kurdish context. It sheds critical light on forms of politics that would have us believe that once formerly silenced voices are raised, the conditions that have led to experiences of injury and loss will be transformed. The mere fact of audibility today often functions as a symbol for being heard and recognized, as if it were sufficient for settling political demands toward justice and equality. Yet what this book shows—and what the Female Minstrels project points to with particular clarity—is that "giving voice" more often than not leaves untouched the underlying sociopolitical issues that make for systematic structures of silencing and neglect.

As the project unfolded, it thus became clear that granting audibility to Kurdish and Armenian voices was hardly sufficient for bringing about the envisioned cross-cultural understanding. Just as it took an enormous amount of labor and investment to bring into harmony separately consolidated Kurdish and Armenian musical repertoires, so did Kurdish-Armenian social interactions during the project struggle with the weight imposed by a history of genocide and expulsion. The fact that Kurdish populations today claim as their own territories that until 1915 used to be densely populated by Armenians, and that certain Kurdish tribes were willing collaborators in the Armenian extinction, haunts these communities' relationship. As a result, the performance of a Kurdish song by an Armenian choir in Yerevan turned into a moment of glaring discomfort when the Kurdish visitors were rebuked for assuming that their own suffering was comparable to that of Armenians, given that they were occupying lands that used to be Armenian property. The project's celebrated intercultural understanding similarly unraveled when the Kurdish participants proudly showed their Armenian visitors a church in Wan's countryside that was, unlike so many other ruined ones, well preserved because a Kurdish family used it as an annex to their house. What to the Kurdish hosts indicated an act of care for Armenian property was for the Armenians an act of desecration and theft.

What these tense encounters highlight is that the mere fact of making voices resonate with each other acoustically does not automatically translate into resonance on sociopolitical grounds. Legacies of violence and genocide do not disappear once voices are granted audibility. This is not to deny the power of the voice, but rather to acknowledge that for voices to carry out their social labor, reducing them to symbolic indices of participation and empowerment will not suffice. Voices are embedded in historical legacies; it is these pathways that endow them with force. (Neo)liberal policies that champion the voice as a transparent medium of communication easily forget, if not actively neglect, this fact. By turning silenced and subaltern voices into sites of symbolic and financial profit and return, they risk failing to address the political structures and historical legacies that allow some voices to be heard while foreclosing reception for others.

Back in 2014, when the Female Minstrels project took place, the pluralist tolerance of Turkish politics had already begun to crack. Now, as I write this conclusion in late 2021, it has all but crumbled. Since the peace negotiations between the Turkish state and the PKK leadership collapsed in the summer of 2015, warfare has returned to the country. Kurdish politics, both legal and extralegal, are under massive attack. New forms of Turkish imperialism have taken war beyond the country's borders, with the Turkish army now occupying Kurdish areas in northern Syria. These forces seriously imperil Kurdish aspirations for autonomy in the region, which had garnered unprecedented global attention as Rojava—the Syrian self-administered Kurdish regions—became a signifier for a different way of organizing society while propelling Kurdish women onto the covers of Western magazines.

Writing about the power of the voice seems banal, if not politically naïve, in the face of this onslaught. How can voices matter when bodies are crushed, maimed, and assaulted? While the period that I describe in this book—with its timid hope for new patterns of public audibility—might be irretrievably over, it has created legacies that will not be easy to erase. The voices that Turkish governance summoned in the name of its ambiguous politics of cultural appeasement continue to haunt it. They have indelibly shaped subjects that lay insistent claim to forms of voice explicitly understood to indicate political agency and will. The Kurdish voice has risen to become an object of desire, profit, and investment. Like the spirits conjured by the apprentice of Goethe's sorcerer, the Kurdish voices called forth by successive Turkish regimes will not be easily stifled. Their reverberations are certain to be felt throughout a region in upheaval.

Acknowledgments

Books incur debts, voices create reverberations. Here, I would like to acknowledge both as I set out to trace the manifold relations that have gone into the making of this monograph.

First, I must express my deepest gratitude to Gazîn, whose voice drew me into this research project and has accompanied it throughout. I am indebted to her not only for being an immensely inspiring research companion, interlocutor, and friend, but also for gifting me with a home and a family in Wan, and for being there in those days when the ground literally slipped away under our feet. Gazîn always dreamed of seeing her voice printed in a book. I wish she could have witnessed the publication of *Voices That Matter*, but she passed much too early. It may be only a small gesture, but I hope that this book can contribute to keeping alive the reverberations of her voice.

I also owe enormous thanks to the numerous other Kurdish women who have agreed to share their voices, histories, and experiences with me over the years. In order to preserve their anonymity, I will not provide full names here. These include the women at the Women Dengbêjs Association in Wan, with whom I was fortunate to establish close bonds and undertake many a journey. Many others welcomed me into their homes, agreed to host me, and shared their company with me. I thank them all for teaching me about the force of women's voices, for being patient and trusting with me, for nurturing and nourishing me with plenty of tea, food, and stories. I wish to extend my gratitude equally to all the women working and volunteering at Wan's different women's associations. They received me with open arms, never tired of my questions, and provided help and guidance throughout. My fieldwork would have been impossible without them. I would also like to thank my host family in Wan for their boundless hospitality and lasting friendship. I am particularly indebted to Xalê Hiseyin for welcoming me into the family, to Gamze for putting up with me in her room, to Zozan and Ali for always welcoming me upstairs, to Gulan for providing a home in Tatwan. In Mûş, I was lucky to find a friend and guide in Necmiye and to be welcomed by her family.

This book began its life at the University of Cambridge. I am deeply indebted to Yael Navaro for her intellectual guidance and generosity throughout the years. She has taught me about the value of ethnography and the challenge of theory—gifts that are invaluable. Esra Özyürek has provided equally steadfast guidance. I thank her for the confidence she has placed in me, and for the invaluable hints and tips she has directed my way. My thanks also go to Harri Englund for his valuable feedback and for asking the right questions at the right time. In Cambridge, I was lucky to enjoy the company of a supportive and stimulating scholarly community. My thanks go in particular to Lys Alcayna-Stevens, Romelia Calin, Ryan Davey, Marilena Frisone, Anna Grigoryeva, Paolo Heywood, Sazana Jayadeva, Yu Qiu, Sertaç Sehlikoğlu, Felix Stein, and Fiona Wright.

While in Brussels, conversations with David Berliner have been guiding and encouraging, as has been his feedback on my writing, for which I am grateful. Exchanges with Laurent Legrain have been equally stimulating; I thank him for that. I am grateful to everyone at the Laboratoire d'Anthropologie des Mondes Contemporains (LAMC) of the Université Libre de Bruxelles for welcoming me so kindly into their midst. At LAMC I also met Marco Di Nunzio, who has been a most helpful guide on this academic journey.

At the Orient-Institut in Istanbul, Martin Greve's generous support and feedback have extended well beyond my time as a doctoral fellow there. I thank him in particular for his commitment to archiving and digitizing the voices and repertoires that form the core of this book.

While a postdoctoral fellow at Ghent University, I was lucky to work with Chris Parker. I thank him for many inspiring conversations and for teaching me to see beyond my own discipline. To Koen Bogaert, Nida Alahmad, Vjosa Musliu, and Charlotte Vekemans: thanks for being such wonderful companions in the office and beyond, providing good spirits and helpful reflection during times when much of this book was written. At Ghent University I am also grateful to the Centre for Research on Culture and Gender, where Chia Longman and Carine Plancke gave me the opportunity to present my work. In addition, I would like to thank Katrien Pype, Victoria Bernal, and Sasha Newell for feedback during (and outside) our Brussels anthropology reading group sessions.

For inviting me to present in their seminar series on Kurdish oral heritage, language, and art hosted by Jagiellonian University Kraków I further thank Joanna Bocheńska and Farangis Ghaderi.

For her faith in this project and for her support at crucial junctures throughout the publishing journey I owe much gratitude to Nancy Rose Hunt. Jonathan Glasser has likewise helped me navigate the world of book publishing and provided encouragement and critical feedback from early on.

I am honored to have been selected to hold the Evans-Pritchard Lectureship in 2021 at All Souls College in Oxford, where I presented part of this book's manuscript. I thank David Gellner for making my stay possible and for his warm welcome when pandemic restrictions finally allowed for traveling. At All Souls, Rima Dapous and her team did a fabulous job organizing my stay. For their generous feedback and questions, I am grateful to the audience who joined the lectures week after week and probed me on ethnography and argument. And for making my Oxford stay all the more pleasurable I would like to thank Akanksha Awal, Miriam Driessen, Zuzanna Olszewska, and Ina Zharkevich.

At Utrecht University, where I carried out the final work on the manuscript before submission and during production, I am grateful to everyone at the Department of Cultural Anthropology for providing me with a warm welcome and a new, inspiring intellectual home.

For engaging with my work at different stages and for providing comments, feedback, and critique on earlier drafts of various chapters I would like to thank Estelle Amy de la Bretèque, Nicholas Argenti, Alice von Bieberstein, Romelia Calin, Esin Düzel, Çiçek İlengiz, Banu Karaca, Margot Luyckfasseel, Ewa Majczak, Hişyar Özsoy, Anoush Suni, Charlotte Vekemans, Jeremy Walton, Fiona Wright, and Aslı Zengin. Alice Wilson has been a stupendous writing and reading companion and given tremendous support. Andrew Bush has likewise been an invaluable critic and friend, whose guidance has been immensely helpful, while Argun Çakır provided crucial last-minute feedback, for which I am truly grateful. For being a wonderful friend and fellow traveler ever since our chance encounter years ago on the Black Sea coast, my thanks go to Caterina Scaramelli. Veronica Buffon provided shelter and comfort during early days in the field, as did Alice von Bieberstein later on in Mûş; I feel indebted to both. I will never forget Susan Benson-Sökmen's warm hospitality in Bazîd, including excellent coffee with a view on Mount Ararat. Ergin Öpengin not only expertly helped me with the transcription and translation of the oral repertoires that appear in this book, but his enthusiasm for this project also provided crucial encouragement.

At the University of Chicago Press, I am grateful to my editor, Mary Al-Sayed, for believing in this project and expertly shepherding it through review and production, and to Tristan Bates for her generous assistance. This book would not be what it is without the critical feedback of the two anonymous reviewers, to whom I am indebted for their careful engagement and encouraging words. I further wish to thank everyone involved in the press's production team for so professionally bringing this book into existence. Both Charlotte Weber and Marian Rogers provided invaluable support in editing the text, catching inconsistencies, and reining in my linguistic escapades. My thanks also go to Serra Akcan and Braxton Hood for allowing me to use their photographs in this book.

The fieldwork and writing of this book would not have been possible without the generous financial support of a number of institutions. I would like to thank the Studienstiftung des deutschen Volkes, Trinity Hall College, Cambridge's Richards and Henry Ling Roth Funds, the Wiener-Anspach Foundation, the Orient-Institut Istanbul, the Research Foundation Flanders (FWO), and the British Academy.

Many dear friends have made all the difference throughout the years this book was in the making. At the risk of being incomplete, I would like to mention Aylin Çelik, whose unwavering friendship and fierce humor have been a gift. Çiçek İlengiz has been there throughout, an extraordinary companion at every juncture. Julia Strutz and Erbatur Çavuşoğlu have provided steady friendship over the years, from Istanbul to Brussels and Berlin. Akın Arslan, Dilan and Berivan Avcı, Fulya Doğan, Mehtap Doğan, Hürü Kaya, Çiğdem Sarısaltık, Anoush Suni, and Gamze Toksoy have been wonderful friends in Wan and beyond. I am grateful to Ergun Sibel Yücel for her wisdom and hospitality, and for all those shared trips between Wan and Istanbul. Braxton Hood has been a dear companion ever since that first hike to the top of the castle in Wan, and I am incredibly grateful for the last-minute nighttime work she put into getting my images ready for publication. In Istanbul, dinners at Klemuri with Elif, Yasemin, and Nilüfer Taşkın, Basri Çağlayan, Deniz Mardin, and Alev Kuruoğlu will not be forgotten. Filiz Çelik, Özgür Karakaya, and Roni Hartmann saw me through those years of writing up in Cambridge. One of the beautiful outcomes of this project has certainly been the encounter of Leonie Schiffauer and Mustafa Gündoğan. In Brussels, I thank Tilmann Heil and Ewa Majczak for the many walks, park runs, dinners, and conversations that have provided crucial sustenance. Finally, I thank my parents for their support in all I have undertaken. And Alan, for everything.

A previous version of chapter 5 was published as "'It Used to be Forbidden': Kurdish Women and the Limits of Gaining Voice," *Journal of Middle East Women's Studies* 14, no. 1 (2018): 3–24. It is republished here with permission of Duke University Press.

Notes

Introduction

1. Shahrzad Mojab (2001) has written about Kurdish women bearing "the solitude of the stateless." Kurdish women, she notes, "remain at the margins of feminist knowledge" (16), a fact that further nurtures the dominance of nation and patriarchy in their lives.

2. A number of authors have highlighted how Western media coverage of Kurdish women fighting the Islamic State (IS) rehashed problematic stereotypes about passive and oppressed Muslim women to which women in Kurdistan seemed to constitute an admirable exception. See Dirik (2014) and Toivanen and Baser (2016). On the ways in which Western media portrayed Kurdish-speaking Yezidi women during IS's genocidal campaign in Sinjar in 2014 through a prism of victimhood based on Orientalist tropes, see Buffon and Allison (2016).

3. Ana María Ochoa Gautier (2014) shows how the differential hearing of voice has been foundational to divisions between "civilized" settlers and "animal-like" indigenous and enslaved populations in (post)colonial Latin America. Both Matt Sakakeeny's (2013) work on brass bands in New Orleans and Nina Sun Eidsheim's (2019) work on black opera singers in the US demonstrate how voices contribute to configuring race as they become matched to racialized bodies. The work of Aaron A. Fox (2004), in turn, sheds light on the making of class through musical and vocal sound.

4. Both Anne Carson (1995) and Mary Beard (2017) document the prevalence of these perceptions of female voices since antiquity.

5. For detailed discussions of this shift, see Kunreuther (2010), Schlichter (2014), and Weidman (2014b, 2021).

6. John Durham Peters (2004) provides a systematic overview of "voice" as a metaphor of power, a medium of communication, and a site of desire. On the voice as a sonic-material object, see Cox (2011); and on its embodied qualities, see Schlichter (2011).

7. Janice Boddy's (1989) account of the *zār* cult in Sudan, for example, shows how possessed women's voices become vehicles for transgressing gendered social norms. In Mozambique, on the other hand, the voices of possessed individuals are able to pronounce otherwise illicit knowledge about collaboration and co-optation during the civil war (Igreja 2018).

8. Anthropological accounts of the social significance of the aesthetic that have inspired my own approach include Gell (1998), Hobart and Kapferer (2005), Meyer (2009), and Pinney (2005).

9. See, for instance, Erlmann (2004), Kahn (1992), Samuels et al. (2010), and Sterne (2003).

10. I draw in particular on Beard (2017), Dunn and Jones (1994), Ehrick (2015a, b), Lentjes (2019), and Thorkelson (2020).

11. The anthropological literature on sound mediation is vast. Most influential for my thinking have been Bessire and Fisher (2012b), Fisher (2016), Larkin (2008), Porcello (2002), Sterne (2003), and Weheliye (2005).

12. See, for instance, Caton (1990), Liebhaber (2018), Miller (2005), Reynolds (1995), and Shryock (1997). On women's poetry, see Abu-Lughod (1986), Miller (2002), and Olszewska (2015).

13. For a critical review of this literature with a specific focus on the politics of poetry, see Bush (2015).

14. On popular discourses that play on images of "saving" Muslim women from the alleged backwardness of their own communities, see Abu-Lughod (2013).

15. Scholarship in this vein includes, for example, Ahmed (2006), Boddy (1989), and Lazreg (1994).

16. For an astute critique of attempts seeking to recover an "African voice," particularly within the realm of oral history, see Cohen, Miescher, and White (2001).

17. My approach is in that sense similar to Sertaç Sehlikoğlu's (2020) account of Muslim Istanbulite women's engagement in sports, in which she sees evidence of a new desiring female subjectivity that is neither mimicking Western models nor situated in a radically different space of Muslim ethics.

18. Suad Joseph defines patriarchy in the context of Middle Eastern kinship arrangements as "the privileging of males and seniors and the deployment of familial structures, morality and idioms to institutionalize and legitimate gender and age hierarchy" (2005, 84).

19. I am not able to do full justice here to the complex history of gender relations in the Ottoman Empire and adjacent areas before the nineteenth century. Accounts that delineate the homosocial logics at play in these contexts include Andrews and Kalpaklı (2005), Najmabadi (2005), and Schick (2010).

20. Studies that show how veiling practices are tied to homosocial logics and patriarchal concerns about female visibility include Abu-Lughod (1986), Hoek (2009), and Sehlikoğlu (2015).

21. For detailed accounts of these historical transformations and an analysis of how they have shaped gender relations in Middle Eastern countries, see Abu-Lughod (1998), Kandiyoti (1991), and Najmabadi (2005).

22. Detailed accounts of the Turkish republic's policies governing gender and sexuality include Arat (1998), Durakbaşa (1998), Kandiyoti (1987, 1998), Sirman (2000, 2004), and White (2003).

23. There exists a vast literature on the politics of women's veiling in Turkey, including the seminal work of Nilüfer Göle (1996, 2002), in which she emphasizes the centrality of the gaze in the making of secular modernity and how it demands women's visibility in public. Sertaç Sehlikoğlu (2015) similarly highlights the gaze as a structuring principle in the making of Islamicate intimacies.

24. On the ways in which Kurdish women have featured as subjects in need of "saving" by Turkish republican modernity and its state feminists, see Arat-Koç (2007), Kogacioglu (2004), and Turkyilmaz (2016).

25. For detailed accounts of the history and ideology of the Kurdish women's movement, including the struggles women have had to wage within the Kurdish political movement and the dilemmas they have encountered, see Açık (2013), Bozgan (2011), Çağlayan (2007, 2012), Dirik (2022), Duzel (2018), Üstündağ (2019b), and Weiss (2010).

26. Andrew Bush (2020) has written a beautiful account of how political shifts in the Kurdish autonomous region in the north of Iraq, particularly as they concern the situation of religion in public and domestic life, have registered in poetry written in the region's Sorani dialect of Kurdish.

27. Detailed historical accounts of how the Turkish nation-building effort sought to systematically erase Kurdish difference include Aslan (2015), Cagaptay (2006), McDowall (2004), and Üngör (2011). On the colonial character of these attempts, see Beşikçi (2013), Duruiz (2020), Ünlü (2016), Yarkın (2019), and Zeydanlıoğlu (2008).

28. Scholars have referred to the attempts at containing Kurdish speech and language as an outright "linguicide." For more details, see Fernandes (2012), Haig (2004), Hassanpour (1992), and Zeydanlıoğlu (2012).

29. The early republic also mobilized civil society in its attempt to make Turkish the hegemonic language of public interaction. An example is the "Citizen, Speak Turkish!" campaign, initiated by students in Istanbul in 1928, which urged people to speak Turkish, via banners displayed in public space and mass transportation (Aslan 2007).

30. In his 1934 report *De la question kurde* (Of the Kurdish Question), Celadet Bedirkhan—son of a prominent family of Kurdish notables and a major figure in the articulation of Kurdish cultural nationalism—writes of ten Kurdish singers being arrested and exiled following armed clashes between state and Kurdish forces, on the grounds that their epic songs provoked Kurdish nationalist sentiment (Yüksel 2011, 66).

31. Orhan Balkılıç (2009), Koray Degirmenci (2006), Necdet Hasgül (1996), Martin Stokes (1992), and Orhan Tekelioğlu (1996, 2001) examine in detail the efforts that went into the crafting of a repertoire of Turkish folk music and its role in the formation of the Turkish nation-state. In a similar vein, Arzu Öztürkmen (1998, 2001) documents the labor the early republic invested in establishing a repertoire of national folkloric dances, which simultaneously stage the diversity of folk traditions in Turkey while emphasizing their common national character.

32. While proficiency in Kurdish has been steadily declining as a result of expanded public schooling, rural-to-urban migration, and the unquestioned role of Turkish as the language of public conduct, Kurdish has also reentered political and cultural spheres in a conscious attempt to counter Turkish language policies. The resulting sociolinguistic landscape is complex. For detailed studies, see Jamison (2015) and Öpengin (2012).

33. For a comprehensive critique of Turkey's pluralist cultural policies, with particular focus on its Greek communities, see Iğsız (2018). Kabir Tambar (2014) and Eray Çaylı (2021) both focus on how Alevi communities have sought to acquire public presence under Turkey's pluralist turn. On the shift toward more plural forms of public memory since the 1990s, see Özyürek (2007).

34. Banu Karaca (2019) outlines how the AKP's alleged willingness to break with Turkey's official memory regimes by acknowledging ethnic and religious diversity fails to adequately acknowledge past state violence and to work toward a more just future. Tambar (2014), too, provides a critical account of the AKP's pluralist turn by interrogating how pluralism works as "a new mode of regulating social difference" (8). Marlies Casier, Joost Jongerden, and Nic Walker (2013), in turn, show how the measures the AKP passed as part of the so-called Kurdish opening in 2009/10 were part of a policy of containment that sought to undermine the Kurdish political movement's voter bases in southeast Turkey rather than bring greater liberties.

35. See, for instance, Brown (2006), Comaroff and Comaroff (2009), Hale (2005), Mahmood (2016), and Povinelli (2002).

36. For more details on the history and demography of Wan in the nineteenth and early twentieth centuries, see Çağlayan (2019), Karayan (2000), Leupold (2020), and Minassian

(2000). Yektan Turkyilmaz (2011) details the history of the Armenian uprising against the Ottoman genocidal regime in 1915. Both Anoush Suni (2019) and David Leupold (2020) show how Wan's Armenian past reverberates in both Kurdish and Armenian lives today.

37. For detailed accounts of the peace process and its collapse, see Hakyemez (2017) and Yeğen (2015).

38. See the report by the International Crisis Group (2017) for an evaluation of the urban warfare that engulfed Kurdish towns in 2015 and 2016.

39. There have been many cases of violent attacks against individuals in western Turkey simply for speaking Kurdish or listening to Kurdish music. During the 2019 Turkish invasion of Kurdish-ruled territory in northern Syria, an elderly man was attacked for speaking Kurdish to his wife while in hospital in the western Turkish town of Çanakkale (see Seçkin Sağlam, "Çanakkale'de Kürtçe konuşan yaşlı adama saldırı!," *Evrensel*, October 15, 2019, https://www.evrensel.net/haber/388931 /canakkalede-kurtce-konusan-yasli-adama-saldiri). In 2020, twenty-year-old Barış Çakan was reportedly fatally stabbed for listening to Kurdish music in Ankara (see "20 yaşındaki Barış Çakan kalbinden bıçaklanarak öldürüldü," *gazeteDuvaR.*, June 1, 2020, https://www.gazeteduvar.com.tr /gundem/2020/06/01/20-yasindaki-baris-cakan-kalbinden-bicaklanarak-olduruldu), while in the summer of 2021 imprisoned Kurdish politician Leyla Güven was disciplined along with fellow inmates for singing in Kurdish (described as an "incomprehensible language" in prison documents). See "HDP's Leyla Güven, Eight Other Prisoners Investigated for Singing Kurdish Songs," *bianet* (English edition), August 23, 2021, https://bianet.org/english/human-rights/249178-hdp-s-leyla -guven-eight-other-prisoners-investigated-for-singing-kurdish-songs.

Chapter One

1. *Dengbêj* is a compound of *deng*, Kurdish for "news, word, or repute," and *-bêj*, the present stem of the verb *gotin*, Kurdish for "say, speak, or tell." While *dengbêj* refers to the performer of sung narrative, the abstract noun *dengbêjî* refers to the practice of performing such narratives.

2. The province of Agirî (Tk. Ağrı), where Bazîd is located, is among the provinces with the lowest Human Development Index and GDP per capita in Turkey. While according to the 2004 UNDP Human Development Report of Turkey the average GDP per capita for Turkey was $5,194, that of Agirî province was $1,803 (Yadirgi 2017, 234). In his detailed study of the political economy of Turkey's Kurdish regions, Veli Yadirgi (2017) shows how these numbers are the result of deliberate de-development policies undertaken by the Turkish state in regions with predominantly Kurdish population.

3. During the 1990s, the Turkish state evacuated and destroyed thousands of Kurdish villages as part of its counterinsurgency strategy that sought to cut support to PKK guerrillas by draining the countryside of sympathetic villagers. Many were given the choice of either leaving their villages or enrolling as paid paramilitary forces (so-called village guards or *korucu*s) to support the military in its fight against the PKK insurgency. Official figures suggest that a total of 3,215 rural settlements were evacuated and destroyed, amounting to over a quarter of all rural settlements in southeast Turkey. Human rights organizations estimate that overall as much as 3 to 4 million people were displaced (Jongerden 2010). The countryside surrounding Bazîd was heavily affected. In 1994 alone, the Ministry of Defence announced that fifty villages on the slopes of the Ararat (Tk. Ağrı) and Tendurek (Tk. Tendürek) mountains with a population of nearly 10,000 were to be evacuated and the areas to be declared a "forbidden military zone" (*askeri yasak bölge*) (Bruinessen 1995).

4. The life expectancy of PKK guerrilla fighters is short. The average PKK militant dies before the age of twenty-four and typically spends five years in the guerrilla before their death (Tezcür 2016).

5. One main reason why assuming that *deng* in *dengbêj* should mean "voice" seems doubtful is the fact that other Kurdish designations for performers of sung narrative, such as *stranbêj, beytbêj,* or *lawjebêj,* always contain as first component a term indicating the genre that the performer (i.e., the teller, -*bêj*) specializes in (here *stran, beyt,* or *lawje*). Based on this pattern, it seems highly likely that *deng* in *dengbêj* indicates a genre. As Mezlûm Doxan (n.d.) suggests, *deng* may be a short form of *deng-û-behs,* a compound that, as is common in Kurdish, is made up of two largely synonymous terms, with both *deng* and *behs* here meaning "news, rumor, or talk." The dengbêj would from this perspective also be a *behsbêj,* which is to say, someone who tells stories and news, someone who spreads the word about events, occurrences, and personalities (see also Çakır 2020).

6. See, for instance, Bloch (1975), Keane (1997b), and Rosaldo (1980, 177–220).

7. Badînî (also Bahdînî or Bahdini) is a variation of Kurmanji Kurdish spoken in the region of Badînan (also Bahdinan), roughly comprising the area of the governorate of Duhok in northern Iraq and adjacent areas of Turkey's Hekarî (Tk. Hakkâri) province.

8. In the Serhed region, by contrast, *beyt* generally refers to oral repertoires with religious content.

9. Detailed accounts of the various (sub)genres of Kurdish oral tradition and their regional variation include Allison (2001), Blum, Christensen, and Shiloah (2001), Çelebi, Yıldırım, and Ataş (2006), Hamelink (2016), Nezan et al. (1996), and Öztürk (2012).

10. This section draws heavily on Estelle Amy de la Bretèque's (2012, 2013, 2016) work on the oral repertoires of Kurmanji-speaking Yezidi communities in Armenia. My own observations as well as the existing literature on Kurdish oral traditions suggest that her insights hold to a great extent true for the Kurmanji-speaking world beyond the Armenian context.

11. These melismatic embellishments are in Kurdish sometimes referred to with onomatopoetic expressions like *xelxelaye* or *xulxulandin* (Öztürk 2012, 12).

12. Not to be confused with the Badînî *stran,* which resembles what I refer to following Serhedî terminology as *kilam.*

13. The way in which musical elements become mapped onto opposing sentiments and emotions here resembles how Denise Gill (2017, 136) describes the difference between melancholic and joyful pieces in Turkish classical music. Making a musical piece melancholic, Gill writes, involves musicians drawing on a tool kit that includes pulling words apart into vowels and ornaments that are heavily ornamented, employing melismas on the last foot of poetic lines, and employing strategic silences. Joyful music, by contrast, is less ornamented, follows a quicker pace, includes no silences or intentional pauses, and does not separate consonants from vowels.

14. Outstanding analyses of this kind include Hamelink and Barış (2014) and Yüksel (2011).

15. Among Yezidis in Armenia, lamentations are simply a subgroup of the wider genre kilam, specified as *kilamê ser şînê* (lit. "*kilam*s on mourning") or *kilamê miriya* (lit. "*kilam*s of the dead") (Amy de la Bretèque, pers. comm.).

16. Women's feelings of estrangement in their husband's household are often expressed through the concept of *xerîb,* meaning "exile or separation," which forms a key trope to communicate feelings of longing and loss not only in lullabies but in a wide range of oral traditions, including the kilam (Amy de la Bretèque 2013, 147–172).

17. Such associations are not particular to the Kurdish cultural sphere, but shared by other Middle Eastern and circum-Mediterranean societies in which the "work of pain" (Magrini 2008)

is similarly a realm of female labor. See, for example, Abu-Lughod (1986) and Seremetakis (1991). In the field of Turkish classical music, too, women are seen as particularly receptive to suffering and pain and to expressing it in music (Gill 2017, 140). Turkish classical music as a whole is, in fact, sometimes described as feminine because of its melancholic and sentimental "feel" (Gill 2017, 143). This does not mean that men do not experience grief and bereavement or that they do not express it. Allison (2001, 171–175) quotes at length from a kilam she collected among the Yezidi community of northern Iraq, in which a man laments the death of his young wife, employing much of the same imagery of bereavement that is associated with the female voice.

18. This observation is confirmed by Amy de la Bretèque (2016, 51), who notes that melodized speech is gendered with regard to the degree of personal involvement. Whereas Kurmanji-speaking women tend to use melodized speech to express what they have personally experienced, men recount historical events that do not make claims to personal experience. According to Christine Allison (2001, 169), the Russian Kurdologist Margaret Rudenko similarly noted that "men's ceremonial laments concentrate on heroic and epic elements, such as valour and battle, whereas those of women are more emotional and lyrical."

19. Thousands of Kurdish politicians, human rights activists, and journalists have been extrajudicially killed by state-sponsored units since the 1990s. Most perpetrators have never been brought to justice, having been declared "unknown" (*faili meçhul*) by state authorities. The killings were at their height in the first half of the 1990s (Bruinessen 1996).

20. The Kurdish original is from Kevirbirî (2004, 85–86). The English translation is my own.

21. The Kurdish text is from Amy de la Bretèque (2010, 135–136). The English translation is my own.

22. Pain is here imagined as a burning force, in a way similar to what Nadia Seremetakis (1991, 115) describes in her work on the Inner Mani region in Greece.

23. See Hamelink (2016, 70–74) for both the Kurdish text and its English translation. The Kurdish text originally appeared in Zal (2011, 98–99). It is a transcription of the kilam as sung by Dengbêj Cahîdo (*1960).

24. On the genre of *uzun hava*, see Saygun (1976) and K. Reinhard (1976), both of whom elaborate on the material collected and analyzed by Béla Bartók, as well as U. Reinhard (2002). For the *mawwal*, see Reynolds (1995).

25. Detailed analyses of how the musical features of Arabic melody modes (*maqām*) are linked to states of emotional affection include Jarjour (2015), Kligman (2011), and Shannon (2003).

26. In thinking about the iterability of affect I draw on Kabir Tambar's (2011) exploration of Alevi mourning rituals' (in)capacity to make affects of sadness and grief palpable in repeated and predictable ways among young Alevis in contemporary Turkey, given the context of secular governance in the Turkish republic and the kinds of affective dispositions it cultivates.

27. See Bloch (1975), Keane (1997b), and Stasch (2011, 164–165).

Chapter Two

1. Anthropologist Alfred Gell's (1992, 1998) concept of art as a technology of enchantment resonates with my use of technology of affect here insofar as Gell, too, is interested in the potency of material objects beyond the symbolic meanings ascribed to them.

2. Even a "natural" voice emerges as a result of the extraordinarily complex interplay of membranes, muscles, and nerves that make up our vocal cords and the medium—gas, liquid, or solid—through which the sound waves that these cords produce travel (Eidsheim 2015). The

voice's uptake, moreover, will inevitably be shaped by equally complex bodily organs as well as prevailing linguistic ideologies and social institutions that suggest what voices mean and how they ought to be understood (Bessire and Fisher 2012a, 22; Harkness 2013).

3. Similarly to how Fadime went about assembling her kilams for her clients, these women also begin their task by collecting information about the deceased's life story and the circumstances of death from family, friends, or other acquaintances ahead of the mourning ceremonies, which they then elaborate into a lament using the pool of stock melodic and poetic formulas provided by the genre. For Kurmanji-speaking Yezidi lamenters in southern Kurdistan (northern Iraq), compare Allison (2001, 177–180). Concerning northern Kurdistan, Hamelink (2016, 79n41) notes that male dengbêjs, too, were occasionally approached by family members to make laments for a deceased and went about a comparable methodology of collecting information. In chapter 1, Asya similarly described how making her lamentation for Hozan Feraşîn involved finding out factual information first, before then setting it to a fitting melody and lyrics.

4. Christine Allison (2001, 179, 197) similarly observes that among Kurdish-speaking Yezidi communities in Iraq semiprofessional female lamenters are commissioned at funerals because guided lamentations allow mourners to "manage" their grief, which would otherwise make them feel "upset" (aciz).

5. Schafer employs the term "schizophonia" to refer to the split between a sound from its original source as a result of electroacoustic reproduction. The term is supposed to convey the sense of "aberration and drama" brought about by modern sound technologies, which create "a synthetic soundscape in which natural sounds are becoming increasingly unnatural while machine-made substitutes are providing the operative signals directing modern life" (Schafer 1977, 91). As much as I argue against a distinction between "natural" and "unnatural" voices, the notion of "schizophonia" usefully highlights how modern sound technologies pose acute questions and anxieties about the efficacy of the mediated voice, particularly in Euro-American contexts.

6. Alexander Weheliye (2005, 7–8) argues from a similar vantage point that the phonograph did not create the same anxieties among African American communities as it did in mainstream, white American culture because the alphabetic script never constituted the primary mode of cultural transmission for African Americans, who were as a result much more ready to experiment with the split between sound and source produced by the phonograph. Amanda Weidman (2021), too, shows how South Indian Tamil cinema has creatively exploited the disjuncture between audible voice and visible body enabled by modern recording technologies. Here, rather than seeking to create the illusion that the bodies visible on screen and the voices animating them belong to the same person, playback singing has itself become a celebrated art form.

7. Sîpanê Xelatê or Mount Sipan is situated immediately north of Lake Wan and is one of the highest mountain peaks in the region. It is the setting of the Kurdish epic Siyabend û Xecê and appears in much Kurdish (oral) literature.

8. The sixteenth-century Tower of Belek (Birca Belek) forms part of the castle and city walls of Cizîr (Tk. Cizre) situated on the banks of the Tigris River, close to the Turkish-Syrian border.

9. There exists considerable scholarship that investigates the ways in which sound technologies create novel forms of intimacy between voices and listeners. Martin Stokes (2009), for instance, writes about the microphone as a technology that allows voices to circulate in ways that are both highly interiorized and highly public (see also Connor 2004; Durham Peters 2004). Other scholars have similarly emphasized how sound technologies create new forms of private and public experience (Larkin 2008; Mrázek 1997; Weheliye 2005).

10. Studies of the radio's role in fashioning a sense of national, ethnic, or racial community include Ahıska (2010), Bolton (1999), Kunreuther (2006), Moorman (2019), and Spitulnik (1997, 1998, 2002).

11. As Christine Allison (2013) underlines, Anderson's model of imagined communities arising from the reading publics brought about by print capitalism does not fit the Kurdish case, where forms of oral discourse and musical sound, including the radio, have been much more influential in the making of collective identity.

12. For a detailed account of the Kurdish section at Radio Baghdad and how it allowed Kurdish musicians to defy the colonial border regimes imposed on them, see Bullock (2021).

13. Lissant Bolton (1999) similarly recounts how Vanuatu residents showed interest in the radio less for national or international news broadcasts than for the traditional songs and stories it transmitted. She notes how this interest was nourished by forms of cultural exchange between different islands that preceded colonization and the installation of the radio as a central mediator of a common Vanuatu identity.

14. This recalls Peter Bloom's (2014) account of how the English radio voice in colonial Ghana, seemingly coming out of nowhere, created an effect of authority that complemented and sustained British colonial sovereignty. Yet while Radio Yerevan's voice might have similarly commanded authority, as a sonic assertion working against the colonial control of the Turkish state over its Kurdish citizens, its authority needs to be seen as more akin to the way in which the phantom-like quality of the voice on revolutionary Algerian radio projected the power of the Algerian uprising (Fanon 1965). As Kamran Elend (2021, 190–194) writes, by elevating Kurdish to the language of official broadcasting, Radio Yerevan for the first time endowed Kurdish with a sense of authority that was crucial in countering ideas about the natural inferiority of the Kurdish language and culture as projected by the Turkish state.

15. Birgit Meyer (2009) has coined the notion of "aesthetic formation" to draw attention to how Anderson's imagined communities rely on embodied and material forms of mediation in order to become experienced as real.

16. Lissant Bolton (1999) and Deborah Spitulnik (1997) similarly observe how in Vanuatu and Zambia, respectively, the radio simultaneously facilitated the imagination of an overarching community and the exploration of local differences within that community. Kamran Elend (2021), too, makes this point with regard to Radio Yerevan and the formation of a Kurdish imagined community.

17. Both Amanda Weidman (2014b, 2021) and Lotte Hoek (2009) discuss similar concerns in the South Indian and Bangladeshi contexts, respectively, where playback singing in cinema allows separating the female voice from the exposed dancing/acting body on screen. By preventing voices from becoming associated with an identifiable body, this separation allows women to circumvent forms of exposure that would easily compromise female respectability.

18. The term was coined by Micaela Di Leonardo (1987, 442) to describe the work of "conception, maintenance, and ritual celebration of cross-household kin ties" that women carry out in American households, for example, by sending cards, planning holidays, or organizing meals with relatives. I use it here to highlight the way in which kinship relations, particularly in contexts of dispersal and forced migration, require constant social investment in order to be maintained.

19. Laura Kunreuther (2006) similarly shows how FM radio has been crucial for consolidating an understanding of the Nepalese diaspora as a collective subject, which the radio at once constructs and promises to make accessible to listeners through forms of technological mediation.

20. The main tagline of Podcast Kurdî (The Kurdish Podcast, http://www.podcastkurdi .com) is "Guhdarên ezîz, ev der Podcast Kurdî ye!" (Dear listeners, this is the Kurdish Podcast!), which Kurds in Turkey would immediately recognize as a play on the famous opening line of Radio Yerevan's Kurdish broadcast.

Chapter Three

1. *Hunermend* is literally translated as "artist" (from *huner*, meaning "art or craft"). But because in English "artist" carries connotations of originality and creativity that the term *hunermend* as used in this context opposes, I translate it here as "performer" instead.

2. Nurcan Baysal (2014) has collected oral history accounts of this armed evacuation of Çorsin, during which the village's headman was brutally murdered and his body mutilated in front of his family and other villagers.

3. Amy de la Bretèque (2013, 136–137) notes a comparable understanding of pain among Kurdish-speaking Yezidi female lamenters in Armenia who describe their burning hearts as the principal force that pushes them to sing kilams. Stefania Pandolfo (1997, 280–281) similarly writes about how poetry in Morocco is understood as a force that the poet needs to learn to inhabit, since it is the words that possess agency rather than the poet.

4. Similar dynamics of how female selves become extended through patriarchally structured networks of kin and affines have been documented by anthropologists for communities across the Mediterranean, the Middle East, and South Asia. See, for instance, Abu-Lughod (1986), Ahmed (2006), Grima (1992), Jean-Klein (2000), Seremetakis (1991), and Wadley (1994).

5. The Kurdish transcription is based on the performance by Salihê Qubînî, available at https://www.youtube.com/watch?v=-vWkGdMaXB4 (last accessed October 9, 2021). Slightly different versions can be found in Hamelink (2016, 127–128) and Kevirbirî (2004, 66–68).

6. Hesîn is another of Perîxan's sons.

7. This is a fate shared by the families of many fallen PKK guerrilla fighters. The Turkish army typically seizes the bodies of fallen fighters, and only some are handed over to their families. Particularly in the 1990s many bodies were buried by Turkish authorities in undisclosed mass graves. For a perceptive analysis of this necropolitical violence, see Bargu (2016). When bodies remain within the hands of the PKK, too, they are often buried quickly right on the spot where combat has taken place. Since fellow guerrilla fighters are not always able to mark the location of buried bodies, many families are unable to locate their fallen relatives.

8. I draw mainly from Eyşe Şan's biography prepared by Kakşar Oremar (2012), which was published by the municipality of Diyarbekir.

9. Since the attempted military coup in 2016, Turkish authorities have replaced nearly all Kurdish-led municipalities with government-appointed trustees (*kayyum*). Many Kurdish civil society organizations, too, were shut down in the aftermath of the coup attempt.

Chapter Four

1. For detailed scholarship of the cultural politics that accompanied early Kurdish nationalism and particularly the place accorded to oral traditions, see Fuccaro (2003, 206–209), Strohmeier (2003, 151–154), and Yüksel (2011, 239–267).

2. *Roja Nû*, a journal run by Kamuran Bedirkhan, featured transcriptions of a number of performances by a dengbêj called Ehmedê Ferman (Yüksel 2011, 65).

3. The peace process (*barış süreci* or *çözüm süreci*, "resolution process") was part of a broader range of policies launched as a "democratic initiative" (*demokratik açılım*) package by Turkey's AKP government in 2009. The process involved, on the one hand, the implementation of legal reforms with a view to recognizing the Kurdish population's cultural and political rights and, on the other hand, negotiations between the Turkish secret service and the PKK leadership that probably began in 2009 and were made public in 2012. The negotiations resulted in the announcement of a ceasefire in 2013 and the partial withdrawal of PKK forces from Turkey to northern Iraq. Throughout, the terms of the peace process remained unclear, and the Kurdish side found the steps taken by the government to be insufficient. The negotiating parties never established a legal framework or interim agreement, rendering the process extremely fragile. Following the AKP's defeat in local elections in July 2015, the process finally collapsed, leading to renewed full-scale warfare in the Kurdish regions. For detailed accounts of the process and its end, see Hakyemez (2017), and Yeğen (2015).

4. The Siyah Bant (Black Ribbon) Project, a nongovernmental platform reporting on instances of cultural and artistic censorship in Turkey, wrote in their 2013 Report on Freedom of Expression in the Arts and Censorship in Turkey's Kurdish Regions that "all cultural (e.g. language) and artistic expression within the Kurdish rights struggle can be construed as illegitimate 'separatist propaganda' and hence outside of the protection of freedom of expression and the arts." They further note that "artistic production in the Kurdish region remains under generalized suspicion of being or aiding terrorist activities" (Siyah Bant 2013).

5. See Oktay Candemir, "Kürtçe Şarkıdan Bir Yıl Hapis," *bianet*, October 10, 2011, https://m .bianet.org/bianet/ifade-ozgurlugu/133320-kurtce-sarkidan-bir-yil-hapis.

6. These intellectuals included figures like Kendal Nezan, Rojen Barnas, Mehemed Malmîsanij, Celîlê Celîl, Mehmed Uzun, and Şerefxan Cizîrî (Çakır 2019, 60; Scalbert-Yücel 2009).

7. These would not be the same individuals, however, as Kurdish society remains deeply divided over whom to support in the conflict, meaning that there is great social pressure to "take sides" (see Schäfers 2020). While it may not be surprising that dengbêjs have centrally featured within the cultural politics of the Kurdish movement, it is particularly in the Kurdish regions, where the Turkish state seeks to prove its pluralist tolerance to the public, that dengbêjs are prominently endorsed by state institutions. In May 2012, for instance, I attended a conference to commemorate Dengbêj Reso that was organized by the Directorate of Culture and Tourism of the province of Mûş and featured a number of dengbêjs from the region. More recently, in April 2019, the University of Şırnak organized an academic symposium on dengbêjs that was prominently endorsed and promoted by the province's governorate (*valilik*): http://dengbejliks empozyumu.sirnak.edu.tr/# (last accessed April 4, 2019).

8. The Diyarbekir-based Mesopotamia Foundation (Weqfa Mezopotamyayê) has been organizing courses aimed at training individuals in the collection of Kurdish oral genres since 2020 with the stated aim of giving collection endeavors a "scientific" (*zanistî*) base and ultimately allowing for lasting archiving and documentation efforts. See https://www.wmezopotamyaye.org /ku/d/naveroken/38-daxuyani-ji-bo-kursa-canda-devki-u-berhevkariya-berhemen-folklore .html (last accessed July 30, 2021).

9. For how genealogical principles organize the transmission of tribal poetry and Islamic knowledge in Yemen, see Caton (1990) and Messick (1996), respectively. Engseng Ho (2006) masterfully depicts how patrilineal genealogies have shaped Yemen's Hadrami diaspora, while Diane King (2008) outlines how patriliny is foundational to statecraft in the Kurdish autonomous region in Iraq.

10. The stanza makes reference to reports widely circulating on social media after the earthquakes, which claimed that volunteers had found letters with nationalist slogans, Turkish flags, and stones in packages that were sent as aid to Wan's Kurdish earthquake victims. The stones allude to the image perpetuated in mainstream Turkish media of Kurdish youth as "stone-throwing children" (*taş atan çocuklar*) who keep provoking Turkish security forces.

Chapter Five

1. See, for instance, Asad (2003), Furani (2012), and Hirschkind (2006).

2. *Jinên Dengbêj/Women Dengbêj*, documentary, 2007, DV, 30 minutes; Kurdish, Turkish, English subtitled; director: Melek Özman, Atölyemor Collective; producer: Filmmor Women's Cooperative.

3. A detailed study conducted by Hacettepe University (Yüksel Kaptanoğlu, Çavlin, and Akadlı Ergöçmen 2015) found that 38 percent of women in Turkey have experienced physical or sexual violence at least once at the hands of their male partners. Numbers have been hovering around this mark since the 1990s. A 1994 study found 34 percent to have been victims of physical violence by their partners, while a 2008 study put the number at 39 percent. According to the 2016 Global Gender Gap Index of the World Economic Forum, Turkey ranks 130 out of 144 countries. For more details, see UN Women's Turkey page: http://eca.unwomen.org/en/where -we-are/turkey (last accessed July 8, 2019).

4. Solitary confinement (*tecrit*) refers to the conditions of detention of PKK leader Abdullah Öcalan, who serves a life sentence on the prison island of Imralı in the Marmara Sea and has mostly been kept in solitary confinement since his arrest in 1999.

5. The party has since been renamed and is now called the Democratic People's Party (Halkların Demokratik Partisi, HDP).

6. Other versions say: *Ez ê ne pariyê devê mirdarê fena te me* (I am not a bite for your dirty mouth). See, for instance, the version sung by Rojda, available online: https://www.youtube .com/watch?v=rdBlDOqykis.

7. *Qam kinikê* is clearly a mistake, as it means "short posture" and would thus directly contradict the previous expression *bej bilind*, meaning "tall posture." During other performances, Gazîn instead sang *meş werdekê*, meaning "duck-like walk," which coincides with most versions by other performers. Duck attributes are a feminine beauty ideal. The girl herself is called Werdem, probably from *werdek*, "duck."

8. While Gazîn's version suggests that Cemîl imagines Werdem descending onto his chest, other versions have the messenger of damned fate descend on him: *Wê çaxê li ser singe min peya be qasidê mîrata kor felekê.* Compare the version sung by Rojda: https://www.youtube.com /watch?v=rdBlDOqykis.

9. Other versions suggest the inverse, that the father is of Ajam origin (referring to Azeris and Persians from Iran) and the mother Christian, which is more likely, given prevailing cross-confessional marriage patterns. Compare the version sung by Rojda: https://www.youtube.com /watch?v=rdBlDOqykis.

10. The literature on the complex relation between feminism and nationalism is vast. Literature that highlights the tendency of nationalist movements to sideline women's concerns and agendas includes Altınay (2004), Aretxaga (1997), Enloe (2014, 83–124), and McClintock (1991).

11. For more details on the Kurdish women's movement ideology and practice, including how both have changed over time, see Açık (2013), Çağlayan (2007, 2012), Dirik (2022), Duzel (2018), Grojean (2013), Özgür Kadın Akademisi (2015), and Shahvisi (2018).

Conclusion

1. Similar to the Kurdish dengbêj, the Armenian *ashugh* is a performer of sung narrative, including epics and oral histories. The ashugh is closely related to the Turkish *aşık* and similar traditions in the Caucasus and Iran. Like dengbêjs, the most prominent ashughs have in the past mainly been men. Ashughs would often accompany themselves on musical instruments like the *kemançe* (also *kamancheh*, a spike fiddle that resembles an upwardly held violin) or a small hand-held frame drum (*def*). Different from dengbêjs, many of their repertoires have been transmitted through written documents rather than orally.

2. Janet Klein (2011) outlines how certain Kurdish tribes became enrolled with the Hamidiye cavalry units established by the Ottoman sultan Abdulhamid II in 1891. The units played a prominent role in the oppression and massacre of Armenian and other non-Muslim populations in the period leading up to and during the 1915 genocide.

3. For details on Kurdish attitudes toward the Armenian genocide and ideas about shared victimhood, see Çelik and Dinç (2015), Çelik and Öpengin (2016), Leupold (2020), and Suni (2019).

4. The idea arose back in 2012, when Gazîn and I attended a concert in Wan that was organized by Anadolu Kültür on the occasion of the liturgical service celebrated at the Armenian Cathedral of the Holy Cross, a medieval church and former apostolic seat situated on Akhtamar Island in Lake Wan. In disuse and exposed to vandalism after 1915, the church was restored between 2005 and 2006 and subsequently turned into a museum. In 2010 the Turkish authorities first granted permission to hold a liturgical service, which has since been organized annually (though suspended from 2015 to 2018), attracting thousands of Armenian visitors from all over the world. In 2012, the service was accompanied by a number of artistic events celebrating the spirit of cultural rapprochement and interreligious dialogue that pervaded the period. When we attended the large concert by the lakeside in the evening, Gazîn was stunned by the proximity of Armenian and Kurdish repertoires. Able to sing along in Kurdish to most of the Armenian pieces performed that night, she was convinced that it was worth exploring further the acoustic resonances between two peoples who share a history yet remain divided by international borders and a legacy of genocidal violence. With the help of friends and contacts in Istanbul, we proposed the idea of an exchange project between Armenian and Kurdish women singers to Anadolu Kültür later that year, who agreed to include it in their portfolio of activities.

5. See "Female Minstrels Project Kicks Off in Yerevan," Support to the Armenia-Turkey Normalisation Process, May 25, 2014, http://www.armenia-turkey.net/en/from-van-to-yerevan -concert-in-yerevan.

6. See, for instance, the popular version by Kurdish artist Nizamettin Ariç, available online: https://www.youtube.com/watch?v=fsZL5-4rA6o.

Bibliography

Abu-Lughod, Lila. 1986. *Veiled Sentiments: Honor and Poetry in a Bedouin Society*. Berkeley: University of California Press.

Abu-Lughod, Lila. 1998. "Introduction: Feminist Longings and Postcolonial Conditions." In *Remaking Women: Feminism and Modernity in the Middle East*, edited by Lila Abu-Lughod, 3–31. Princeton, NJ: Princeton University Press.

Abu-Lughod, Lila. 2000. "Modern Subjects: Egyptian Melodrama and Postcolonial Difference." In *Questions of Modernity*, edited by Timothy Mitchell, 87–114. Minneapolis: University of Minnesota Press.

Abu-Lughod, Lila. 2013. *Do Muslim Women Need Saving?* Cambridge, MA: Harvard University Press.

Açık, Necla. 2013. "Re-Defining the Role of Women within the Kurdish National Movement in Turkey in the 1990s." In *The Kurdish Question in Turkey: New Perspectives on Violence, Representation, and Reconciliation*, edited by Cengiz Gunes and Welat Zeydanlıoğlu, 114–135. Abingdon: Routledge.

Ağçakaya, Nevzat. 2019. "1960 Sonrası Van'da İskân Politikaları: Dönerdere Örneği." In *"Dünyada Van": Nüfus, Etnisite, Tarih ve Toplum*, edited by Ercan Çağlayan, 87–105. Istanbul: İletişim.

Ağcakulu, Ali. 2012. "Ortadoğu'da Kürtçe Radyo Yayınları: Erivan Radyosu Örneği (1955–1990)." Master's thesis, Marmara University.

Agha, Asif. 2005. "Voice, Footing, Enregisterment." *Journal of Linguistic Anthropology* 15 (1):38–59. https://doi.org/10.1525/jlin.2005.15.1.38.

Ahıska, Meltem. 2010. *Occidentalism in Turkey: Questions of Modernity and National Identity in Turkish Radio Broadcasting*. London: I.B. Tauris.

Ahmed, Amineh. 2006. *Sorrow and Joy among Muslim Women: The Pukhtuns of Northern Pakistan*. Cambridge: Cambridge University Press.

Ahmed, Sara. 2004. *The Cultural Politics of Emotion*. New York: Routledge.

Ahmetbeyzade, Cihan. 2007. "Negotiating Silences in the So-Called Low-Intensity War: The Making of the Kurdish Diaspora in Istanbul." *Signs* 33 (1):159–182.

Akkaya, Ahmet Hamdi, and Joost Jongerden. 2012. "Reassembling the Political: The PKK and the Project of Radical Democracy." *European Journal of Turkish Studies* 14. https://doi.org/10.4000/ejts.4615.

Aksoy, Ozan E. 2006. "The Politicization of Kurdish Folk Songs in Turkey in the 1990s." *Music and Anthropology: Journal of Musical Anthropology of the Mediterranean* 11. http://www.levi .provincia.venezia.it/ma/index/number11/aksoy/ak_0.htm.

Alê, Hesenê. N.d. *Dengbêj û Stranên Me, Destan û Folklora Me.* Stockholm. https://www.scribd .com/doc/204178582/Hemu-stranen-Kurdi-An-Anthology-of-Kurdish-Songs-by-Hesene -Ale-Stran-A-K-Hesene-Ale.

Allison, Christine. 2001. *The Yezidi Oral Tradition in Iraqi Kurdistan.* Richmond: Curzon Press.

Allison, Christine. 2010. "Kurdish Oral Literature." In *Oral Literature of Iranian Languages: Kurdish, Pashto, Balochi, Ossetic, Persian, and Tajik: Companion Volume II*, edited by Philip G. Kreyenbroek and Ulrich Marzolph. London: I.B. Tauris.

Allison, Christine. 2013. "From Benedict Anderson to Mustafa Kemal: Reading, Writing, and Imagining the Kurdish Nation." In *Joyce Blau: L'éternelle chez les Kurdes*, edited by Hamit Bozarslan and Clémence Scalbert-Yücel, 101–133. Paris: Institut Kurde de Paris.

Altınay, Ayşe Gül. 2004. *The Myth of the Military Nation: Militarism, Gender, and Education in Turkey.* New York: Palgrave Macmillan.

Amy de la Bretèque, Estelle. 2010. "Des Affects Entre Guillemets: Mélodisation de la Parole chez les Yézidis d'Arménie." *Cahiers d'Ethnomusicologie* 23: 131–145. http://ethnomusicologie.re vues.org/pdf/978.

Amy de la Bretèque, Estelle. 2012. "Voices of Sorrow: Melodized Speech, Laments, and Heroic Narratives among the Yezidis of Armenia." *Yearbook for Traditional Music* 44: 129–148. https://doi.org/10.5921/yeartradmusi.44.0129.

Amy de la Bretèque, Estelle. 2013. *Paroles Mélodisés: Récits Épiques et Lamentations chez les Yézidis d'Arménie.* Paris: Classiques Garnier.

Amy de la Bretèque, Estelle. 2016. "Self-Sacrifice, Womanhood, and Melodized Speech: Three Case Studies from the Caucasus and Anatolia." *Asian Music* 47 (1): 29–63. https://doi.org /10.1353/amu.2016.0008.

Amy de la Bretèque, Estelle, Boris Doval, Lionel Feugère, and Louis Moreau-Gaudry. 2017. "Liminal Utterances and Shapes of Sadness: Local and Acoustic Perspectives on Vocal Production among the Yezidis of Armenia." *Yearbook for Traditional Music* 49:129–148. https://doi .org/10.5921/yeartradmusi.49.2017.0129.

Anderson, Benedict. 2006. *Imagined Communities: Reflections on the Origin and Spread of Nationalism.* London: Verso.

Andrews, Walter G., and Mehmet Kalpaklı. 2005. *The Age of Beloveds: Love and the Beloved in Early-Modern Ottoman and European Culture and Society.* Durham, NC: Duke University Press.

Arat, Zehra F. 1998. "Educating the Daughters of the Republic." In *Deconstructing Images of the Turkish Woman*, edited by Zehra F. Arat, 157–180. Basingstoke: Macmillan.

Arat-Koç, Sedef. 2007. "(Some) Turkish Transnationalism(s) in an Age of Capitalist Globalization and Empire: 'White Turk' Discourse, the New Geopolitics, and Implications for Feminist Transnationalism." *Journal of Middle East Women's Studies* 3 (1):35–57.

Aretxaga, Begoña. 1997. *Shattering Silence: Women, Nationalism, and Political Subjectivity in Northern Ireland.* Princeton, NJ: Princeton University Press.

Argenti-Pillen, Alex. 2003. *Masking Terror: How Women Contain Violence in Southern Sri Lanka.* Philadelphia: University of Pennsylvania Press.

Asad, Talal. 2000. "Agency and Pain: An Exploration." *Culture and Religion* 1 (1):29–60.

Asad, Talal. 2003. *Formations of the Secular: Christianity, Islam, Modernity.* Stanford, CA: Stanford University Press.

Aslan, Senem. 2007. "'Citizen, Speak Turkish!': A Nation in the Making." *Nationalism and Ethnic Politics* 13 (2):245–272. https://doi.org/10.1080/13537110701293500.

Aslan, Senem. 2015. *Nation-Building in Turkey and Morocco: Governing Kurdish and Berber Dissent.* Cambridge: Cambridge University Press.

Ayata, Bilgin, and Serra Hakyemez. 2013. "The AKP's Engagement with Turkey's Past Crimes: An Analysis of PM Erdoğan's 'Dersim Apology.'" *Dialectical Anthropology* 37 (1):131–143. https://doi.org/10.1007/s10624-013-9304-3.

Bakhtin, Mikhail. 1981a. "Discourse in the Novel." In *The Dialogic Imagination,* edited by Michael Holquist, 262–349. Austin: University of Texas Press.

Bakhtin, Mikhail. 1981b. "Epic and Novel: Toward a Methodology for the Study of the Novel." In *The Dialogic Imagination,* edited by Michael Holquist, 3–40. Austin: University of Texas Press.

Bakhtin, Mikhail. 1984. *Problems of Dostoevsky's Poetics.* Translated by Caryl Emerson. Minneapolis: University of Minnesota Press.

Bakker Kellogg, Sarah. 2015. "Ritual Sounds, Political Echoes: Vocal Agency and the Sensory Cultures of Secularism in the Dutch Syriac Diaspora." *American Ethnologist* 42 (3):431–445. https://doi.org/10.1111/amet.12139.

Balkılıç, Özgür. 2009. *Cumhuriyet, Halk ve Müzik: Türkiye'de Müzik Reformu, 1922–1952.* Istanbul: Tan.

Barber, Karin. 2007. *The Anthropology of Texts, Persons, and Publics: Oral and Written Culture in Africa and Beyond.* Cambridge: Cambridge University Press.

Bargu, Banu. 2016. "Another Necropolitics." *Theory & Event* 19 (1). muse.jhu.edu/article/610222.

Barthes, Roland. 1977. "The Death of the Author." In *Image-Music-Text,* 142–148. London: Fontana Press.

Bauman, Richard, and Charles L. Briggs. 2003. *Voices of Modernity: Language Ideologies and the Politics of Inequality.* Cambridge: Cambridge University Press.

Baysal, Nurcan. 2014. *O Gün.* Istanbul: İletişim.

Beard, Mary. 2017. *Women & Power: A Manifesto.* London: Profile Books, London Review of Books.

Beeman, William O. 2005. "Making Grown Men Weep." In *Aesthetics in Performance: Formations of Symbolic Construction and Experience,* edited by Angela Hobart and Bruce Kapferer, 23–42. New York: Berghahn Books.

Behrent, Michael C. 2013. "Foucault and Technology." *History and Technology* 29 (1):54–104. https://doi.org/10.1080/07341512.2013.780351.

Benjamin, Walter. 2007a. "The Storyteller: Reflections on the Works of Nikolai Leskov." In *Illuminations,* edited by Hannah Arendt, 83–109. New York: Schocken Books.

Benjamin, Walter. 2007b. "Theses on the Philosophy of History." In *Illuminations,* edited by Hannah Arendt, 253–264. New York: Schocken Books.

Berlant, Lauren. 2008. *The Female Complaint: The Unfinished Business of Sentimentality in American Culture.* Durham, NC: Duke University Press.

Berlant, Lauren. 2011. *Cruel Optimism.* Durham, NC: Duke University Press.

Beşikçi, İsmail. 2013. *Devletlerarası Sömürge Kürdistan.* Istanbul: İsmail Beşikçi Vakfı.

Bessire, Lucas, and Daniel Fisher. 2012a. "Introduction: Radio Fields." In *Radio Fields: Anthropology and Wireless Sound in the 21st Century,* edited by Lucas Bessire and Daniel Fisher, 1–47. New York: New York University Press.

Bessire, Lucas, and Daniel Fisher. 2012b. *Radio Fields: Anthropology and Wireless Sound in the 21st Century.* New York: New York University Press.

Biagioli, Mario, and Peter Galison. 2003a. "Introduction." In *Scientific Authorship: Credit and Intellectual Property in Science*, edited by Mario Biagioli and Peter Galison, 1–9. New York: Routledge.

Biagioli, Mario, and Peter Galison. 2003b. *Scientific Authorship: Credit and Intellectual Property in Science*. New York: Routledge.

Bilal, Melissa, and Estelle Amy de la Bretèque. 2013. "The Oror and the Lorî: Armenian and Kurdish Lullabies in Present-Day Istanbul." In *Remembering the Past in Iranian Societies*, edited by Christine Allison and Philip G. Kreyenbroek, 125–139. Wiesbaden: Harrassowitz.

Bilik, Mehmet Baki. 2019. "Van'ın Değişen Yüzleri: Kentte Demografik Dönüşümler ve Küresünniler." In *"Dünyada Van": Nüfus, Etnisite, Tarih ve Toplum*, edited by Ercan Çağlayan, 107–126. Istanbul: İletişim.

Bloch, Maurice, ed. 1975. *Political Language and Oratory in Traditional Society*. London: Academic Press.

Bloom, Peter J. 2014. "Elocution, Englishness, and Empire: Film and Radio in Late Colonial Ghana." In *Modernization as Spectacle in Africa*, edited by Peter J. Bloom, Stephan F. Miescher, and Takyiwaa Manuh, 136–156. Bloomington: Indiana University Press.

Blum, Stephen, Dieter Christensen, and Amnon Shiloah. 2001. "Kurdish Music." *Grove Music Online*. https://doi.org/10.1093/gmo/9781561592630.article.15686.

Blum, Stephen, and Amir Hassanpour. 1996. "'The Morning of Freedom Rose Up': Kurdish Popular Song and the Exigencies of Cultural Survival." *Popular Music* 15 (3):325–343. https://doi.org/10.1017/S026114300000831X.

Boddy, Janice. 1989. *Wombs and Alien Spirits: Women, Men, and the Zār Cult in Northern Sudan*. Madison: University of Wisconsin Press.

Bohlman, Andrea F., and Peter McMurray. 2017. "Tape: Or, Rewinding the Phonographic Regime." *Twentieth-Century Music* 14 (1):3–24. https://doi.org/10.1017/S1478572217000032.

Bolton, Lissant. 1999. "Radio and the Redefinition of *Kastom* in Vanuatu." *Contemporary Pacific* 11 (2): 335–360.

Bonini Baraldi, Filippo. 2013. *Tsiganes, Musique et Empathie*. Paris: Éditions de la Maison des Sciences de l'Homme.

Booth, Marilyn. 2013. "Locating Women's Autobiographical Writing in Colonial Egypt." *Journal of Women's History* 25 (2):36–60. https://doi.org/10.1353/jowh.2013.0019.

Bozgan, Dilan Özgen. 2011. "Kürt Kadın Hareketi Üzerine Bir Değerlendirme." In *Birkaç Arpa Boyu . . . 21. Yüzyıla Girerken Türkiye'de Feminist Çalışmalar*, vol. 2, edited by Serpil Sancar, 757–799. Istanbul: Koç Üniversitesi Yayınları.

Briggs, Charles L., and Richard Bauman. 1992. "Genre, Intertextuality, and Social Power." *Journal of Linguistic Anthropology* 2 (2):131–172. https://doi.org/10.1525/jlin.1992.2.2.131.

Brown, Wendy. 2006. *Regulating Aversion: Tolerance in the Age of Identity and Empire*. Princeton, NJ: Princeton University Press.

Bruinessen, Martin van. 1995. *Forced Evictions and Destruction of Villages in Dersim (Tunceli) and the Western Part of Bingöl, Turkish Kurdistan, September–November 1994*. Amsterdam: Stichting Nederland Koerdistan.

Bruinessen, Martin van. 1996. "Turkey's Death Squads." *Middle East Report* 199:20–23. https://doi.org/10.2307/3012887.

Bryant, Rebecca. 2005. "The Soul Danced into the Body: Nation and Improvisation in Istanbul." *American Ethnologist* 32 (2):222–238. https://doi.org/10.1525/ae.2005.32.2.222.

Buch Segal, Lotte. 2016. *No Place for Grief: Martyrs, Prisoners, and Mourning in Contemporary Palestine*. Philadelphia: University of Pennsylvania Press.

Buffon, Veronica, and Christine Allison. 2016. "The Gendering of Victimhood: Western Media and the Sinjar Genocide." *Kurdish Studies* 4 (2):176–195. https://doi.org/10.33182/ks.v4i2.427.

Bullock, Jon. 2021. "Decolonizing the Boundaries: Indigenous Musical Discourse in the History of Kurdish Radio Baghdad." *IASPM Journal* 11 (2):22–38. https://doi.org/10.5429/2079 -3871(2021v11i2.3en.

Bush, J. Andrew. 2015. "The Politics of Poetry." In *A Companion to the Anthropology of the Middle East*, edited by Soraya Altorki, 187–204. Hoboken, NJ: Wiley Blackwell.

Bush, J. Andrew. 2020. *Between Muslims: Religious Difference in Iraqi Kurdistan*. Stanford, CA: Stanford University Press.

Butler, Judith. 1997. *Excitable Speech: A Politics of the Performative*. New York: Routledge.

Cagaptay, Soner. 2006. *Islam, Secularism, and Nationalism in Modern Turkey: Who Is a Turk?* London: Routledge.

Çağlayan, Ercan, ed. 2019. *"Dünyada Van": Nüfus, Etnisite, Tarih ve Toplum*. Istanbul: İletişim.

Çağlayan, Handan. 2007. *Analar, Yoldaşlar, Tanrıçalar: Kürt Hareketinde Kadınlar ve Kadın Kimliğinin Oluşumu*. Istanbul: İletişim Yayınları.

Çağlayan, Handan. 2012. "From Kawa the Blacksmith to Ishtar the Goddess: Gender Constructions in Ideological-Political Discourses of the Kurdish Movement in Post-1980 Turkey." *European Journal of Turkish Studies* 14. https://doi.org/10.4000/ejts.4657.

Çakır, Argun Nihat. 2011. "The Representation of the Dengbêj Tradition in Kurdish Contemporary Popular Discourse." Master's thesis, University of Exeter.

Çakır, Argun Nihat. 2019. "From Charity-Seeking to Music-Making: An Ethnography of Perpatetic Adaptation in the Mêrdîn (Mardin) Area, Southeastern Turkey." PhD diss., University of Exeter.

Çakır, Argun Nihat. 2020. "İdealize Edilmiş Yekpare Dengbêjlik Karşısında Dengbêj-Tipi Icracıların Bölgesel Çeşitliği." *Politik Art* 286:4–5.

Campbell, Matthew. 2012. "Affective Traces: Sounds of Intimacy and the Phenomenology of the Voice in Amateur Tape Exchange during the Vietnam Conflict." Paper presented at Making Sound Objects: British Forum for Ethnomusicology's Annual One Day Conference, Oxford, November 24, 2012. https://makingsoundobjects.wordpress.com/2012/11/05 /campbell-matthew/.

Carson, Anne. 1995. "The Gender of Sound." In *Glass, Irony, and God*, 119–141. New York: New Directions.

Caruth, Cathy. 1996. *Unclaimed Experience: Trauma, Narrative, and History*. Baltimore: Johns Hopkins University Press.

Casier, Marlies, Joost Jongerden, and Nic Walker. 2013. "Turkey's Kurdish Movement and the AKP's Kurdish Opening: Kurdish Spring or Fall?" In *The Kurdish Spring: Geopolitical Changes and the Kurds*, edited by Mohammed M. A. Ahmed and Michael Gunter, 135–162. Costa Mesa, CA: Mazda.

Caton, Steven C. 1990. *"Peaks of Yemen I Summon": Poetry as Cultural Practice in a North Yemeni Tribe*. Berkeley: University of California Press.

Cavarero, Adriana. 2005. *For More Than One Voice: Towards a Philosophy of Vocal Expression*. Stanford, CA: Stanford University Press.

Çaylı, Eray. 2021. *Victims of Commemoration: The Architecture and Violence of Confronting the Past in Turkey*. Syracuse, NY: Syracuse University Press.

Çelebi, Nezan Newzat, Vedat Yıldırım, and Aytekin G. Ataş. 2006. "Geleneksel Kürt Müziğine Genel Bir Bakış." *Artizan*. https://www.art-izan.org/artizan-arsivi/geleneksel-kurt-muzigine -genel-bir-bakis/.

Çelik, Adnan, and Namık Kemal Dinç. 2015. *Yüz Yıllık Ah! Toplumsal Hafızanın İzinde 1915 Diyarbekir*. Istanbul: İsmail Beşikçi Vakfı.

Çelik, Adnan, and Ergin Öpengin. 2016. "The Armenian Genocide in the Kurdish Novel: Restructuring Identity through Collective Memory." *European Journal of Turkish Studies*. https://doi.org/10.4000/ejts.5291.

Chakrabarty, Dipesh. 2000. *Provincializing Europe: Postcolonial Thought and Historical Difference*. Princeton, NJ: Princeton University Press.

Chartier, Roger. 2003. "Foucault's Chiasmus: Authorship between Science and Literature in the Seventeenth and Eighteenth Centuries." In *Scientific Authorship: Credit and Intellectual Property in Science*, edited by Mario Biagioli and Peter Galison, 13–31. New York: Routledge.

Chikowero, Mhoze. 2014. "Is Propaganda Modernity? Press and Radio for 'Africans' in Zambia, Zimbabwe, and Malawi during World War II and Its Aftermath." In *Modernization as Spectacle in Africa*, edited by Peter J. Bloom, Stephan F. Miescher, and Takyiwaa Manuh, 112–135. Bloomington: Indiana University Press.

Chion, Michel. 1982. *La Voix au Cinéma*. Paris: Éditions de l'Étoile.

Christensen, Dieter. 1975. "On Variability in Kurdish Dance Songs." *Asian Music* 6 (1/2):1–6.

Christensen, Dieter. 2002. "Kurdistan." In *Garland Encyclopedia of World Music*, vol. 6, *The Middle East*, edited by Virginia Danielson, Marcus Scott, and Dwight Reynolds, 739–752. New York: Routledge.

Clark, Jessie Hanna. 2015. "Green, Red, Yellow, and Purple: Gendering the Kurdish Question in South-East Turkey." *Gender, Place & Culture* 22 (10):1463–1480. https://doi.org/10.1080/096 6369X.2014.991701.

Cohen, David William, Stephan F. Miescher, and Luise White. 2001. "Introduction: Voices, Words, and African History." In *African Words, African Voices: Critical Practices in Oral History*, edited by Luise White, Stephan F. Miescher, and David William Cohen, 1–30. Bloomington: Indiana University Press.

Comaroff, John L., and Jean Comaroff. 2009. *Ethnicity, Inc.* Chicago: University of Chicago Press.

Connor, Steven. 2004. "Edison's Teeth: Touching Hearing." In *Hearing Cultures: Essays on Sound, Listening, and Modernity*, edited by Veit Erlmann, 153–172. Berg: Oxford.

cooke, miriam. 2007. "The Muslimwoman." *Contemporary Islam* 1 (2):139–154. https://doi.org /10.1007/s11562-007-0013-z.

Coombe, Rosemary J. 1998. *The Cultural Life of Intellectual Properties: Authorship, Appropriation, and the Law*. Durham, NC: Duke University Press.

Coşkun, Vahap, Şerif M. Derince, and Nesrin Uçarlar. 2011. *Scar of Tongue: Consequences of the Ban on the Use of Mother Tongue in Education and Experiences of Kurdish Students in Turkey*. Diyarbakır: Diyarbakır Institute for Political and Social Research.

Couldry, Nick. 2010. *Why Voice Matters: Culture and Politics after Neoliberalism*. Los Angeles: SAGE.

Cox, Christoph. 2011. "Beyond Representation and Signification: Toward a Sonic Materialism." *Journal of Visual Culture* 10 (2):145–161. https://doi.org/10.1177/1470412911402880.

Cusick, Suzanne G. 2008. "Musicology, Torture, Repair." *Radical Musicology* 3. http://www .radical-musicology.org.uk/2008/Cusick.pdf.

Das, Veena. 1997. "Language and Body: Transactions in the Construction of Pain." In *Social Suffering*, edited by Arthur Kleinman, Veena Das, and Margaret M. Lock, 67–91. Berkeley: University of California Press.

Das, Veena. 2000. "The Act of Witnessing: Violence, Poisonous Knowledge, and Subjectivity." In *Violence and Subjectivity*, edited by Veena Das, Arthur Kleinman, Mamphela Ramphele, and Pamela Reynolds, 205–225. Berkeley: University of California Press.

Das, Veena. 2007. *Life and Words: Violence and the Descent into the Ordinary*. Berkeley: University of California Press.

Das, Veena, Arthur Kleinman, Margaret Lock, and Pamela Reynolds, eds. 2001. *Remaking a World: Violence, Social Suffering, and Recovery*. Berkeley: University of California Press.

Das, Veena, Arthur Kleinman, Mamphela Ramphele, and Pamela Reynolds, eds. 2000. *Violence and Subjectivity*. Berkeley: University of California Press.

Deeb, Lara. 2009. "Piety Politics and the Role of a Transnational Feminist Analysis." *Journal of the Royal Anthropological Institute*, n.s., 15 (1):S112–S126. https://doi.org/10.1111/j.1467 -9655.2009.01545.x.

Degirmenci, Koray. 2006. "On the Pursuit of a Nation: The Construction of Folk and Folk Music in the Founding Decades of the Turkish Republic." *International Review of the Aesthetics and Sociology of Music* 37 (1):47–65.

DeNora, Tia. 2000. *Music in Everyday Life*. Cambridge: Cambridge University Press.

Derrida, Jacques. 1977. "Signature Event Context." In *Limited Inc*, 1–23. Evanston, IL: Northwestern University Press.

Derrida, Jacques. 1998a. *Archive Fever: A Freudian Impression*. Chicago: University of Chicago Press.

Derrida, Jacques. 1998b. *Of Grammatology*. Baltimore: Johns Hopkins University Press.

Di Leonardo, Micaela. 1987. "The Female World of Cards and Holidays: Women, Families, and the Work of Kinship." *Signs* 12 (3):440–453.

Dirik, Dilar. 2014. "Western Fascination with 'Badass' Kurdish Women." *Al Jazeera*, October 29, 2014. https://www.aljazeera.com/indepth/opinion/2014/10/western-fascination-with-badas -201410211241052736.html.

Dirik, Dilar. 2022. *The Kurdish Women's Movement: History, Theory, Practice*. London: Pluto Press.

Doxan, Mazlûm. N.d. "Tirkîfîkasyona Xwemalî Di Zimanê Medyaya Kurdî De Li Bakurê Kurdistanê." http://www.zazaki.net/file/tirkifikasyon-.pdf.

Duncan, Michelle. 2004. "The Operatic Scandal of the Singing Body: Voice, Presence, Performativity." *Cambridge Opera Journal* 16 (3):283–306. https://doi.org/10.1017/S0954586704001879.

Dunn, Leslie C., and Nancy A. Jones. 1994. *Embodied Voices: Representing Female Vocality in Western Culture*. Cambridge: Cambridge University Press.

Durakbaşa, Ayşe. 1998. "Kemalism as Identity Politics in Turkey." In *Deconstructing Images of the Turkish Woman*, edited by Zehra F. Arat, 139–156. Basingstoke: Macmillan.

Durham Peters, John. 2004. "The Voice and Modern Media." In *Kunst-Stimmen*, edited by Doris Kolesch and Jenny Schrödl, 85–100. Berlin: Theater der Zeit.

Duruiz, Deniz. 2020. "Tracing the Conceptual Genealogy of Kurdistan as International Colony." *Middle East Report* 295. https://merip.org/2020/08/tracing-the-conceptual-genealogy -of-kurdistan-as-international-colony/.

Duzel, Esin. 2018. "Fragile Goddesses: Moral Subjectivity and Militarized Agencies in Female Guerrilla Diaries and Memoirs." *International Feminist Journal of Politics* 20 (2):1–16. https:// doi.org/10.1080/14616742.2017.1419823.

Ehrick, Christine. 2015a. *Radio and the Gendered Soundscape: Women and Broadcasting in Argentina and Uruguay, 1930–1950*. New York: Cambridge University Press.

Ehrick, Christine. 2015b. "Vocal Gender and the Gendered Soundscape: At the Intersection of Gender Studies and Sound Studies." *Sounding Out!* https://soundstudiesblog.com /2015/02/02/vocal-gender-and-the-gendered-soundscape-at-the-intersection-of-gender -studies-and-sound-studies/.

Eidsheim, Nina Sun. 2015. *Sensing Sound: Singing and Listening as Vibrational Practice*. Durham, NC: Duke University Press.

Eidsheim, Nina Sun. 2019. *The Race of Sound: Listening, Timbre, and Vocality in African American Music*. Durham, NC: Duke University Press.

Eisenlohr, Patrick. 2018. *Sounding Islam: Voice, Media, and Sonic Atmospheres in an Indian Ocean World*. Oakland: University of California Press.

Elend, Kamran. 2021. *Kimliği Terennüm Etmek: Erivan Radyosu Kürtçe Yayını*. Istanbul: İletişim.

Elias, Nicolas. 2016. "This Is Not a Festival: Transhumance-Based Economies on Turkey's Upland Pastures." *Nomadic Peoples* 20 (2):265–286. https://doi.org/10.3197/np.2016.200206.

Enloe, Cynthia. 2014. *Bananas, Beaches, and Bases: Making Feminist Sense of Internationalist Politics*. 2nd ed. Berkeley: University of California Press.

Erlmann, Veit, ed. 2004. *Hearing Cultures: Essays on Sound, Listening, and Modernity*. Berg: Oxford.

Fanon, Frantz. 1965. "This Is the Voice of Algeria." In *A Dying Colonialism*, 69–97. New York: Grove Press.

Fassin, Didier, and Richard Rechtman. 2009. *The Empire of Trauma: An Inquiry into the Condition of Victimhood*. Princeton, NJ: Princeton University Press.

Feld, Steven. 1982. *Sound and Sentiment: Birds, Weeping, Poetics, and Song in Kaluli Expression*. Philadelphia: University of Pennsylvania Press.

Feld, Steven, and Aaron A. Fox. 1994. "Music and Language." *Annual Review of Anthropology* 23:25–53. https://doi.org/10.1146/annurev.an.23.100194.000325.

Feld, Steven, Aaron A. Fox, Thomas Porcello, and David Samuels. 2004. "Vocal Anthropology: From the Music of Language to the Language of Song." In *A Companion to Linguistic Anthropology*, edited by Alessandro Duranti, 321–345. Oxford: Blackwell.

Felman, Shoshana, and Dori Laub. 1992. *Testimony: Crises of Witnessing in Literature, Psychoanalysis, and History*. New York: Routledge.

Fernandes, Desmond. 2012. "Modernity and the Linguistic Genocide of Kurds in Turkey." *International Journal of the Sociology of Language* 217:75–98. https://doi.org/10.1515/ijsl-2012-0050.

Fisher, Daniel. 2016. *The Voice and Its Doubles: Media and Music in Northern Australia*. Durham, NC: Duke University Press.

Foucault, Michel. 1977. "What Is an Author?" In *Michel Foucault: Language, Counter-Memory, Practice: Selected Essays and Interviews*, edited by Donald F. Bouchard, 113–138. Ithaca, NY: Cornell University Press.

Foucault, Michel. 1998. *The History of Sexuality, Volume I: The Will to Knowledge*. London: Penguin.

Fox, Aaron A. 2004. *Real Country: Music and Language in Working-Class Culture*. Durham, NC: Duke University Press.

Fuccaro, Nelida. 2003. "Kurds and Kurdish Nationalism in Mandatory Syria: Politics, Culture, and Identity." In *Essays on the Origins of Kurdish Nationalism*, edited by Abbas Vali, 191–217. Costa Mesa, CA: Mazda.

Furani, Khaled. 2012. *Silencing the Sea: Secular Rhythms in Palestinian Poetry*. Stanford, CA: Stanford University Press.

Gal, Susan. 1989. "Between Speech and Silence: The Problematics of Research on Language and Gender." *IPrA Papers in Pragmatics* 3 (1):1–38.

Gell, Alfred. 1992. "The Technology of Enchantment and the Enchantment of Technology." In *Anthropology, Art, and Aesthetics*, edited by Jeremy Coote and Anthony Shelton, 40–63. Oxford: Clarendon Press.

Gell, Alfred. 1998. *Art and Agency: An Anthropological Theory*. Oxford: Clarendon Press.

Ghazaryan, Gayane. 2019. "The Kurdish Voice of Radio Yerevan." *EVN Report*, January 24, 2019. https://www.evnreport.com/evn-youth-report0/the-kurdish-voice-of-radio-yerevan.

Ghazaryan, Gayane. 2020. "The Kurdish Voice of Radio Yerevan." Bachelor's thesis, American University of Armenia.

Gill, Denise. 2017. *Melancholic Modalities: Affect, Islam, and Turkish Classical Musicians*. New York: Oxford University Press.

Gill-Gürtan, Denise. 2011. "Performing Meşk, Narrating History: Legacies of Transmission in Contemporary Turkish Musical Practices." *Comparative Studies of South Asia, Africa and the Middle East* 31 (3):615–630. https://doi.org/10.1215/1089201x-1426773.

Gitelman, Lisa. 1999. *Scripts, Grooves, and Writing Machines: Representing Technology in the Edison Era*. Stanford, CA: Stanford University Press.

Glasser, Jonathan. 2016. *The Lost Paradise: Andalusi Music in Urban North Africa*. Chicago: University of Chicago Press.

Glastonbury, Nicholas. 2018. "'They Imprisoned the Radios': Materiality, Circulation, and the Social Life of Radio in Kurdistan." Paper presented at the Annual Meeting of the American Anthropological Association, San Jose, CA, November 16, 2018.

Goffman, Erving. 1979. "Footing." *Semiotica* 25 (1–2):1–30. https://doi.org/10.1515/semi.1979.25.1-2.1.

Göle, Nilüfer. 1996. *The Forbidden Modern: Civilization and Veiling*. Ann Arbor: University of Michigan Press.

Göle, Nilüfer. 2002. "Islam in Public: New Visibilities and New Imaginaries." *Public Culture* 14 (1):173–190. https://doi.org/10.1215/08992363-14-1-173.

Good, Byron. 1977. "The Heart of What's the Matter: The Semantics of Illness in Iran." *Culture Medicine and Psychiatry* 1 (1):25–58. https://doi/.org/10.1007/BF00114809.

Goodman, Jane E. 2002. "'Stealing Our Heritage?': Women's Folksongs, Copyright Law, and the Public Domain in Algeria." *Africa Today* 49 (1):85–97. https://doi.org/10.1353/at.2002.0006.

Göral, Özgür Sevgi, Ayhan Işık, and Özlem Kaya. 2013. *The Unspoken Truth: Enforced Disappearances*. Istanbul: Truth Justice Memory Center (Hafıza Merkezi).

Grabolle-Çeliker, Anna. 2013. *Kurdish Life in Contemporary Turkey: Migration, Gender, and Ethnic Identity*. London: I.B. Tauris.

Gray, Lila Ellen. 2013. *Fado Resounding: Affective Politics and Urban Life*. Durham, NC: Duke University Press.

Grima, Benedicte. 1992. *The Performance of Emotion among Paxtun Women: "The Misfortunes Which Have Befallen Me."* Austin: University of Texas Press.

Grojean, Olivier. 2013. "Théorie et Construction des Rapports de Genre dans la Guérilla Kurde de Turquie." *Critique Internationale* 60 (3): 21–35.

Güneş, Ömer, and İbrahim Şahin. 2018. *Antolojiya Dengbêjan*. Vol. 1, *Dengbêj Reso*. Istanbul: Nûbihar.

Habermas, Jürgen. 1990. *Strukturwandel der Öffentlichkeit: Untersuchungen zu einer Kategorie der bürgerlichen Gesellschaft*. Frankfurt am Main: Suhrkamp.

Haig, Geoffrey. 2004. "The Invisibilisation of Kurdish: The Other Side of Language Planning in Turkey." In *Die Kurden: Studien zu ihrer Sprache, Geschichte und Kultur*, edited by Stephan Conermann and Geoffrey Haig, 121–150. Hamburg: EB-Verlag.

Hakyemez, Serra. 2017. "Turkey's Failed Peace Process with the Kurds: A Different Explanation." In *Middle East Brief* no. 111, 1–9. Waltham, MA: Crown Center for Middle East Studies, Brandeis University.

Hale, Charles R. 2005. "Neoliberal Multiculturalism: The Remaking of Cultural Rights and Racial Dominance in Central America." *PoLAR: Political and Legal Anthropology Review* 28 (1):10–28. https://doi.org/10.1525/pol.2005.28.1.10.

Hamelink, Wendelmoet. 2016. *The Sung Home: Narrative, Morality, and the Kurdish Nation*. Leiden: Brill.

Hamelink, Wendelmoet, and Hanifi Barış. 2014. "Dengbêjs on Borderlands: Borders and the State as Seen through the Eyes of Kurdish Singer-Poets." *Kurdish Studies* 2 (1):34–60.

Harkness, Nicholas. 2013. *Songs of Seoul: An Ethnography of Voice and Voicing in Christian South Korea*. Berkeley: University of California Press.

Hasgül, Necdet. 1996. "Cumhuriyet Dönemi Müzik Politikaları." *Dans, Müzik, Kültür: Folklora Doğru* 62:27–49.

Hassanpour, Amir. 1992. *Nationalism and Language in Kurdistan, 1918–1985*. San Francisco: Mellen Research University Press.

Hassanpour, Amir. 2020a. *Essays on Kurds: Historiography, Orality, and Nationalism*. New York: Peter Lang.

Hassanpour, Amir. 2020b. "Orality and Nationalism." In *Essays on Kurds: Historiography, Orality, and Nationalism*, 3–38. New York: Peter Lang.

Henning, Barbara. 2018. *Narratives of the History of the Ottoman-Kurdish Bedirhani Family in Imperial and Post-Imperial Contexts*. Bamberg: University of Bamberg Press.

Henriques, Julian. 2010. "The Vibrations of Affect and Their Propagation on a Night out on Kingston's Dancehall Scene." *Body & Society* 16 (1):57–89. https://doi.org/10.1177/1357034 X09354768.

Hirschkind, Charles. 2006. *The Ethical Soundscape: Cassette Sermons and Islamic Counterpublics*. New York: Columbia University Press.

Hirschkind, Charles. 2021. *The Feeling of History: Islam, Romanticism, and Andalusia*. Chicago: University of Chicago Press.

Hobart, Angela, and Bruce Kapferer, eds. 2005. *Aesthetics in Performance: Formations of Symbolic Construction and Experience*. New York: Berghahn Books.

Hoek, Lotte. 2009. "'More Sexpression Please!' Screening the Female Voice and Body in the Bangladesh Film Industry." In *Aesthetic Formations: Media, Religion, and the Senses*, edited by Birgit Meyer, 71–90. New York: Palgrave.

Hunt, Nancy Rose. 2016. *A Nervous State: Violence, Remedies, and Reverie in Colonial Congo*. Durham, NC: Duke University Press.

Igreja, Victor. 2018. "'What Made the Elephant Rise Up from the Shade?' Relationships in Transition and Negotiating Silence in Mozambique." In *Truth, Silence, and Violence in Emerging States: Histories of the Unspoken*, edited by Aidan Russell, 88–110. London: Routledge.

Iğsız, Aslı. 2018. *Humanism in Ruins: Entangled Legacies of the Greek-Turkish Population Exchange*. Stanford, CA: Stanford University Press.

Impey, Angela. 2013. "Keeping in Touch via Cassette: Tracing Dinka Songs from Cattle Camp to Transnational Audio-Letter." *Journal of African Cultural Studies* 25 (2):197–210. https://doi .org/10.1080/13696815.2013.775038.

İnanç, Zeri. 2016. *Di Radyoya Êrîvanê De Dengê Kurdî/Erivan Radyosunda Kürt Sesi*. Istanbul: İsmail Beşikçi Vakfı.

Inoue, Miyako. 2003. "The Listening Subject of Japanese Modernity and His Auditory Double: Citing, Sighting, and Siting the Modern Japanese Woman." *Cultural Anthropology* 18 (2):156–193. https://doi.org/10.1525/can.2003.18.2.156.

International Crisis Group. 2017. *Managing Turkey's PKK Conflict: The Case of Nusaybin*. Brussels: International Crisis Group. https://www.crisisgroup.org/europe-central-asia/western -europemediterranean/turkey/243-managing-turkeys-pkk-conflict-case-nusaybin.

Irvine, Judith T. 1990. "Registering Affect: Heteroglossia in the Linguistic Expression of Emotion." In *Language and the Politics of Emotion*, edited by Lila Abu-Lughod and Catherine A. Lutz, 126–161. Cambridge: Cambridge University Press.

Jakobson, Roman. 1960. "Closing Statement: Linguistics and Poetics." In *Style in Language*, edited by T. A. Sebeok, 350–377. Cambridge: MIT Press.

Jamison, Kelda. 2015. "Making Kurdish Public(s): Language Politics and Practice in Turkey." PhD diss., University of Chicago.

Jamison, Kelda. 2016. "Hefty Dictionaries in Incomprehensible Tongues: Commensurating Code and Language Community in Turkey." *Anthropological Quarterly* 89 (1):31–62.

Jarjour, Tala. 2015. "Ḥasho: Music Modality and the Economy of Emotional Aesthetics." *Ethnomusicology Forum* 24 (1):51–72. https://doi.org/10.1080/17411912.2015.1018918.

Jaszi, Peter, and Martha Woodmansee. 2003. "Refiguring Rights in Traditional Culture and Bioknowledge." In *Scientific Authorship: Credit and Intellectual Property in Science*, edited by Mario Biagioli and Peter Galison, 195–223. New York: Routledge.

Jean-Klein, Iris. 2000. "Mothercraft, Statecraft, and Subjectivity in the Palestinian Intifada." *American Ethnologist* 27 (1):100–127.

Jongerden, Joost. 2010. "Village Evacuation and Reconstruction in Kurdistan (1993–2002)." *Études Rurales* 186:77–100. https://doi.org/10.4000/etudesrurales.9241.

Joseph, Suad. 1993. "Connectivity and Patriarchy among Urban Working-Class Arab Families in Lebanon." *Ethos* 21 (4):452–484.

Joseph, Suad. 2005. "Learning Desire: Relational Pedagogies and the Desiring Female Subject in Lebanon." *Journal of Middle East Women's Studies* 1 (1):79–109. https://doi.org/10 .1215/15525864-2005-1005.

Kadioglu, Ayse. 2007. "Denationalization of Citizenship? The Turkish Experience." *Citizenship Studies* 11 (3):283–299. https://doi.org/10.1080/17450100701381839.

Kahn, Douglas. 1992. "Introduction: Histories of Sound Once Removed." In *Wireless Imagination: Sound, Radio, and the Avant-Garde*, edited by Douglas Kahn, 1–29. Cambridge: MIT Press.

Kandiyoti, Deniz. 1987. "Emancipated but Unliberated? Reflections on the Turkish Case." *Feminist Studies* 13 (2):317–338.

Kandiyoti, Deniz, ed. 1991. *Women, Islam, and the State*. Philadelphia: Temple University Press.

Kandiyoti, Deniz. 1998. "Some Awkward Questions on Women and Modernity in Turkey." In *Remaking Women: Feminism and Modernity in the Middle East*, edited by Lila Abu-Lughod, 270–287. Princeton, NJ: Princeton University Press.

Karaca, Banu. 2009. "Governance of or through Culture? Cultural Policy and the Politics of Culture in Europe." *Focaal* 55:27–40. https://doi.org/10.3167/fcl.2009.550103.

Karaca, Banu. 2011. "Images Delegitimized and Discouraged: Explicitly Political Art and the Arbitrariness of the Unspeakable." *New Perspectives on Turkey* 45:155–183. https://doi.org /10.1017/S0896634600001345.

Karaca, Banu. 2013. "Europeanization from the Margins? Istanbul's Cultural Capital Initiative and the Formation of European Cultural Policies." In *The Cultural Politics of Europe: European Capitals of Culture and European Union since the 1980s*, edited by Kiran Klaus Patel, 157–176. London: Routledge.

Karaca, Banu. 2019. "'When Everything Has Been Said before . . .': Art, Dispossession, and the Economies of Forgetting in Turkey." In *Women Mobilizing Memory*, edited by Ayşe Gül Altınay, María José Contrerars, Marianne Hirsch, Jean Howard, Banu Karaca, and Alisa Solomon, 285–303. New York: Columbia University Press.

Karakaş, Berrin. 2012. "Zincirleri Koparıp Gelmişiz." *Radikal*, March 8, 2012. http://www.radikal .com.tr/yazarlar/berrin-karakas/zincirleri-koparip-gelmisiz-1081055/.

Karasu, Doğan, Ahmet Hülakü, Orhan Korkmazcan, Devrim Güleryüz, and Özlem Güngör, eds. 2007. *Bingöl Dengbêjleri*. Istanbul: Peri.

Karayan, Sarkis Y. 2000. "Demography of Van Province, 1844–1914." In *Armenian Van/Vaspurakan*, edited by Richard G. Hovannisian, 195–208. Costa Mesa, CA: Mazda.

Kaya, Duygu Gül. 2015. "Coming to Terms with the Past: Rewriting History through a Therapeutic Public Discourse in Turkey." *International Journal of Middle East Studies* 47 (4):681–700. https://doi.org/10.1017/S0020743815000938.

Keane, Webb. 1991. "Delegated Voice: Ritual Speech, Risk, and the Making of Marriage Alliances in Anakalang." *American Ethnologist* 18 (2):311–330. https://doi.org/10.1525/ae.1991 .18.2.02a00070.

Keane, Webb. 1997a. "From Fetishism to Sincerity: On Agency, the Speaking Subject, and Their Historicity in the Context of Religious Conversion." *Comparative Studies in Society and History* 39 (4):674–693. https://doi.org/10.1017/S0010417500020855.

Keane, Webb. 1997b. *Signs of Recognition: Powers and Hazards of Representation in an Indonesian Society*. Berkeley: University of California Press.

Keane, Webb. 2002. "Sincerity, 'Modernity,' and the Protestants." *Cultural Anthropology* 17 (1):65–92. https://doi.org/10.1525/can.2002.17.1.65.

Keil, Charles. 1966. *Urban Blues*. Chicago: University of Chicago Press.

Kevirbirî, Salih. 2002. *Karapetê Xaço: Bir Çığlığın Yüzyılı*. Istanbul: Sî Yayınları.

Kevirbirî, Salih. 2004. *Filitê Quto: Yirmi Olay, Yirmi Kılam*. Translated by Mazlum Doğan. Istanbul: Evrensel.

King, Diane E. 2008. "The Personal Is Patrilineal: *Namus* as Sovereignty." *Identities: Global Studies in Culture and Power* 15:317–342. https://doi.org/10.1080/10702890802073266.

Kittler, Friedrich A. 1985. *Aufschreibesysteme 1800/1900*. Munich: Wilhelm Fink.

Kittler, Friedrich A. 1999. *Gramophone, Film, Typewriter*. Stanford, CA: Stanford University Press.

Klein, Janet. 2000. "Proverbial Nationalism: Proverbs in Kurdish Nationalist Discourse of the Late Ottoman Period." *International Journal of Kurdish Studies* 14 (1/2):7–26.

Klein, Janet. 2011. *The Margins of Empire: Kurdish Militias in the Ottoman Tribal Zone*. Stanford, CA: Stanford University Press.

Kleinman, Arthur, Veena Das, and Margaret M. Lock, eds. 1997. *Social Suffering*. Berkeley: University of California Press.

Kligman, Mark. 2011. "The Bible, Prayer, and Maqām: Extra-Musical Associations of Syrian Jews." *Ethnomusicology* 45 (3):443–479.

Kogacioglu, Dicle. 2004. "The Tradition Effect: Framing Honor Crimes in Turkey." *Differences: A Journal of Feminist Cultural Studies* 15 (2):119–151. https://doi.org/10.1215/10407391-15-2-118.

Kunreuther, Laura. 2006. "Technologies of the Voice: FM Radio, Telephone, and the Nepali Diaspora in Kathmandu." *Cultural Anthropology* 21 (3):323–353. https://doi.org/10.1525/can .2006.21.3.323.

Kunreuther, Laura. 2010. "Transparent Media: Radio, Voice, and Ideologies of Directness in Postdemocratic Nepal." *Journal of Linguistic Anthropology* 20 (2):334–351. https://doi.org/10 .1111/j.1548-1395.2010.01073.x.

Kunreuther, Laura. 2018. "Sounds of Democracy: Performance, Protest, and Political Subjectivity." *Cultural Anthropology* 33 (1):1–31. https://doi.org/10.14506/ca33.1.01.

Kuruoğlu, Alev P., and Güliz Ger. 2015. "An Emotional Economy of Mundane Objects." *Consumption Markets & Culture* 18 (3):209–238.

Larkin, Brian. 2008. *Signal and Noise: Media, Infrastructure, and Urban Culture in Nigeria*. Durham, NC: Duke University Press.

Lazreg, Marnia. 1994. *The Eloquence of Silence: Algerian Women in Question*. New York: Routledge.

Lentjes, Rebecca. 2016. "Gendered Sonic Violence, from the Waiting Room to the Locker Room." *Sounding Out!* October 31, 2016. https://soundstudiesblog.com/2016/10/31/gendered-sonic -violence-from-the-waiting-room-to-the-locker-room/.

Lentjes, Rebecca. 2019. "Sonic Patriarchy in the Neoliberal University." Former blog post. March 27, 2019. http://www.rebeccalentjes.com/?p=788.

Leupold, David. 2020. *Embattled Dreamlands*. New York: Routledge.

Liebhaber, Samuel. 2018. *When Melodies Gather: Oral Art of the Mahra*. Stanford, CA: Stanford University Press.

Lovell, Stephen. 2015. *Russia in the Microphone Age: A History of Soviet Radio, 1919–1970*. Oxford: Oxford University Press.

Luhrmann, T. M., R. Padmavati, H. Tharoor, and A. Osei. 2015. "Differences in Voice-Hearing Experiences of People with Psychosis in the USA, India, and Ghana: Interview-Based Study." *British Journal of Psychiatry* 206 (1):41–44. https://doi.org/10.1192/bjp.bp.113.139048.

Magrini, Tullia. 2008. "Women's 'Work of Pain' in Christian Mediterranean Europe." *Music & Anthropology: Journal of Musical Anthropology of the Mediterranean* 3. http://umbc.edu /MA/index/number3/magrini/magr0.htm.

Mahmood, Saba. 2001. "Feminist Theory, Embodiment, and the Docile Agent: Some Reflections on the Egyptian Islamic Revival." *Cultural Anthropology* 16 (2):202–236. https://doi .org/10.1525/can.2001.16.2.202.

Mahmood, Saba. 2005. *Politics of Piety: The Islamic Revival and the Feminist Subject*. Princeton, NJ: Princeton University Press.

Mahmood, Saba. 2016. *Religious Difference in a Secular Age: A Minority Report*. Princeton, NJ: Princeton University Press.

Maisel, Sebastian, ed. 2018. *The Kurds: An Encyclopedia of Life, Culture, and Society*. Santa Barbara: ABC-CLIO, LLC.

Mauss, Marcel. 1921. "L'Expression Obligatoire des Sentiments (Rituels Oraux Funéraires Australiens)." *Journal de Psychologie* 18:425–434. Electronic version by Jean-Marie Tremblay, Chicoutimi, Québec, 2002. http://classiques.uqac.ca/classiques/mauss_marcel/essais_de_socio /T3_expression_sentiments/expression_sentiments.html.

Mazzarella, William. 2004. "Culture, Globalization, Mediation." *Annual Review of Anthropology* 33:345–367. https://doi.org/10.1146/annurev.anthro.33.070203.143809.

McClintock, Anne. 1991. "'No Longer in a Future Heaven': Women and Nationalism in South Africa." *Transition* 51:104–123. https://doi.org/10.2307/2935081.

McDowall, David. 2004. *A Modern History of the Kurds*. 3rd rev. and updated ed. London: I.B. Tauris.

Messick, Brinkley. 1996. *The Calligraphic State: Textual Domination and History in a Muslim Society*. Berkeley: University of California Press.

Meyer, Birgit. 2009. "From Imagined Communities to Aesthetic Formations: Religious Mediations, Sensational Forms, and Styles of Binding." In *Aesthetic Formations: Media, Religion, and the Senses*, edited by Birgit Meyer, 1–28. New York: Palgrave Macmillan.

Miller, W. Flagg. 2002. "Public Words and Body Politics: Reflections on the Strategies of Women Poets in Rural Yemen." *Journal of Women's History* 14 (1):94–122. https://doi.org/10.1353/jowh.2002.0024.

Miller, W. Flagg. 2005. "Of Songs and Signs: Audiocassette Poetry, Moral Character, and the Culture of Circulation in Yemen." *American Ethnologist* 32 (1):82–99. https://doi.org/10.1525/ae.2005.32.1.82.

Minassian, Anahide Ter. 2000. "The City of Van at the Turn of the Twentieth Century." In *Armenian Van/Vaspurakan*, edited by Richard G. Hovannisian, 171–193. Costa Mesa, CA: Mazda.

Mojab, Shahrzad. 2001. "The Solitude of the Stateless: Kurdish Women at the Margins of Feminist Knowledge." In *Women of a Non-state Nation: The Kurds*, edited by Shahrzad Mojab, 1–22. Costa Mesa, CA: Mazda.

Mojab, Shahrzad. 2021. "Part I: The Making of the Bibliography." In *Women of Kurdistan: A Historical and Bibliographic Study*, edited by Shahrzad Mojab and Amir Hassanpour, 7–66. London: Transnational Press London.

Moorman, Marissa J. 2019. *Powerful Frequencies: Radio, State Power, and the Cold War in Angola, 1931–2002*. Athens: Ohio University Press.

Morris, Rosalind C. 2000. *In the Place of Origins: Modernity and Its Mediums in Northern Thailand*. Durham, NC: Duke University Press.

Mrázek, Rudolf. 1997. "'Let Us Become Radio Mechanics': Technology and National Identity in Late-Colonial Netherlands East Indies." *Comparative Studies in Society and History* 39 (1):3–33. https://doi.org/10.1017/S0010417597000017.

Mueggler, Erik. 2014. "'Cats Give Funerals to Rats': Making the Dead Modern with Lament." *Journal of the Royal Anthropological Institute* 20 (2):197–217. https://doi/.org/10.1111/1467-9655.12100.

Najmabadi, Afsaneh. 2005. *Women with Mustaches and Men without Beards*. Berkeley: University of California Press.

Nezan, Kendal, Mehrdad R. Izady, Ayako Tatsumura, Erol Mutlu, Christian Poche, Dieter Christensen, and Archimandrite Komitas. 1996. *Kürt Müziği*. Istanbul: Avesta.

Nichanian, Marc. 2003. "Catastrophic Mourning." In *Loss: The Politics of Mourning*, edited by David L. Eng and David Kazanjian, 99–124. Berkeley: University of California Press.

Öcalan, Abdullah. 1993. *Kürdistan'da Kadın ve Aile*. Cologne: Weşanên Serxwebûn.

Ochoa Gautier, Ana María. 2014. *Aurality: Listening & Knowledge in Nineteenth-Century Colombia*. Durham, NC: Duke University Press.

Öktem, Kerem. 2008. "The Nation's Imprint: Demographic Engineering and the Change of Toponymes in Republican Turkey." *European Journal of Turkish Studies* 7. https://doi.org/10.4000/ejts.2243.

Olszewska, Zuzanna. 2015. *The Pearl of Dari: Poetry and Personhood among Young Afghans in Iran*. Bloomington: Indiana University Press.

Olszewska, Zuzanna. 2019. "Claiming an Individual Name: Revisiting the Personhood Debate with Afghan Poets in Iran." In *The Scandal of Continuity in Middle East Anthropology: Form, Duration, Difference*, edited by Judith Scheele and Andrew Shryock, 163–186. Bloomington: Indiana University Press.

Öncü, Ayşe. 2011. "Representing and Consuming 'the East' in Cultural Markets." *New Perspectives on Turkey* 45:49–73.

Öpengin, Ergin. 2012. "Sociolinguistic Situation of Kurdish in Turkey: Sociopolitical Factors and Language Use Patterns." *International Journal of the Sociology of Language* 217:151–180. https://doi.org/10.1515/ijsl-2012-0053.

Oremar, Kakşar. 2012. *Prensesa bê Tac û Text: Eyşe Şan*. Diyarbakır: Weşanên Şaredariya Bajarê Mezin a Amedê.

Oushakine, Serguei. 2009. *The Patriotism of Despair: Nation, War, and Loss in Russia*. Ithaca, NY: Cornell University Press.

Özgür Kadın Akademisi, ed. 2015. *Jineoloji Tartışmaları*. Diyarbakır: Aram.

Öztürk, Selda. 2012. "Kadın Kimliği Bağlamında Kültürel Bellek Ve Van Merkezdeki Kadın Dengbêjliği Yansımaları." Master's thesis, Istanbul Technical University.

Öztürkmen, Arzu. 1998. *Türkiye'de Folklor ve Milliyetçilik*. Istanbul: İletişim Yayınları.

Öztürkmen, Arzu. 2001. "Politics of National Dance in Turkey: A Historical Reappraisal." *Yearbook for Traditional Music* 33:139–143. https://doi.org/10.2307/1519638.

Özyürek, Esra, ed. 2007. *The Politics of Public Memory in Turkey*. Syracuse, NY: Syracuse University Press.

Pandolfo, Stefania. 1997. *Impasse of the Angels: Scenes from a Moroccan Space of Memory*. Chicago: University of Chicago Press.

Pinney, Christopher. 2005. "Things Happen: Or, from Which Moment Does That Object Come?" In *Materiality*, edited by Daniel Miller, 256–272. Durham, NC: Duke University Press.

Porcello, Thomas. 2002. "Music Mediated as Live in Austin: Sound, Technology, and Recording Practice." *City and Society* 14 (1):69–86. https://doi.org/10.1525/city.2002.14.1.69.

Posel, Deborah. 2008. "History as Confession: The Case of the South African Truth and Reconciliation Commission." *Public Culture* 20 (1):119–141. https://doi.org/10.1215/08992363-2007-019.

Povinelli, Elizabeth A. 2002. *The Cunning of Recognition: Indigenous Alterities and the Making of Australian Multiculturalism*. Durham, NC: Duke University Press.

Racy, A. J. 2004. *Making Music in the Arab World: The Culture and Artistry of Tarab*. Cambridge: Cambridge University Press.

Rancière, Jacques. 2010. *Dissensus: On Politics and Aesthetics*. Translated by Steven Corcoran. London: Bloomsbury.

Rangan, Pooja. 2017a. "Audibilities: Voice and Listening in the Penumbra of Documentary; An Introduction." *Discourse: Journal for Theoretical Studies in Media and Culture* 39 (3):279–291. https://doi.org/10.13110/discourse.39.3.0279.

Rangan, Pooja. 2017b. *Immediations: The Humanitarian Impulse in Documentary*. Durham, NC: Duke University Press.

Reigle, Robert F. 2013. "A Brief History of Kurdish Music Recordings in Turkey." *Hellenic Journal of Music, Education, and Culture* 4 (1). http://hejmec.eu/journal/index.php/HeJMEC/index.

Reinhard, Kurt. 1976. "Afterword." In *Turkish Folk Music from Asia Minor by Béla Bartók*, edited by Béla Bartók and Benjamin Suchoff, 255–270. Princeton, NJ: Princeton University Press.

Reinhard, Ursula. 2002. "Turkey: An Overview." In *The Garland Encyclopedia of World Music*, vol. 6, *The Middle East*, edited by Virginia Danielson, Marcus Scott, and Dwight Reynolds, 759–777. New York: Routledge.

Reynolds, Dwight Fletcher. 1995. *Heroic Poets, Poetic Heroes: The Ethnography of Performance in an Arabic Oral Epic Tradition*. Ithaca, NY: Cornell University Press.

Rosaldo, Michelle Z. 1980. *Knowledge and Passion: Ilongot Notions of Self and Social Life*. New York: Cambridge University Press.

Rosaldo, Michelle Z. 1984. "Words That Are Moving: The Social Meanings of Ilongot Verbal Art." In *Dangerous Words: Language and Politics in the Pacific*, edited by Donald Brenneis and Fred R. Myers, 131–160. New York: New York University Press.

Rose, Mark. 1993. *Authors and Owners: The Invention of Copyright*. Cambridge, MA: Harvard University Press.

Ross, Fiona C. 2003. *Bearing Witness: Women and the Truth and Reconciliation Commission in South Africa*. London: Pluto.

Sakakeeny, Matt. 2013. *Roll with It: Brass Bands in the Streets of New Orleans*. Durham, NC: Duke University Press.

Samuels, David W., Louise Meintjes, Ana Maria Ochoa, and Thomas Porcello. 2010. "Soundscapes: Toward a Sounded Anthropology." *Annual Review of Anthropology* 39 (1):329–345. https://doi.org/10.1146/annurev-anthro-022510-132230.

Savcı, Evren. 2021. *Queer in Translation: Sexual Politics under Neoliberal Islam*. Durham, NC: Duke University Press.

Saygun, Ahmed A. 1976. "Uzun Hava." In *Béla Bartók's Folk Music Research in Turkey*, edited by Béla Bartók, Ahmed A. Saygun, and Laszlo Vikár, 212–224. Budapest: Akadémiai Kiadó.

Scalbert-Yücel, Clémence. 2009. "The Invention of a Tradition: Diyarbakır's Dengbêj Project." *European Journal of Turkish Studies* 10. https://doi.org/10.4000/ejts.4055.

Schafer, R. Murray. 1977. *The Soundscape: Our Sonic Environment and the Tuning of the World*. Rochester: Destiny.

Schäfers, Marlene. 2015. "Being Sick of Politics: The Production of Dengbêjî as Kurdish Cultural Heritage in Contemporary Turkey." *European Journal of Turkish Studies* 20. https://doi.org/10.4000/ejts.5200.

Schäfers, Marlene. 2019. "Archived Voices, Acoustic Traces, and the Reverberations of Kurdish History in Modern Turkey." *Comparative Studies in Society and History* 61 (2):447–473. https://doi.org/10.1017/S0010417519000112.

Schäfers, Marlene. 2020. "Walking a Fine Line: Loyalty, Betrayal, and the Moral and Gendered Bargains of Resistance." *Comparative Studies of South Asia, Africa and the Middle East* 40 (1):119–132. https://doi.org/10.1215/1089201X-8186126.

Schick, Irvin Cemil. 2010. "The Harem as Gendered Space and the Spatial Reproduction of Gender." In *Harem Histories: Envisioning Places and Living Spaces*, edited by Marilyn Booth, 69–84. Durham, NC: Duke University Press.

Schlichter, Annette. 2011. "Do Voices Matter? Vocality, Materiality, Gender Performativity." *Body & Society* 17 (1):31–52. https://doi.org/10.1177/1357034X10394669.

Schlichter, Annette. 2014. "Un/Voicing the Self: Vocal Pedagogy and the Discourse-Practices of Subjectivation." *Postmodern Culture* 24 (3). https://doi.org/10.1353/pmc.2014.0011.

Schmidt, Leigh Eric. 2000. *Hearing Things: Religion, Illusion, and the American Enlightenment*. Cambridge, MA: Harvard University Press.

Sehlikoğlu, Sertaç. 2015. "The Daring *Mahrem*: Changing Dynamics of Public Sexuality in Turkey." In *Gender and Sexuality in Muslim Cultures*, edited by Gul Ozyegin, 235–252. London: Ashgate.

Sehlikoğlu, Sertaç. 2020. *Working Out Desire: Women, Sport, and Self-Making in Istanbul.* Syracuse, NY: Syracuse University Press.

Seremetakis, C. Nadia. 1991. *The Last Word: Women, Death, and Divination in Inner Mani.* Chicago: University of Chicago Press.

Shahvisi, Arianne. 2018. "Beyond Orientalism: Exploring the Distinctive Feminism of Democratic Confederalism in Rojava." *Geopolitics* 26(4):998–1022. https://doi.org/10.1080/1465 0045.2018.1554564.

Shannon, Jonathan H. 2003. "Emotion, Performance, and Temporality in Arab Music: Reflections on Tarab." *Cultural Anthropology* 18 (1):72–98. https://doi.org/10.1525/can.2003.18.1.72.

Sharifi, Amir, and Zuzan Barwari. 2020. "The Oral Tradition of Dengbêjî: A Kurdish Genre of Verbal Art and Reported Speech." In *Kurdish Art and Identity: Verbal Art, Self-Definition, and Recent History*, edited by Philip G. Kreyenbroek, 136–168. Berlin: De Gruyter.

Shryock, Andrew. 1997. *Nationalism and the Genealogical Imagination: Oral History and Textual Authority in Tribal Jordan.* Berkeley: University of California Press.

Silverstein, Michael, and Greg Urban, eds. 1996. *Natural Histories of Discourse.* Chicago: University of Chicago Press.

Simpson, Audra. 2007. "On Ethnographic Refusal: Indigeneity, 'Voice,' and Colonial Citizenship." *Junctures* 9:67–80.

Sinha, Mrinalini. 1996. "Gender in Critiques of Colonialism and Nationalism: Locating the 'Indian Woman.'" In *Feminism and History*, edited by Joan Wallach Scott, 477–504. New York: Oxford University Press.

Sirman, Nükhet. 2000. "Writing the Usual Love Story: The Fashioning of Conjugal and National Subjects in Turkey." In *Gender, Agency, and Change: Anthropological Perspectives*, edited by Victoria A. Goddard, 202–219. London: Routledge.

Sirman, Nükhet. 2004. "Kinship, Politics, and Love: Honour in Post-Colonial Contexts—the Case of Turkey." In *Violence in the Name of Honour: Theoretical and Political Challenges*, edited by Shahrzad Mojab and Nahla Abdo, 39–56. Istanbul: İstanbul Bilgi University Press.

Siyah Bant. 2013. *Siyah Bant Research Reports, Report II: Freedom of Expression in the Arts and Censorship in Kurdish Region Diyarbakir, Batman.* Siyah Bant. http://www.siyahbant.org /wp-content/uploads/2014/01/SiyahBant_Arastirma_Raporlari_2013.pdf.

Slotta, James. 2015. "Phatic Rituals of the Liberal Democratic Policy: Hearing Voices in the Hearings of the Royal Commission on Aboriginal Peoples." *Comparative Studies in Society and History* 57 (1):130–160. https://doi.org/10.1017/S0010417514000620.

Spitulnik, Debra. 1997. "The Social Circulation of Media Discourse and the Mediation of Communities." *Journal of Linguistic Anthropology* 6 (2):161–187. https://doi.org/10.1525/jlin.1996 .6.2.161.

Spitulnik, Debra. 1998. "Mediated Modernities: Encounters with the Electronic in Zambia." *Visual Anthropology Review* 14 (2):63–84. https://doi.org/10.1525/var.1998.14.2.63.

Spitulnik, Debra. 2002. "Mobile Machines and Fluid Audiences: Rethinking Reception through Zambian Radio Culture." In *Media Worlds: Anthropology on New Terrain*, edited by Faye D. Ginsburg, Lila Abu-Lughod, and Brian Larkin, 337–354. Berkeley: University of California Press.

Spivak, Gayatri Chakravorty. 1988. "Can the Subaltern Speak?" In *Marxism and the Interpretation of Culture*, edited by Cary Nelson and Lawrence Grossberg, 271–313. Urbana: University of Illinois Press.

Stasch, Rupert. 2011. "Ritual and Oratory Revisited: The Semiotics of Effective Action." *Annual Review of Anthropology* 40 (1):159–174. https://doi.org/10.1146/annurev-anthro-081309-145623.

Steingo, Gavin. 2017. "The Inaudible Nation: Music and Sensory Perception in Postapartheid South Africa." *Cultural Critique* 95:71–100. https://doi.org/10.5749/culturalcritique.95.2017.0071.

Sterne, Jonathan. 2003. *The Audible Past: The Cultural Origins of Sound Reproduction*. Durham, NC: Duke University Press.

Stewart, Kathleen. 2011. "Atmospheric Attunements." *Environment and Planning D: Society and Space* 29 (3):445–453. https://doi.org/10.1068/d9109.

Stoichita, Victor Alexandre. 2008. *Fabricants d'Émotion: Musique et Malice dans un Village Tsigane en Roumanie*. Nanterre: Société d'Ethnologie.

Stokes, Martin. 1992. *The Arabesk Debate: Music and Musicians in Modern Turkey*. Oxford: Clarendon Press.

Stokes, Martin. 2009. " 'Abd Al-Halim's Microphone." In *Music and the Play of Power in the Middle East, North Africa, and Central Asia*, edited by Laudan Nooshin, 55–73. Surrey: Ashgate.

Stokes, Martin. 2010. *The Republic of Love: Cultural Intimacy in Turkish Popular Music*. Chicago: University of Chicago Press.

Stokes, Martin. 2015. "The Politics of Aesthetics in the Muslim Middle East." In *A Companion to the Anthropology of the Middle East*, edited by Soraya Altorki, 91–106. Hoboken, NJ: Wiley Blackwell.

Strathern, Marilyn. 1996. "Cutting the Network." *Journal of the Royal Anthropological Institute* 2 (3):517–535.

Strathern, Marilyn. 1999. *Property, Substance, and Effect: Anthropological Essays on Persons and Things*. London: Athlone Press.

Strathern, Marilyn. 2005. *Kinship, Law, and the Unexpected: Relatives Are Always a Surprise*. Cambridge: Cambridge University Press.

Strohmeier, Martin. 2003. *Crucial Images in the Presentation of a Kurdish National Identity: Heroes and Patriots, Traitors and Foes*. Leiden: Brill.

Suni, Anoush. 2019. "Palimpsests of Violence: Ruination and the Politics of Memory in Anatolia." PhD diss., UCLA.

Tahaoğlu, Çiçek. 2012. "Kadınlar Söylemiş, Erkeklere Malolmuş." *Bianet*, March 8, 2012. http://bianet.org/bianet/sanat/136758-kadinlar-soylemis-erkeklere-malolmus.

Tambar, Kabir. 2010. "The Aesthetics of Public Visibility: Alevi Semah and the Paradoxes of Pluralism in Turkey." *Comparative Studies in Society and History* 52 (3):652–679. https://doi.org/10.1017/S0010417510000344.

Tambar, Kabir. 2011. "Iterations of Lament: Anachronism and Affect in a Shi'i Islamic Revival in Turkey." *American Ethnologist* 38 (3):484–500. https://doi.org/10.1111/j.1548-1425.2011.01318.x.

Tambar, Kabir. 2014. *The Reckoning of Pluralism: Political Belonging and the Demands of History in Turkey*. Stanford, CA: Stanford University Press.

Tejel Gorgas, Jordi. 2007. *Le Mouvement Kurde de Turquie en Exil: Continuités et Discontinuités du Nationalisme Kurde sous le Mandat Français en Syrie et au Liban (1925–1946)*. Bern: Peter Lang.

Tekelioğlu, Orhan. 1996. "The Rise of a Spontaneous Synthesis: The Historical Background of Turkish Popular Music." *Middle Eastern Studies* 32 (2):194–215. https://doi.org/10.1080/00263209608701111.

Tekelioğlu, Orhan. 2001. "Modernizing Reforms and Turkish Music in the 1930s." *Turkish Studies* 2 (1):93–109. https://doi.org/10.1080/14683849.2001.11009175.

Tezcür, Güneş Murat. 2016. "Ordinary People, Extraordinary Risks: Participation in an Ethnic Rebellion." *American Political Science Review* 110 (2):247–264. https://doi.org/10.1017/S0003055416000150.

Thorkelson, Eli. 2020. "Sonic Patriarchy in a Left-Wing French Philosophy Department." *Feminist Anthropology* 1 (1): 56–70. https://doi.org/10.1002/fea2.12008.

Toivanen, Mari, and Bahar Baser. 2016. "Gender in the Representations of an Armed Conflict: Female Kurdish Combatants in French and British Media." *Middle East Journal of Culture and Communication* 9 (3):294–314. https://doi.org/10.1163/18739865-00903007.

Trawick, Margaret. 2017. *Death, Beauty, Struggle: Untouchable Women Create the World*. Philadelphia: University of Pennsylvania Press.

Turkyilmaz, Yektan. 2011. "Rethinking Genocide: Violence and Victimhood in Eastern Anatolia, 1913–1915." PhD diss., Duke University.

Turkyilmaz, Zeynep. 2016. "Maternal Colonialism and Turkish Woman's Burden in Dersim: Educating the 'Mountain Flowers' of Dersim." *Journal of Women's History* 28 (3):162–186. https://doi.org/10.1353/jowh.2016.0029.

UNESCO and EQUALS Skills Coalition. 2019. *I'd Blush If I Could: Closing Gender Divides in Digital Skills through Education*. EQUALS and UNESCO. https://unesdoc.unesco.org/ark:/48223/pf0000367416.page=1.

Üngör, Uğur Ümit. 2011. *The Making of Modern Turkey: Nation and State in Eastern Anatolia, 1913–1950*. Oxford: Oxford University Press.

Ünlü, Barış. 2016. "The Kurdish Struggle and the Crisis of the Turkishness Contract." *Philosophy & Social Criticism* 42 (4–5):397–405. https://doi.org/10.1177/0191453715625715.

Urban, Greg. 1988. "Ritual Wailing in Amerindian Brazil." *American Anthropologist* 90 (2):385–400. https://doi.org/10.1525/aa.1988.90.2.02a00090.

Üstündağ, Nazan. 2019a. "Antigone as Kurdish Politician: Gendered Dwellings in the Limit between Freedom and Peace." *History of the Present* 9 (2):113–141. https://doi.org/10.5406/historypresent.9.2.0113.

Üstündağ, Nazan. 2019b. "Mother, Politician, and Guerilla: The Emergence of a New Political Imagination in Kurdistan through Women's Bodies and Speech." *differences* 30 (2):115–145. https://doi.org/10.1215/10407391-7736077.

Uzun, Mehmed. 1991. *Rojek Ji Rojên Evdalê Zeynikê*. Istanbul: Doz.

Uzun, Mehmed. 2008. *Dengbêjlerim*. Istanbul: İthaki.

Volpp, Leti. 2000. "Blaming Culture for Bad Behavior." *Yale Journal of Law and the Humanities* 12:89–116.

Wadley, Susan S. 1994. *Struggling with Destiny in Karimpur, 1925–1984*. Berkeley: University of California Press.

Walton, Jeremy F. 2013. "Confessional Pluralism and the Civil Society Effect: Liberal Mediations of Islam and Secularism in Contemporary Turkey." *American Ethnologist* 40 (1):182–200.

Watts, Nicole F. 2010. *Activists in Office: Kurdish Politics and Protest in Turkey*. Seattle: University of Washington Press.

Weheliye, Alexander G. 2005. *Phonographies: Grooves in Sonic Afro-Modernity*. Durham, NC: Duke University Press.

Weidman, Amanda J. 2003. "Gender and the Politics of Voice: Colonial Modernity and Classical Music in South India." *Cultural Anthropology* 18 (2):194–232. https://doi.org/doi.org/10.1525/can.2003.18.2.194.

Weidman, Amanda J. 2006. *Singing the Classical, Voicing the Modern: The Postcolonial Politics of Music in South India*. Durham, NC: Duke University Press.

Weidman, Amanda J. 2014a. "Anthropology and Voice." *Annual Review of Anthropology* 43:37–51. https://doi.org/10.1146/annurev-anthro-102313-030050.

Weidman, Amanda J. 2014b. "Neoliberal Logics of Voice: Playback Singing and Public Female-ness in South India." *Culture, Theory and Critique* 55 (2):175–193. https://doi.org/10.1080/1 4735784.2014.899883.

Weidman, Amanda J. 2021. *Brought to Life by the Voice: Playback Singing and Cultural Politics in South India*. Oakland: University of California Press.

Weiss, Nerina. 2010. "Falling from Grace: Gender Norms and Gender Strategies in Eastern Turkey." *New Perspectives on Turkey* 42:55–76. https://doi.org/10.1017/S0896634600000574.

White, Jenny B. 2003. "State Feminism, Modernization, and the Turkish Republican Woman." *NWSA Journal* 15 (3):145–159. https://doi.org/10.1353/nwsa.2004.0024.

White, Luise. 2000. *Speaking with Vampires: Rumor and History in Colonial Africa*. Berkeley: University of California Press.

Wilce, James M. 1998. *Eloquence in Trouble: The Poetics and Politics of Complaint in Rural Bangladesh*. New York: Oxford University Press

Yadirgi, Veli. 2017. *The Political Economy of the Kurds of Turkey: From the Ottoman Empire to the Turkish Republic*. Cambridge: Cambridge University Press.

Yarkın, Güllistan. 2019. "İnkâr Edilen Hakikat: Sömürge Kuzey Kürdistan." *Kürd Araştırmaları* 1:45–69.

Yeğen, Mesut. 2015. "The Kurdish Peace Process in Turkey: Genesis, Evolution, and Prospects." In *Global Turkey in Europe III: Democracy, Trade, and the Kurdish Question in Turkey-EU Relations*, edited by Senem Aydın-Düzgit, Daniela Huber, Meltem Müftüler-Baç, Fuat E. Keyman, Michael Schwarz, and Nathalie Tocci, 157–184. Rome: Edizioni Nuova Cultura.

Yıldırım, Umut. 2021. "Spaced-Out States: Decolonizing Trauma in a War-Torn Middle Eastern City." *Current Anthropology* 62 (6):717–740. https://doi.org/10.1086/718206.

Yükseker, Deniz, and Dilek Kurban. 2009. *Permanent Solution to Internal Displacement? An Assessment of the Van Action Plan for IDPs*. Istanbul: TESEV.

Yüksel, Metin. 2011. "Dengbêj, Mullah, Intelligentsia: The Survival and Revival of the Kurdish-Kurmanji Language in the Middle East, 1925–1960." PhD diss., University of Chicago.

Yüksel Kaptanoğlu, İlknur, Alanur Çavlin, and Banu Akadlı Ergöçmen. 2015. *Research on Domestic Violence against Women in Turkey*. Ankara: Hacettepe University, Nüfus Etütleri Enstitüsü. http://hdl.handle.net/11655/23338.

Zal, Azad, ed. 2011. *Antolojiya Dengbêjan*. Vol. 1. Diyarbakır: Şaredariya Bajarê Mezin a Diyarbekirê.

Zeydanlıoğlu, Welat. 2008. " 'The White Turkish Man's Burden': Orientalism, Kemalism, and the Kurds in Turkey." In *Neo-Colonial Mentalities in Contemporary Europe? Language and Discourse in the Construction of Identities*, edited by Guido Rings and Anne Ife, 155–174. Newcastle upon Tyne: Cambridge Scholars Publishing.

Zeydanlıoğlu, Welat. 2012. "Turkey's Kurdish Language Policy." *International Journal of the Sociology of Language* 217:99–125. https://doi.org/10.1515/ijsl-2012-0051.

Index

Printed in Great Britain
by Amazon